Shakespeare through Islamic Worlds investigates the peculiar absence of Islam and Muslims from Shakespeare's canon. While many of Shakespeare's plays were set in the Mediterranean, a geography occupied by Muslim empires and cultures, his work eschews direct engagement with the religion and its people. This erasure is striking given the popularity of this topic in the plays of Shakespeare's contemporaries.

By exploring the limited ways in which Shakespeare uses Islamic and Muslim tropes and topoi, Ambereen Dadabhoy argues that Islam and Muslim cultures function as an alternate or shadow text in his works, ranging from his staged Mediterranean plays to his histories and comedies. By consigning the diverse cultures of the Islamic regimes that occupied and populated the early modern Mediterranean, Shakespeare constructs a Europe and Mediterranean freed from the presence of non-white, non-European, and non-Christian Others, which belied the reality of the world in which he lived.

Focusing on the Muslims at the margins of Shakespeare's works, Dadabhoy reveals that Islam and its cultures informed the plots, themes, and intellectual investments of Shakespeare's plays. She puts Islam and Muslims back into the geographies and stories from which Shakespeare had evacuated them. This innovative book will be of interest to all those working on race, religion, global and cultural exchange within Shakespeare, as well as people working on Islamic, Mediterranean, and Asian studies in literature and the early modern period.

Ambereen Dadabhoy is Associate Professor of Literature at Harvey Mudd College, USA. She is the coauthor of *Anti-Racist Shakespeare* (with Nedda Mehdizadeh, 2023) and several articles on race and religion in Shakespeare and the early modern English literature.

Spotlight on Shakespeare
Series Editors: John Garrison and Kyle Pivetti

Spotlight on Shakespeare offers a series of concise, lucid books that explore the vital purchase of the modern world on Shakespeare's work. Authors in the series embrace the notion that emergent theories, contemporary events, and movements can help us shed new light on Shakespeare's work and, in turn, his work can help us better make sense of the contemporary world. The aim of each volume is two-fold: to show how Shakespeare speaks to questions in our world and to illuminate his work by looking at it through new forms of human expression. *Spotlight on Shakespeare* will adopt fresh scholarly trends as contemporary issues emerge, and it will continually prompt its readers to ask, "What can Shakespeare help us see? What can he help us do?"

Spotlight on Shakespeare invites scholars to write non-exhaustive, pithy studies of very focused topics—with the goal of creating books that engage scholars, students, and general readers alike.

Available in this series:

Shakespeare on Consent
Amanda Bailey

Shakespeare through Islamic Worlds
Ambereen Dadabhoy

For more information about this series, please visit: www. routledge.com/Spotlight-on-Shakespeare/book-series/ SOSHAX

AMBEREEN DADABHOY

Shakespeare
through Islamic Worlds

Routledge
Taylor & Francis Group

LONDON AND NEW YORK

Designed cover image: GavinD, Getty

First published 2024
by Routledge
4 Park Square, Milton Park, Abingdon, Oxon OX14 4RN

and by Routledge
605 Third Avenue, New York, NY 10158

Routledge is an imprint of the Taylor & Francis Group, an informa business

British Library Cataloguing-in-Publication Data
A catalogue record for this book is available from the British Library

ISBN: 978-1-032-10088-3 (hbk)
ISBN: 978-1-032-10084-5 (pbk)
ISBN: 978-1-003-21358-1 (ebk)

DOI: 10.4324/9781003213581

Typeset in Joanna MT
by Newgen Publishing UK

For my family

Contents

Acknowledgments

Books are simultaneously the culmination and continuation of scholarly conversations. In this regard, I have been fortunate to have had many incredible conversationalists and interlocutors who have guided, challenged, and supported me as I navigated through the thickets of this project. *Shakespeare through Islamic Worlds* would not exist without my incredible dissertation advisor Constance Jordan, whose twin commitments to rigor and ethics I hope to embody in all of my work. Constance taught me how to think about Shakespeare in new ways and very early on encouraged me to explore the presence and politics of Islamicate cultures in the period. She set me on this path, for which I am eternally grateful. I have been fortunate to have found mentors in Shakespeare studies who have recognized, affirmed, and sustained my work, giving generously of their time and offering invaluable feedback and support. I am particularly indebted to Kim F. Hall, whose scholarship has always been a model and whose friendship and generosity show her to be a true leader and community builder in this field. Not only has Bernadette Andrea's scholarship influenced my own but also she has offered guidance and resources over many years. Likewise Patricia Parker continuously exhibits intellectual generosity, particularly through her commitment to advancing the work of junior scholars. What can I say about Margo Hendricks that will adequately express her fierce advocacy of Premodern Critical Race Studies and the scholars of color who do this work, other than that I'm glad she's on my side. To this list of powerhouse scholars, mentors, and friends I would like to add Lori Anne Ferrell, Jean Howard, Farah Karim-Cooper, Joyce Green MacDonald, Lena Cowen Orlin, Jyotsna Singh, Ayanna Thompson, and Lehua Yim who have all offered generously of themselves.

My work has benefited tremendously from being in conversation with early modern scholars of color, PCRS scholars, and the #ShakeRace community. In particular, I want to acknowledge the scholars who are also my dear friends, generous readers, and rigorous critics. I and this book have been rewarded by their sage advice, deep knowledge of the field, and discerning vision. In particular, I want to thank Nedda Mehdizadeh, Leticia García; Brandi K. Adams, Vanessa Corredera, Kim F. Hall, Debapriya Sarkar, Kathryn Vomero-Santos, Miles P. Grier, Mary Rambaran-Olm, Erik Wade, Carol Mejia-LaPerle, Mira 'Assaf Kafantaris, Sharon Becker, and Ellen Scheible for their love, care, and friendship which has energized me and enriched my work. In addition, Patricia Akhimie, Abdulhamit Arvas, Dennis Britton, Jerry Brotton, Jonathan Burton, Urvashi Chakravarty, Eric De Barros, Ruben Espinosa, Rebecca Fall, Megan Gallagher, Kate Gillen, Yasmine Hachimi, Robert Hornback, Jennifer Jared, Erika Lin, Kathleen Lynch, M. Bilal Nasir, Noémie Ndiaye, Michael Neill, Jennifer Park, Marc Redfield, Benedict Robinson, Emma Smith, Ian Smith, Daniel Vitkus, Owen Williams, Nora Williams, and Kathryn Wolford have all inspired my thinking, shared material and ephemeral resources, and been sounding boards—large and small acts from which I have benefited tremendously.

I want to give special thanks to my friends and colleagues who read the draft chapters of this book and gave me invaluable feedback, which I tried to adequately address. The brilliance is theirs and the errors are mine. My appreciation to Debapriya Sarkar, Mira 'Assaf-Kafantaris, Vanessa Corredera, Andrea Moore, David Seitz, Ellen Scheible, Mary Rambaran-Olm, and Erik Wade. Additionally, Kavita Mudan Finn's incisive reading, copy editing, and engagement with my manuscript made this book both sharper and better.

I would also like to extend my thanks to Kyle Pivetti and John Garrison for inviting me to write for this series back in 2018. It took several years for this book to materialize, but Kyle and John were unwavering in their support of the different manifestations of this project from the proposal to the final draft. Chris Ratcliffe at Routledge was tremendously helpful and patient in the final stages of preparing this manuscript.

Our students are why we do what we do, and I want to thank my brilliant and curious students at Harvey Mudd College who have always been willing and game to try new things with me. I would also like to thank my colleagues at HMC for their mentorship, friendship, and support: Bill Alves, Isabel Balseiro, Marianne De Laet, Erika Dyson, Ken Fandell, Alfred Flores, Anup Gampa, Sharon Gerbode, Jeff Groves, Vivien Hamilton, Patrick Little, Rachel Mayeri, Wendy Menefee-Libey, Salvador Placencia, David Seitz, Brian Shuve, Paul Steinberg, Lisa Sullivan, Darryl Wright, and Darryl Yong. There is no other computer scientist I would teach Shakespeare with than my intrepid and fearless friend and colleague, Ben Wiedermann. I am incredibly grateful for the research funding I received from HMC, which supported this project in its final stages. Teaching at Harvey Mudd College has allowed me to stretch my research in unimaginable ways.

I am very fortunate to work and think alongside these incredible colleagues and students.

Finally, my most profound appreciation goes to my family who have unwaveringly and patiently supported me on this path. I would not have been able to accomplish anything in this career or my life without their love and understanding. My parents, Abdul Rashid and Abeda Dadabhoy, instilled a love of knowledge in me that I continue to pursue. My sisters, Asya, Fatima, and Nausheen, have been my inspiration, built-in friends, and support system. I would be nothing without them, and I am so lucky to stand beside these talented and accomplished women. Our ancestors would be so proud of us. DadaGirls doing DadaGiri for life. Last but not least, much of this book was written with a cat either on my lap or beside my laptop or on my books, offering encouragement, love, and furry distractions. I will miss the love of my beautiful Luci who was with me at every stage of this book, except this last. Without these incredible people and felines, this book would not exist. With gratitude, I will let Shakespeare have the last word, "I can no other answer make but thanks, and thanks, and ever thanks."

Introduction

Where Are All My Muslims At or Shakespearean Erasures

Shakespeare through Islamic Worlds addresses a simple question: What did William Shakespeare have to say about Islam? The short answer is, not much. Out of the hundreds of characters he created, and the disparate and distant settings of his plays, there are only one or two figures who we can definitely (maybe) call Muslim. Both characters, the Prince of Morocco and Othello, are African, and their geographic origin as well as the epithet applied to (one of) them, "Moor," hints at rather than confirms their religious identity. Beyond these two characters, Shakespeare's works contain fleeting references to "Turks," "Arabians," "Sophys," "scimitars," "turbans," and one meager mention of "Mahomet."[1] These scant textual traces appear to corroborate the caustic words of one particularly hostile writer that Shakespeare "wasn't even Islamo-curious," a dismissal designed to marginalize the religion, its peoples, and their culture through Shakespeare's cultural capital, deployed here as his perceived disinterest in the matter.[2] Shakespeare's indifference to Islamic culture was, however, an aberration, rather than the norm for his period. The early modern English stage was fascinated by Islam's cultures and geographies, particularly those in the Mediterranean and further east including India, Iran (Persia), and east Asia. Between 1579 and 1642—during what we might call the height of early modern English drama—the

Introduction

DOI: 10.4324/9781003213581-1

prolific output of Shakespeare's contemporaries on this subject numbered somewhere between 32 and 50 plays that featured Islam, Muslim, or "Oriental," characters.[3] The popularity of such material offers strong evidence that Islam was an object of great curiosity on London stages and for London audiences.

Shakespeare's corpus, with its sparse references to Islam and Muslims, deviates from the trend popularized by his contemporaries. Only two out of thirty-seven extant plays, *The Merchant of Venice* (1597) and *Othello* (1603) seem to broach and engage with the culture in a substantive manner. In *Merchant* one of Portia's doomed suitors, the Prince of Morocco, originates from a geography that in the period—and even now—signals Islamic cultural and religious affiliation. *Othello* offers a more complex genealogy for its titular character, an African origin, a conversion, and the epithet of "Moor" point to a possible Muslim backstory, but they can suggest other confessional and cultural sources of ancestry as well.[4] Matthew Dimmock has pointed out that neither of these plays explicitly references Islam, and so Shakespeare leaves the matter of his engagement opaque through omission.[5] It is worth considering what explicit references to Islam look like in the Shakespearean canon and at what threshold references are considered significant enough to demonstrate Shakespeare's interest in Islam and Muslims. One of the arguments of *Shakespeare through Islamic Worlds* is that the occlusion and repression of Islam and Muslims within Shakespeare's plays, particularly given his Mediterranean settings, demands attending to the implicit, the opaque, the referential, the absent-present, and the repressed. Following bell hooks's theorization of the margin as a location from which to interrogate the power relations that cohere within the center, looking both from and at the margins illuminates those elements of Shakespeare's worldmaking that deliberately excise Islamic culture from the purview of the plays.[6] Such hermeneutical practice simultaneously questions how scholars measure the significance of Shakespeare's engagement, which they locate in explicit, material presence, and seem to dismiss in other rhetorical or allusive gestures. My argument rests on the notion that the Muslim presence in Shakespeare is conjured through tropes and topoi commonly associated with Islam in the early modern period, which were often rooted in and routed through geography and the fantasy wherein Islam and its cultures occupied a different or Other geographic sphere from Christians and Europeans, despite the fact of Umayyad Arab and North African conquest of Iberia (711–1492) and Ottoman occupation of Byzantium (1453) and much of Europe.[7]

A significant majority of William Shakespeare's plays have settings in or adjacent to the Mediterranean. The geography of the "middle sea," which connects Africa, Asia, Europe, and the Atlantic cinched the known world, facilitating various encounters between people of different confessional and cultural traditions as well as those of diverse ethnic and racial backgrounds. The Mediterranean formed a meeting ground, "contact zone," and theater of cultural exchange, which was as often friendly as it was contentious.[8] Inhabited as the region was by various competing political and imperial interests, the Mediterranean offered a geographic setting through which cultural plurality could be discursively and dramatically depicted, where multiple forms of border-crossing were encouraged, adopted, and ultimately contained. For the English, who were on the periphery of this hotbed of cross-cultural activity, the remote geography of the Mediterranean

Figure I.1 *Map of western Mediterranean,* from George Sandys *Relation of a Journey.* LUNA: Folger Digital Image Collection, Folger Shakespeare Library.

provided the opportunity to depict cultural, ethnic, racial, and social differences as a means to entertain and instruct their domestic audiences. These discourses, of which early modern English drama served as a critical element, performed vital ideological work in bringing the foreign home and rendering it legible.

As Mary Louise Pratt has aptly argued, such discourses "created the imperial order for Europeans 'at home' and gave them their place in it."[9] While Pratt's investigation focuses on travel writing, early modern drama, influenced as it was by such news from voyaging abroad, can also be indexed under that rubric. In fact, early modern English drama's pronounced interest in the foreign aligns its commercial and entertainment agendas through English culture's burgeoning enthusiasm for overseas mercantile and imperial expansion.

The preferred Mediterranean setting of early modern English dramas promised a material and figurative geography through which to play with the fears, anxieties, and desires generated by personal, political, and cultural encounters with differences. In her study on "contact zones," Pratt defines such arenas as "social spaces where disparate cultures meet, clash, and grapple with each other, often in highly asymmetrical relations of domination and subordination—such as colonialism and slavery, or their aftermaths as they are lived out across the globe today."[10] While contact zones are organized around and through the relations of power that inhere within those spaces, they can also disrupt those relations, and offer opportunities for encounters that negotiate power rather than simply adhering to the norm. As Pratt discloses, the contact zone is

often synonymous with "colonial frontier." But while the latter term is grounded within a European expansionist perspective (the frontier is a frontier only with respect to Europe), "contact zone" shifts the center of gravity and the point of view. It invokes the space and time where subjects previously separated by geography and history are co-present, the point at which their trajectories now intersect. The term "contact" foregrounds the interactive, improvisational dimensions of imperial encounters so easily ignored or suppressed by accounts of conquest and domination told from the invader's perspective. A "contact" perspective emphasizes how subjects get constituted in and by their relations to each other. It treats the relations among colonizers and colonized, or travelers and "travelees," not in terms of separateness, but in terms of co-presence, interaction, interlocking understandings and practices, and often within radically asymmetrical relations of power.[11]

Pratt's theorization of this geography depends upon active, protean, and fluid negotiations of power, culture, and identity that allow for new and different relations to emerge because of the dynamism fostered by the contact zone. Indeed, the "contact perspective" she advocates is one that facilitates reading and meaning-making practices, and challenges the dominant form of knowledge production because it attends to the fluctuations and instabilities promoted by the contact zone. Pratt's paradigm suggests new interpretive avenues for considering the Mediterranean settings of Shakespeare's plays by highlighting the negotiated, "improvisational" modes that attend to moments of encounter in a geography that facilitates traffic and exchange in peoples, goods, ideas, and ways of being.

To think of Shakespeare's and much of early modern drama's Mediterranean setting as a "contact zone," means thinking spatially or geographically. By this, I do not mean source studies or critical investigations that, at least thus far, have not engaged with the foundational insights offered by the discipline of geography, particularly theories of how space is constituted on a social, lived, and experienced level.[12] Geography, and particularly the subfield of feminist geography, designates not just landscape and topography but the arrangement of space by and for human survival and interaction. Often, scholarly and critical considerations of Shakespeare's geography have framed landscapes and seascapes through an imperial or colonial lens in order to demarcate those topographies. As a discipline, geography is steeped and implicated in such meaning-making practices, which focus on creating totalized knowledge about the world.[13] Feminist geographer Gillian Rose demonstrates how these ideological underpinnings are simultaneously masculinist and imperial, since they assume that "in principle, the world can be fully known and understood. [...] The founding fathers of geography wanted to render the world amenable to the operation of masculinist reason, and thus sought a kind of knowledge that would apply universally."[14] Rose further points out how the desire for such universal knowledge was also created by those who unquestioningly accepted their own position as universal subjects:

> They made no connection between the world as it was seen and the position of the viewer, and the truth of what they saw was established by that claim to objectivity. Their denial of their partiality was both produced by, and reproduced, their power as master subjects. And it is important to note, in the context of the imperialist origins of geography, that not only did a masculinity enable this claim to its exhaustiveness; so too did the whiteness of these geographers.[15]

Thus, the represented world created via the discipline of geography disguised its ideological commitments to the normative, white, masculine, and western subject while purporting to offer control of that world through its universal epistemological practices. Feminist geography's challenge to the discipline is to argue for the necessity of women's partial and subjective knowledge and to focus on how women occupy and experience space. Attending to women as geographers, as agents in theorizing spatial relations, means reevaluating ideas of universality and univocality in what and how geography signifies and creates meaning.

The semiotics and norms of geography are further challenged by investigations that center race within spatial arrangements and argue that spatial relations are racial relations.[16] In "The Space that Race Makes," David Delaney points out that the racialization of space may be easier for the majority culture to observe in constructs like "the inner city" or "ghetto," yet "geographies of race" likewise include "the gated community," "the boardroom," and the "home."[17] The point might seem obvious, but it deserves reiterating because it emphasizes the invisibility of whiteness as a racialized position, while simultaneously mandating an examination of the power that accrues to whiteness because of this invisibility. Expanding this provocation, Delaney contends that racialization affects not only the function of space, but also how space is experienced by white and non-white racialized subjects:

> Spaces may be produced in accordance with ideologies of color-blindness or race consciousness, of integrationism, assimilationism, separatism, or nativism. These race-centered ideologies combine with other ideological elements—such as those centered on public-private, ownership, sexuality, citizenship, democracy, or crime—and with other axes of power to produce the richly textured, highly variegated, and power-laden spatialities of everyday life. The question for geographers might then be: how does the racial formation shape space, give meanings to places, and condition the experience of embodied subjects emplaced in and moving through the material world?[18]

Rather than being value-neutral, geographies are implicated within a network of political relations that include sex, gender, class, and race, which affect their signifying and meaning-making possibilities. As Delaney emphasizes, "elements of the social (race, gender, and so on) are not simply *reflected* in spatial arrangements; rather, spatialities are regarded as *constituting and/or reinforcing* aspects of the social."[19] Delaney's claim underscores how the norms and regulations informing the use and function of geographies allows them to be active agents in creating and administering hegemonic norms. As Black feminist geographer Katherine McKittrick argues, the "naturalization of difference" is a vital part of the intellectual and imperial commitments of geography as a discipline, which seeks to "spatialize" difference in order to locate "where nondominant groups 'naturally' belong."[20] In other words, geographic analysis colludes with other epistemological practices that seek to make difference knowable via strategies of control and domination as well as appeals to a so-called natural order. McKittrick further contends that

> geographic domination, then, is conceptually and materially bound up with racial-sexual displacement and the knowledge-power of a unitary vantage point. It is not a finished or immovable act, but it does signal unjust spatial practices; it is not a natural system, but rather a working system that manages the social world. It is meant to recognize the hierarchies of human and inhuman persons and reveal how this social categorization is also a contested geographic project.[21]

The questions of belonging and displacement that animate McKittrick's analysis of Black women's geographies are also relevant to early modern discourses which fabricate and represent human and geographic difference for their domestic reading and theater-going audiences. By spatializing difference in land and people, early modern writers were also participating in imperial knowledge-making practices; moreover, they were actively constructing race through geography via the expansionist agenda that spurred their overseas ventures in the Mediterranean, the Atlantic, and beyond. To write about the Mediterranean in this period is to contemplate more than a geography that yokes Europe to Africa to Asia, it is to write about the movement of people—free and unfree, coerced and voluntary—within this space. These people and their movements constructed the manifold cultures and norms of the Mediterranean and established the contours of its racial composition and ideologies. Scholars working in and on "the Black Mediterranean" have cogently demonstrated that theorizations of the Mediterranean as *Mare Nostrum*, "the classical, Mediterranean Studies model of the basin as a unitary sea" are rooted in the erasure of the enslaved movement of Black people across this geography, which has a long premodern history and contemporary relevance in the migrant and refugee crisis in Europe.[22] Camilla Hawthorne critiques the popular construction of Mediterranean identity as a model of cultural pluralism, arguing that "political mobilizations of Mediterraneanness are not wholly innocent," because they often "work in practice to *exclude* Blackness," a strategy that relies on "invoking historical relationships with North Africa, while metaphorically severing the deep pan-African ties that traverse the entirety of the Mediterranean basin."[23] For example, Hawthorne points to the Mediterranean as a geography that troubled and disturbed the racial project of Italian unification which sought to harness historical and racial ties to whiteness, but was challenged in this aim because of Africa's proximity to the Italian Peninsula and the longue durée of movement and exchange between peoples. The "Black Mediterranean," thus, signals the historical, material, and political presence of African people in this space and the intimacies of their encounters with and within Europe. For scholars of Shakespeare, Hawthorne's argument opens up an important area of study, since many of his plays are set in an Italy that has often and uncritically been represented as white. Analysis of the uses of geography, particularly the imagined geography of the Mediterranean within Shakespeare's oeuvre, requires attending to these "social" spatial arrangements and the movement of people within these spaces, especially since they inform conditions of encounter in his plays.

I undertake such analysis of Shakespeare's works here and offer interpretations that critically reevaluate the static positioning of this geography as only and always imaginative, classical, or purely European and Eurocentric. The Mediterranean geography of Shakespeare's plays is far removed from the reality of the early modern Mediterranean as a region shaped and dominated by Muslim imperial powers. Examining his representation of that space as deliberate and exclusionary, as part of a project of European worldmaking, reveals the cultural and ideological contours of the plays and their insistence on a Mediterranean void of the religious, racial, and cultural differences that formed its quotidian reality.

Understanding geography as relationally inflected by forms of domination and subordination brings me to another important category of analysis in *Shakespeare through Islamic Worlds*: race. Early modern English and European representations of Islam and Muslims focused on their religious and cultural difference as signs of both alterity and incompatibility with European Christian cultures. This delineation is important because Europeans were beginning to define themselves and their cultural superiority through opposition to Jewish and Muslim identities.[24] In this way, early modern constructions of Muslim identity possess striking resonances to contemporary western prejudices. Marking the shift in racism from the "old," biologically rooted prejudices and bigotries to the "new," Etienne Balibar argues that twentieth- and twenty-first-century Islamophobia is grounded on the idea that Muslims are culturally incommensurate with western traditions and values. Liberal chauvinism facilitates this form of bigotry by instantiating a cultural hierarchy and rendering culture and values through the somatic register.[25] Balibar posits that "the 'different' cultures are those which constitute obstacles, or which are established as obstacles [...] to the acquisition of culture."[26] The unmodified culture of the dominant tradition becomes inherently inaccessible to those belonging to "different" cultures, resulting in the resurgence of pseudo-biological racism. In this analysis, what such ideologies "aim to explain is not the constitution of races, but the vital importance of cultural closures and traditions for the accumulation of individual aptitudes, and, most importantly, the 'natural' biases of xenophobia and social aggression."[27] By erecting protective borders around European or white Christian culture, such strategies simultaneously authorize and naturalize bigotry, prejudice, and racism through discourses of cultural belonging. The immediate context of Balibar's study into "the new racism" is contemporary xenophobia driven by increased immigration from the Global South and formerly colonized states to imperialist Global North nations; however, similar ideas about cultural and religious superiority animate early modern representations of Islam, Muslims, and the cultures and geographies that they inhabit.

In early modern Europe, Muslim alterity was frequently rooted in its perceived religious and cultural difference from western European Christian culture, and part of my argument in *Shakespeare through Islamic Worlds* is that this Otherness was functional in the more recognizable formulation of "old racism" as well. By highlighting this element of Islamic representation by non-Muslim European writers and discourses, I want to trouble the distinction that Balibar seeks to make between "new" and "old" racism, not to suggest a continuity of racism that holds steadfast from the early modern period to our own contemporary moment, but rather to enumerate how race and racism are active, dynamic, and fluid ideas, discourses, and structures capable of adapting to the needs and specificities of the dominant order that brings them into being. Indeed, looking at the longue durée of race and racism makes it quite clear that ontological and epistemological conceptions of race have changed over the ensuing centuries, moving from the religious, to the biological, to the social.[28] This shifting or fluid characteristic of race exhibits its malleability, which has allowed it to signify differing relations of power across time and space.

In order to apprehend how race works and how it was and continues to be mobilized, it is important to understand what race is. Commonplace and commonsense definitions of race identify it as a sign of human biological difference, usually observed through physical or bodily markers. While race operates via the visual register, making itself legible through phenotype, it is not simply a matter that is skin deep. By manifesting in the body, race has a "biological referent" that acts as its "guarantor of truth," yet race is also a system of power and subordination wherein bodies are made to signify social, political, moral, and cultural status.[29] Stuart Hall explains that as a "signifier" race carries "discursive power." Race makes no truth claims; rather, it exhibits "what is *made* to be true. Such is the way racial discourses operate."[30] Thus, the differing values that are assigned to certain skin colors, for example, are made "real" through behavior that corroborates those values. Hall elaborates by noting that

> racial discourses produce, mark and fix the infinite differences and diversities of human beings through a rigid binary coding. That logic establishes a chain of correspondences both between the physical and the cultural, between intellectual and cognitive characteristics; it gives legibility to a social system in which it operates; it allows us to decipher different signifiers from the racial fixing of the signifier "race": and through that reading it organizes, regulates, and gives meaning to social practices through the distribution of symbolic and material resources between different groups and the establishment of racial hierarchy.[31]

Hall's articulation of the discursive logics of race and its affordances discloses the system of benefit and advantage that race-based societies construct. By only focusing on the biological and phenotypic, the commonplace understanding obscures race's systemic operations and effects while also fixing its meaning in the body and eliding its relation to the other categories of power and knowledge through which it comes into being. Hall's formulation of race as a discourse illuminates the similarities and differences of racial discourses across time, which, in turn, obviates the need for defining race and racism as either "old" or "new." The character of race

Introduction

is itself fluid and changing according to the social and taxonomic practices that imbue it with meaning.

Early modern racial discourses harness this expansive signifying capacity of race. Rather than exhibiting the scientific, biological, and taxonomic qualities and definitions of race that come to be assigned to it in the wake of seventeenth- and eighteenth-century European imperial plunder, bondage, and enslavement in Africa and the Americas, as well as the Enlightenment's scientific and philosophical revolutions, early modern mobilizations of race demonstrate its dexterity through the flexible ways in which it was being formed.[32] Race was an emergent category of human differentiation and organization in the period that bolstered European overseas imperial expansion. In her magisterial study *Things of Darkness*, Kim F. Hall argues that English colonial projects, which were furthered by mercantile voyages of the early modern period, necessitated social control over domestic subjects, such as women, and required the construction and maintenance of normative identity through "tropes of blackness."[33] In Hall's analysis, "tropes of blackness" were capable of representing a "broad" ensemble of identities that included various groups ranging from Indigenous peoples of the Americas to the Irish yet still acquired "power from England's ongoing negotiations of African difference and from the implied color comparison therein."[34] Hall further develops the connection between race, blackness, and early modern gendered constructions of beauty, uncovering the intersectional register through which race came into being in the period. She establishes the importance of noting the operations of race, racial thinking, and racism in the color-coded aesthetic discourse of the period, highlighting the somatic as a vital schema through which race comes into being and accrues material power in the early modern period.

Representations of Islam and Muslims often accessed this color-coded dimension, particularly on the English stage. As I observed earlier, if we are looking for Muslims in Shakespeare's work, we can definitely (maybe) find them in his "Moors." Somatic, physical, and epidermalized difference is often yoked to religious difference in the period. Even if the characters are not represented as brown and dark-skinned African men (and in my view both the Prince of Morocco and Othello are), the works offer enough evidence to demonstrate the spiritual blackening of Muslims.[35] Early modern European discourses of religious difference often located that difference in the body via blood or through rituals, like circumcision, in which those religions engaged. Thus, both Jewish and Muslim difference from Christianity came to be signaled through forms of racializing that were also embodied. Spain's *limpieza de sangre* or blood purity laws legislated *Converso*, *Marrano*, and *Morisco* as "New Christian" identities, barring Christian descendants of Jews and Muslims from holding certain public offices.[36] Religious identity was being constructed through the body, through blood, and through the heritability of that blood to pass on non-Christian religious and cultural affiliation. At the same time that Europeans were developing racial theories rooted in color, geography, and culture, they were also fabricating race through religion. Iberian blood purity laws are an example of a racial project that promotes the purity of "Old Christian" blood and posits the blood of "New Christians" as polluted, corrupt, and suspect. These laws, then, enforced difference by legislating the social and political life of *Conversos*, based on prior religious affiliation and the underlying notion that Judaism and Islam left traces in the blood that prevented sincere conversion to Christianity.[37] By this logic, non-Christian religion was racialized as impure and Christianity simultaneously racialized as pure. The racialization of religion exhibits the power and malleability of race as discourse and as a system of domination and subordination. As Ania Loomba notes, "religion should not obscure or undermine the place of somatic difference; instead, we need to locate how the two come together and transform each other in the early modern period."[38] Rather than being discrete discourses, then, race and religion often work in tandem to manufacture an alterity that stands outside the bounds of the emerging nation and its preferred normative identity.

As my example of Iberian blood purity legislation and enforcement reveals, Islam and Muslims have been essential to emerging European articulations of race and racialization. In *Terrifying Muslims* Junaid Rana argues that "from the inception of the race concept, Islam has been at the center of creating, representing, and justifying a system of dominance and control that has shifted according to historical context and practice."[39] Tracing his analysis from the early modern period, through the Iberian fabrication of blood as a marker of religion, corruption, or purity, and to more contemporary representations of Muslims as dangerous Others within western national security discourses, Rana contends that

the racialized Muslim developed as a geographically external other that was demonized not only through notions of the body, but also through the superimposition of cultural features onto Muslim and non-Muslim groups. Because this process was not based exclusively on phenotypic or physical difference (although this was often imputed), some have been able to use a strategy of dissimulation—that

is, disguising or concealing religious difference—to keep
themselves from being interpreted in racial terms.[40]

Islam was, then, instrumental to the consolidation of European
white Christianity and empire-building. Soham Patel and
M. Bilal Nassir have argued that

the figure of the Muslim [...] occupies an important racialized
position as a theological and political "other" that the West
continues to draw upon to shape and organize modern
systems of capital accumulation, land dispossession,
warfare, policing, and modern state sovereignty.[41]

The ideological positioning allotted to Islam and Muslims
locates them as different and threatening; moreover, the historical development of racial discourses which were formed
in and through white European Christian contact with and
managing of Islam, racialized both their danger and difference. Consequently, many Islamic studies scholars prefer
the term anti-Muslim racism over Islamophobia because
the former "more accurately reflects the intersection of race
and religion as a reality of structural inequality and violence
rooted in the longer history of U.S. (and European) empire
building," while the latter is framed as a "problem of individual bias or individual fear."[42] They further emphasize that

conceptually, a focus on anti-Muslim racism is connected
to an analysis of history and forms of dominance—from
white supremacy, slavery, and settler colonialism to
multiculturalism and the security logics of war and
imperialism—that produce various forms of racial exclusion
as well as incorporation into racist structures.[43]

Such precision in naming is important because, as Rana notes, many western analyses of race have obfuscated the role of anti-Muslim racism in their accounts of the historical development of racializing discourses in the period. I use both Islamophobia and anti-Muslim racism throughout *Shakespeare through Islamic Worlds* to point to the individual and systemic Othering of Islam in early modern texts. Figuring Muslims as racialized underscores the protean quality of racial discourses in both the early modern period and in our own time, their unending capacity to shift and accommodate the mandates of power.

Part of my argument in *Shakespeare through Islamic Worlds* is that Shakespeare's exclusion of Islam and Muslims in his plays positions them outside of (and as outsiders to) Europe through the interlinking modalities of geography and race, despite the known reality of the Muslim Mediterranean. While this phrasing might strike my readers as an exaggeration, recall that almost the entirety of the eastern Mediterranean was under Ottoman dominion during this period, while the southern Mediterranean was under the control of the so-called Barbary states, which were also Muslim and often allied or affiliated with the Ottoman Empire. Shakespeare's "European" Mediterranean is the stuff of fantasy. It requires the wholesale rejection of history and current events to imagine this geography as being free from Muslim presence or influence. It further requires the idea of a Europe in which Islam has no historical presence, an idea belied by the Arab and North African conquests of Iberia early in the eighth century (711 CE).[44] Those medieval Muslim incursions and settlements created an Islamic culture in Iberia which lasted for centuries, until the joint forces of Castile and Aragon, headed by Ferdinand and Isabella routed the last Muslim kingdom of Grenada on the peninsula

(1492). The construction of Europe as a unified religious culture around Christianity depends upon the Islamic presence in and of Europe. At the same time that Iberia began to construct its identity through the expulsion of Islam from Christian Europe, the Ottomans became a powerful imperial force on the eastern end of the Mediterranean basin. In 1453 Fatih Sultan Mehmet—or Mehmet the Conqueror—successfully laid siege to and captured the capital of Byzantium and the Eastern Roman Empire, Constantinople. This singular, "worldmaking" event announced the Ottoman arrival on the European imperial scene, and resulted in the Ottoman sultans framing themselves as the Caesars of Rome, by virtue of inheritance by conquest.[45] The loss of Constantinople, along with other Ottoman military campaigns into Europe by Mehmet and his successors in the fifteenth and sixteenth centuries, demonstrated European vulnerability to the highly efficient Ottoman military machine, and testified to the longue durée of Muslim peoples' presence in Europe. I draw attention to the European character of Constantinople or Istanbul because I am problematizing how the geopolitical construction "Eastern Europe" has been mobilized in order to exclude Islam and the Ottoman Empire from European dominions proper.[46] In other words, if the Ottoman dominion over Europe can be discursively circumscribed to the geopolitical entity fabricated as "Eastern Europe," then "Western Europe," the seat of so much imperial dominance in later periods, is free from Ottoman influence, control, and "pollution." Such maneuvers are still more discursive strategies that reveal the influence of racism—old and new—and Orientalism within representations of Islam in Europe.

By the time of Shakespeare's writing (from the 1590s to the 1610s), Islam had been in and was an important part of

Europe for many centuries. Christian Europe's familiarity with Islam resulted in the forms of containment that I outlined earlier, such as the geographical and the racial. While it is not fashionable to talk about Orientalism in the context of the early modern period—indeed many of my readers will be tempted to object to the term—it is a framework that unearths the process of Othering of Islam, its peoples, and geographies in order to ideologically, discursively, and materially manage and control them. The bulk of Edward Said's monumental study, *Orientalism* (1978), concerns the high period of European imperial expansion into the Islamicate dominions of the "Near East" and argues that "Orientalism is a style of thought based upon an ontological and epistemological distinction made between 'the Orient' and (most of the time) 'the Occident.'"[47] The geographic distinction between east and west, as well as the critical position, the "style of thought," are vital because they root/route Said's claims about the ideological work that Orientalism does and the material ends it serves. He makes explicit that "the Orient" and "the Occident" are "man-made" constructs, and like "the West itself, the Orient is an idea that has a history and a tradition of thought, imagery, and vocabulary that have given it a reality and presence in and for the West."[48] While the geographies and cultures of the east are real, material, and historical entities, Said's point about the Orient is that it was an ideological construct that served "the Occident"; this "relationship" was one of "power, of domination, of varying degrees of a complex hegemony."[49] In this view, "the Orient was Orientalized not only because it was discovered to be 'Oriental' in all those ways considered commonplace by the average nineteenth-century European, but also because it could be—that is, submitted to being—made Oriental."[50]

Said's focus is on a geographic and ideological locale already under the purview of European colonial domination. That was certainly not the case in the early modern period. Many scholars object to Said's totalizing conception, which fixes Europeans and non-Europeans within an epistemological and ideological frame that does not allow agency or fluidity.[51] Moreover, early modern scholars discount Said's analysis on the basis of periodization.[52] The power dynamics between the imperial regimes of early modern Europe and the "Near East" were quite different from those of the nineteenth century. Rather than being colonized by the British and French—the focus of Said's study—eastern, Islamic powers were often colonizing Europe, as is the case with the Ottoman Empire. Consequently, so the argument goes, material power was differently distributed and the hegemony of thought that Said identifies was not present.

The colonial and imperial arrangements of the early modern period were, indeed, divergent from those of later centuries; however, Said's insights about the discourse that manufactures the Orient to confirm and conform to European ideas and stereotypes remain relevant. It is, in fact, the discursive power of Orientalism that has allowed it to be so enduring, continuing on into our present moment through the logics of the War on Terror and contemporary forms of Islamophobia and anti-Muslim racism. In the premodern, however, this discourse was being formed through the various encounters that European Christians had with Islamicate cultures and Muslim peoples. Said's thesis, that the Orient "is not only adjacent to Europe; it is also the place of Europe's greatest and richest, and oldest colonies, the source of its civilizations and languages, its cultural contestant, and one of its deepest and most recurring images of the Other carries some currency for the early modern period."[53] In particular, the proximity of the Orient to the Occident, the shifting relations of power, and the Orient's fabrication as a site and sight of difference or Otherness through which Europeans constructed their own cultural and individual identities provide an analytic for interpreting early modern Christian European encounters with Islam and Muslims. I rely on Said's theorization of Orientalism in *Shakespeare through Islamic Worlds* because it offers a way of seeing, understanding, and apprehending Islam in early modern English discourses as a racialized Other. Moreover, it exposes the fiction that a lack of material power over Muslims means that demonizing ideologies were absent in works that range from drama to travel literature. Indeed, it seems to me that much of the deliberate occlusions and evasions of Said's method rely on a need to morally secure the early modern period from the imperial degradations that ensue in the following centuries. Thus, we can be said to study texts, authors, and genres that are rhetorically and politically innocent of those implications.

In *Orientalism* Said emphasizes the need to interpret "representations *as representations*, not as 'natural' depictions of the Orient," and requires attention "not [to] the correctness of the representation," but rather to its "exteriority," which "is always governed by some version of the truism that if the Orient could represent itself, it would; since it cannot, the representation does the job."[54] These representations harness a wide range of early modern stereotypes about Islam and Muslims, including but certainly not limited to their perceived violence (as exhibited through their military successes), their sexuality or venality (as illustrated by sites such as the harem),

and their superstitious nature (as embodied by their misbelief).[55] These qualities acquire the status of truth through their
repetition—or citationality as Said calls it—and the geopolitical realities that inform how Islam and Muslims should
be considered, approached, and ultimately managed.[56] Thus,
early modern drama, including Shakespeare's plays exhibit
the values of the culture that produces those artifacts and
discourses and is complicit in "the nexus of knowledge and
power creating 'the Oriental' and in a sense obliterating him
as a human being."[57]

Orientalism as a theory captures many of the geographic
and racial contours of Shakespearean representations of
Islam; further, Orientalism informs how some scholars have
approached this topic in the field of Shakespeare studies. My
readers will have noticed that in this book I consistently use
Islam and Muslims to refer to the religion and its adherents.
This naming convention may not have been the usual practice
in the early modern period, wherein the prejudicial terms
"Mahometanism" and "Mahometan" were commonly but not
always employed. In fact, Samuel Purchas in his Purchas, His
Pilgrimage, or, Relations of the World (1614) uses "Muhammed"
to refer to the prophet in his discussion of the Arab Muslim
conquests of North Africa.[58] This section is replete with historically accurate information about the transmission of political power after the death of the prophet. Purchas's use of
Muhammed here is a claim to authority. It allows him to
demonstrate his capacious and accurate knowledge about
Islam, its history, and practices to his readers. It establishes
his credibility, and so when he then returns to "Mahomet,"
or "Mahumetan," or "Mahometisme" these usages suggest a
return to a vocabulary and idiom that is not about accuracy

but about discrediting the religion and its prophet based on the authority that he has already established.[59] He gets to be the one to name and define Islam and its figurehead. Such a rhetorical move is deeply implicated in religious ideology that seeks to religiously invalidate and Other Islam. These terms are Orientalist, and not usages that are correct or preferred by Muslims.

Scholarly choices to deploy historic and archaic terminology for Islam and Muslims exhibit at best a deep ambivalence toward their object of study and at worst latent, cultural Islamophobia. Scholarship that chooses an inflated and artificial allegiance to historical accuracy by employing descriptors that were current in the period about which they are writing, regardless of the dehumanizing damage they may be doing to their Muslim readers when they encounter these words, is scholarship rooted in Orientalism.[60] It deliberately Others Islam and Muslims now, in the contemporary moment, in order to align with—or remain authentic to—premodern discourses, which, as this scholarship reveals, were often quite hostile to Islam. By using this language, such work corroborates the ideologies within those discourses and reveals its own Orientalist genealogical inheritance and affiliation. It is a mode of citation, announcing the scholar's

strategic location, which is a way of describing the author's position in a text with regard to the Orientalist material he writes about, and strategic formation, which is a way of analyzing the relationship between texts and the way in which groups of texts, types of texts, even textual genres acquire mass density and referential power among themselves and thereafter in the culture at large.[61]

Adherence to such notions of historical purity reveals the ideological underpinnings of the work; further, they announce a deliberate lack of care for a community already demonized and marginalized in western culture at large through the west's War on Terror, whose theater of engagement has been primarily in Muslim-majority countries. On a rhetorical level, it shows that Islam has no place in the study of Shakespeare and early modern literature. It makes it easy to say: "there were no Muslims back then because early modern people did not use that word to describe them." It further negates inquiry into these topics by policing what can and cannot be said about Islam and Muslims through this strict reliance on vocabulary and nomenclature. While Shakespeare and his contemporaries may have lacked this language, we do not. Finally, it is worth repeating that the audience of our scholarship is not living in the early modern period. They are people who will understand that the use of Islam and Muslims may be anachronistic, but it is an ethically sound rhetorical and political choice. I linger on this point because it is vital to examine our own social locations and ideological investments when we are doing scholarly work about communities that have historically been marginalized within the western canon. My call for being deliberate about naming practices is not about stifling speech or "canceling" language, but rather it is about understanding that early modern English and European discourses about Islam secured Christian supremacy. The words they used to describe the religion, its prophet, and its followers expose these religious and cultural investments. Being attentive to these nuances allows us to move beyond the binary of positive or negative images, and to consider the function they serve within the discourses in which they appear, while also advancing our own commitment to an ethics that grants full humanity to Muslims.

Even if the words Islam and Muslims were not *au courant* for early modern Christian European writers, there was no shortage of ink spilled about them. From travel writing to diplomatic accounts to private letters between the queen and the Ottoman sultan's mother, Islamicate cultures were both objects of curiosity and matters of state.[62] The lack of material presence should not, as *Shakespeare through Islamic Worlds* argues, foreclose the possibility of Islam and Muslims being important to the worldmaking projects in which writers like Shakespeare were engaged. My readers might, at this juncture, want to know what kind of knowledge early modern English writers possessed about Islam and Muslims. While news of military conflicts between Muslims and Christians was plentiful, often disseminated from the pulpit, there was a distinct lack of knowledge about Islam as a theology.[63]

Nonetheless, as Matthew Dimmock enumerates the Prophet Muhammad was something of a celebrity in early modern English culture, a "defining and often divisive figure."[64] For Dimmock, the prophet, almost exclusively referred to as "Mahomet," becomes a trope through which the English interrogate notions of religious legitimacy. In these discourses, "Mahomet" was depicted in numerous divergent forms in poetry, drama, and prose of different genres; he was invoked from pulpits, related stories, declaimed by travelers and polemically paralleled with Christ, Luther, various popes, and almost every English monarch in the period. His image appeared in political and religious tracts and pamphlets, in chronicle histories and in English prayerbooks, and hung on the wall of at least one noble household. In early modern and enlightenment England he was ubiquitous to the point that his invocation became a shorthand for a whole range of associations.[65]

Although the Qur'an was available to elite and learned European audiences from the twelfth century onward, through Robert of Ketton's Latin translation, *The Law of the Pseudo-Prophet Muhammad and the Arabic Koran* (1143), there is scant evidence that Shakespeare or his contemporaries were familiar with Islam beyond polemic.[66] As its title suggests, the translation worked to simultaneously make Islam and its theology knowable and to discredit it as any kind of divine truth. It was not until 1649 that Alexander Ross translated the Qur'an into English, not from Arabic but from a French translation.[67] I would hesitate to argue, however, that English knowledge about Islam be measured against the dearth of translations of its holy book.

Many histories of the Ottoman Empire written or translated by English writers frequently included as prefatory material information about the origins of Islam, which featured lurid and sensational accounts of the Prophet Muhammad dying trampled by swine while drunk or training a dove to whisper in his ear, which his misguided followers took to be a miracle confirming his prophethood.[68] These histories usually contained material about rituals and observances such as the five daily prayers required of Muslims, the ablutions performed before prayer, fasting, sex-segregation, and circumcision, and further included knowledge about religious and cultural divisions between Muslim polities, such as sectarian differences between Sunni and Shi'a Islam. Localized within ritual and practice as well as racialized ethnic identities such as "Moor," "Turk," or even the medieval "Saracen," Islam was for early modern Christian Europeans a cultural superstition or misbelief. As Benedict Robinson points out,

> Europe has always refused to treat Islam as a religion at all, preferring to inscribe it into theories of racial, political, and cultural difference, and thereby refusing to acknowledge Islam's own claims to universality while at the same time insisting that it is always the same, across vast reaches of time and space.[69]

European Christian "refusal" of Islam as a confessional or faith tradition does not in any way undermine the status of Islam as a major world religion in the early modern period and in our own time. Indeed, by circumscribing Islam, fixing it, as it were, to certain European understandings, norms, and conditions, European Christian discourses display their ideological investments in bounding a rapidly growing religion and the expansionist empires which espoused this faith. If Islam could be discursively "inscribed"—to borrow Robinson's word—then it could be marked and located, controlled within the matrix of knowledge if not through material power. Such acts are reproduced in Shakespeare's works, which restrict the plurality of identity within the Mediterranean so as to avoid acknowledging the power of Islam and Muslims in that space.

Shakespeare through Islamic Worlds challenges these refusals. This study uncovers the textual traces of Islam and Muslims in Shakespeare's work, while offering a methodology for how to read the Islamic presence through these troped phantasms. While the Islamic worlds of the early modern period were as vast as the worlds of Islam are in our current era, Shakespeare through Islamic Worlds confines its study primarily to the region of the Mediterranean, the common setting for many of Shakespeare's plays. The rationale underpinning the geographical restrictions and limitations of my inquiry is that no study of Islamic cultures can cover them in their entirety. Islam is a global religion, and its cultures are vast, spanning several continents, cultural, linguistic, ethnic, racial, and confessional traditions. Islam as practiced by the Ottomans (Sunni) was different from that practiced in Safavid Iran (Shi'a). The cultures within those two imperial societies were also heterogenous. Therefore, to make grand, sweeping, or totalizing claims about an "Islamic world" would be to fall into an Orientalist critical mode that I have every interest in dismantling. *Shakespeare through Islamic Worlds*, the title of this book, signals my aversion to the quotidian phrase, "the Islamic world," which hegemonizes and homogenizes the spectrum of Muslim cultures under an artificial construct usually deployed to Otherize Islamicate societies from those of the west. Despite the valiant attempts made by early modern English discourses to organize and unify many of the differences they encountered within the Muslim cultures with which they trafficked and exchanged, their understanding of Islamicate societies signaled their plurality. Muslim worlds are vast and this study aims to uncover a sliver of what they encompass.

The premise that guides my investigation—what did Shakespeare have to say about Islam—might suggest that this book is an attempt to elevate Islam and Muslims through Shakespeare's cultural capital, or that it is a "woke" attempt to make Shakespeare diverse and inclusive by forcing Islam on him, or even more insidiously to exhibit Shakespeare's universality by discovering his interest in these matters. None of these reasons underlie my inquiry. The purpose, rather, of *Shakespeare through Islamic Worlds* is to demonstrate how Shakespeare's works deliberately excise and erase the Islamic presence from the geographies to which it belongs. Instead of corroborating the universalist position by showing how Shakespeare's engagement with Islam validates it and Muslims—a culturally chauvinistic and white supremacist attitude—this book argues that Shakespeare's sidelining of Islam and Muslims, his confining them to tropes and topoi, reveals his imaginative investment in European Christian cultural purity. If Shakespeare's universality accords marginalized identities a form of humanity because they are depicted in his oeuvre, what claims to humanity can Muslims make when they are definitely (maybe) removed from them? Universality is damaging when it becomes a cudgel, which is why that is not the critical orientation of this book. *Shakespeare through Islamic Worlds* instead advocates for readings that show how Islamic cultures and their practices formed a shadow, alternate, or Other world through which Shakespeare could experiment with normative and hegemonic identities. Islam was conjured through referents, rituals, practices, racialization, and geography but also banished in favor of a return to the familiar order of things. Indeed, it is not coincidental that Shakespeare's so-called race plays are also the ones that contain characters who are definitely (maybe) Muslims or are set in geographies that facilitate easy cultural contact with Islamicate societies. This connection exhibits the racialized construction and representation of Muslims in the period, while also, then, making it possible to root/route them out of the restored social order that characterizes many of his endings. *Shakespeare through Islamic Worlds* looks for the repressed and hidden Muslim presence in Shakespeare's works in order to show that Shakespeare needed Islam and Muslims more than Islam and Muslims need(ed) Shakespeare.

NOTES

1 *Open Source Shakespeare: Concordance*, s.v. "Turks (n.)," "Arabians (n.)," "Sophys (n.)," "scimitars (n.)," "turbans (n.)," "Mahomet (n.)," www.opensourceshakespeare.org/concordance/

2 A.J. Caschetta, "'No Shakespeare' without Islam?" *The National Review* (June 26, 2022), www.nationalreview.com/2022/06/no-shakespeare-without-islam/

3 See Louis Wann, "The Oriental in Elizabethan Drama," *Modern Philology* 12.7 (1915): 389–456; Jonathan Burton, *Traffic and Turning: Islam and English Drama, 1579–1624* (Newark, DE: University of Delaware Press, 2005).

4 Dennis A. Britton, *Becoming Christian: Race, Reformation, and Early Modern English Romance* (New York: Fordham University Press, 2014).

5 Matthew Dimmock, "Shakespeare's Non-Christian Religions," *Shakespeare and Early Modern Religion*, ed. David Loewenstein and Michael Whitmore (Cambridge: Cambridge University Press, 2015), 297.

6 bell hooks, "Choosing the Margin as a Space of Radical Openness." *Framework: The Journal of Cinema and Media*, 36 (1989): 15–23.

7 I borrow the formulation of roots and routes from Paul Gilroy's *The Black Atlantic*, wherein this rhizomatic structure allows for the assemblage of western hemispheric and afro-diasporic identity and exhibits their influence on western worldmaking projects. Paul Gilroy, *The Black Atlantic: Modernity and Double Consciousness* (Cambridge: Harvard University Press, 1993), 3.

8 Mary Louise Pratt, *Imperial Eyes: Travel Writing and Transculturation* (London: Routledge, 2007).

9 Pratt, *Imperial Eyes*, 3.

10 Pratt, *Imperial Eyes*, 7.

11 Pratt, *Imperial Eyes*, 8.

12 *Narrative and Dramatic Sources of Shakespeare. Vol. 7: Major Tragedies: Hamlet, Othello, King Lear, Macbeth*, ed. Geoffrey Bullough (New York: Columbia University Press, 1975); Jean E. Howard, "Shakespeare, Geography, and the Work of Genre on the Early Modern Stage," *MLQ: Modern Language Quarterly* 64.3 (2003): 299–322; John Gillies, *Shakespeare and the Geography of Difference* (Cambridge: Cambridge University Press,

1994); Sarah Dustagheer, "Shakespeare and the 'Spatial Turn'," *Literature Compass* 10.7 (2013): 570–81.

13 David N. Livingstone. *The Geographical Tradition: Episodes in the History of a Contested Enterprise* (Cambridge, USA: Blackwell, 1993).

14 Gillian Rose, *Feminism & Geography: The Limits of Geographical Knowledge* (Minneapolis: University of Minnesota Press, 1993), 7.

15 Rose, *Feminism & Geography*, 7–8.

16 David Delaney, "The Space that Race Makes," *The Professional Geographer* 54.1 (2002), 8.

17 Delaney, "The Space that Race Makes," 6–7.

18 Delaney, "The Space that Race Makes," 7.

19 Delaney, "The Space that Race Makes," 7.

20 Katherine McKittrick, *Demonic Grounds: Black Women and the Cartographies of Struggle* (Minneapolis: University of Minnesota Press, 2006), xv.

21 McKittrick, *Demonic Grounds*, xvi.

22 Cristina Lombardi-Diop, "Preface," *The Black Mediterranean: Bodies, Borders, and Citizenship*, eds. Gabriele Proglio, et al. (New York: Palgrave MacMillan, 2021), 2–3.

23 Camilla Hawthorne, *Contesting Race and Citizenship: Youth Politics in the Black Mediterranean* (Ithaca: Cornell UP, 2022), 97.

24 I do not want to suggest that early modern Christianity was mono-lithic, in addition to the Protestant Reformation, Christian practice in the east, such as in Byzantium was different from Latin or Roman Catholicism. Rather, I want to emphasize that the idea of a unified Christendom was always at hand and at the ready in the face of Muslim imperial expansion within Europe.

25 Etienne Balibar and Immanuel Wallerstein, *Race, Nation, Class—Ambiguous Identities* (New York: Verso, 1991), 21–26.

26 Balibar and Wallerstein, *Race, Nation, Class*, 25.

27 Balibar and Wallerstein, *Race, Nation, Class*, 26.

28 Michael Omi and Howard Winant, *Racial Formation in the United States* (London: Routledge, 2014), 109–24.

29 Stuart Hall, "Subjects in History," *Selected Writings on Race and Difference*, ed. Paul Gilroy and Ruth Wilson Gilmore (Durham, NC: Duke University Press, 2021), 330.

30 Hall, "Subjects," 330.

31 Hall, "Subjects," 330.

32 Omi and Winant, *Racial Formation*.

33 Kim F. Hall, *Things of Darkness: Economies of Race and Gender in Early Modern England* (Ithaca, NY: Cornell University Press, 1995), 2–23.

34 Hall, *Things of Darkness*, 7.

35 Choosing identity markers in the twenty-first century for people who lived in the early modern period is a fraught process because it can be one of projecting identity onto people who would have defined themselves differently if they could have. In this book I use black, Black, and African in different ways to signal color, culture, and political self-identification. When I am quoting other scholars, I have not amended their use of Black, black, Blackness, or blackness, to signal the shifting political mobilization of these terms. For a more detailed rationale, please see endnote 1 on page 160.

36 Gregory B. Kaplan, "The Inception of *Limpieza de Sangre* (Purity of Blood) and Its Impact in Medieval and Golden Age Spain," *Marginal Voices: Studies in Converso Literature of Medieval and Golden Age Spain*, ed. Amy I. Aronson-Friedman and Gregory B. Kaplan (Leiden: Brill, 2012), 19–41.

37 Janet Adelman, *Blood Relations: Christian and Jew in The Merchant of Venice* (Chicago: University of Chicago Press, 2008).

38 Ania Loomba, *Shakespeare, Race, and Colonialism* (Oxford: Oxford University Press, 2002), 45.

39 Junaid Rana, *Terrifying Muslims: Race and Labor in the South Asian Diaspora*. (Durham: Duke University Press, 2011), 25.

40 Rana, *Terrifying Muslims*, 28.

41 Soham Patel and M. Bilal Nasir, "The Asianist Is Muslim," *Who Is the Asianist: The Politics of Representation in Asian Studies*, eds. Will bridges, Nitasha Tamar Sharma, and Marvin D. Sterling (New York: Columbia University Press, 2022), 79.

42 Junaid Rana, Evelyn Alsultany, Lara Deeb, Carol Fadda, Su'ad Abdul Khabeer, Arshad Ali, Sohail Daulatzai, Zareena Grewal, Juliane Hammer, and Nadine Naber. "Pedagogies of Resistance: Why Anti-Muslim Racism Matters." *Amerasia Journal* 46.1 (2020): 58.

43 Rana, et al., "Pedagogies of Resistance," 58.

44 Ramzi Rouighi, *Inventing the Berbers: History and Ideology in the Maghrib* (Philadelphia: University of Pennsylvania Press, 2019).

45 Jerry Brotton, *Trading Territories: Mapping the Early Modern World* (Ithaca: Cornell University Press, 1998), 92.

Introduction

46 I follow Daniel Goffman's lead in shifting the geographic perspective to consider the Ottoman presence in Europe through models that do not reproduce Orientalist modes of exclusion. See *The Ottoman Empire and Early Modern Europe* (Cambridge: Cambridge University Press, 2002), 6.

47 Edward Said, *Orientalism* (London: Penguin Classics, 2003), 2.

48 Said, *Orientalism*, 5.

49 Said, *Orientalism*, 5.

50 Said, *Orientalism*, 5–6.

51 Robert J.C. Young, *White Mythologies: Writing History and the West* (London: Routledge, 2004).

52 Daniel J. Vitkus, "Early Modern Orientalism: Representations of Islam in Sixteenth- and Seventeenth-Century Europe," *Western Views of Islam in Medieval and Early Modern Europe: Perception of Other*, ed. David R. Blanks and Michael Frassetto (New York: Palgrave Macmillan, 1999), 207–30; *The Dialectics of Orientalism in Early Modern Europe*, ed. Marcus Keller and Javier Irigoyen-García (New York: Palgrave, 2018), 2–3.

53 Said, *Orientalism*, 1.

54 Said, *Orientalism*, 21.

55 Said, *Orientalism*, 27.

56 Said, *Orientalism*, 20.

57 Said, *Orientalism*, 27.

58 Samuel Purchas, *Purchas, His Pilgrimage, or Relation of the World and the Religions Observed in all Ages and Places Discovered, from the Creation unto This Present*. London: William Stansby for Henrie Fetherstone, 1614. STC 20508.5, 635.

59 Purchas, 635.

60 One example of this is in Dimmock, "Shakespeare's Non-Christian Religions."

61 Said, *Orientalism*, 20.

62 Bernadette Andrea, *Women and Islam in Early Modern English Literature* (Cambridge: Cambridge University Press, 2008).

63 Samuel C. Chew, *The Crescent and the Rose: Islam and England during the Renaissance* (Oxford: Oxford University Press, 1937).

64 Matthew Dimmock, *Mythologies of the Prophet Muhammad in Early Modern English Culture* (London: Cambridge University Press, 2013), 7.

65 Dimmock, 7.

66 Bruce Lawrence, *The Qur'an: A Biography* (London: Atlantic Books Ltd, 2014), 31–32.

67 Lawrence, *The Qur'an*, 37.

68 Augustino Curione, Celio, *A Notable Historie of the Saracens Briefly and Faithfully Descrybing the Originall Beginning, Continuaunce and Successe Aswell of the Saracens, as also of Turkes, Souldans, Mamalukes, Assassines, Tartarians and Sophians. with a Discourse of their Affaires and Actes from the Byrthe of Mahomet their First péeuish Prophet and Founder for 700 yéeres Space. VVhereunto is Annexed a Compendious Chronycle of all their Yeerely Exploytes, from the Sayde Mahomets Time Tyll this Present Yeere of Grace. 1575. Drawn Out of Augustine Curio and Sundry Other Good Authours by Thomas Newton* [Sarracenicae historiae libri tres.]. London: 1575; Chew, *Crescent and the Rose*, 398–413.

69 Benedict S. Robinson, *Islam and Early Modern English Literature: The Politics of Romance from Spenser to Milton* (New York: Palgrave, 2007), 5.

REFERENCES

Adelman, Janet. *Blood Relations: Christian and Jew in The Merchant of Venice.* Chicago: University of Chicago Press, 2008.

Andrea, Bernadette. *Women and Islam in Early Modern English Literature.* Cambridge: Cambridge University Press, 2008.

Balibar, Etienne and Immanuel Wallerstein, *Race, Nation, Class—Ambiguous Identities.* New York: Verso, 1991.

Bullough, Geoffrey, ed. *Narrative and Dramatic Sources of Shakespeare, Major Tragedies: Hamlet, Othello, King Lear, Macbeth.* Vol. 7. New York: Columbia University Press, 1975.

Burton, Jonathan. *Traffic and Turning: Islam and English Drama, 1579–1624.* Newark, DE: University of Delaware Press, 2005.

Caschetta, A.J. "'No Shakespeare' Without Islam?" *The National Review.* June 26, 2022. www.nationalreview.com/2022/06/no-shakespeare-with out-islam/

Chew, Samuel C. *The Crescent and the Rose: Islam and England during the Renaissance.* Oxford: Oxford University Press, 1937.

Delaney, David. "The Space that Race Makes." *The Professional Geographer* 54.1 (2002): 6–14.

Dimmock, Matthew. *Mythologies of the Prophet Muhammad in Early Modern English Culture.* London: Cambridge University Press, 2013, 7.

————. "Shakespeare's Non-Christian Religions." *Shakespeare and Early Modern Religion*, edited by David Loewenstein and Michael Witmore, 280–99. Cambridge: Cambridge University Press, 2015.

Dustagheer, Sarah. "Shakespeare and the 'Spatial Turn'." *Literature Compass* 10.7 (2013): 570–81.

Gillies, John. *Shakespeare and the Geography of Difference*. Cambridge: Cambridge University Press, 1994.

Goffman, Daniel. *The Ottoman Empire and Early Modern Europe*. Cambridge: Cambridge University Press, 2002.

Hall, Kim F. *Things of Darkness: Economies of Race and Gender in Early Modern England*. Ithaca, NY: Cornell University Press, 1995.

Hall, Stuart. "Subjects in History." In *Selected Writings on Race and Difference*, edited by Paul Gilroy and Ruth Wilson Gilmore, 329–38. Durham, NC: Duke University Press, 2021.

Howard, Jean E. "Shakespeare, Geography, and the Work of Genre on the Early Modern Stage." *MLQ: Modern Language Quarterly* 64.3 (2003): 299–322.

Kaplan, Gregory B. "The Inception of *Limpieza de Sangre* (Purity of Blood) and Its Impact in Medieval and Golden Age Spain." In *Marginal Voices: Studies in Converso Literature of Medieval and Golden Age Spain*, edited by Amy I. Aronson-Friedman and Gregory B. Kaplan, 19–41. Leiden: Brill, 2012.

Keller, Marcus and Javier Irigoyen-García, eds. *The Dialectics of Orientalism in Early Modern Europe*. New York: Palgrave, 2018.

Lawrence, Bruce B. *The Qur'an: A Biography*. London: Atlantic Books Ltd, 2014.

Lombardi-Diop, Cristina. "Preface," *The Black Mediterranean: Bodies, Borders, and Citizenship*, eds. Gabriele Proglio, et al., New York: Palgrave MacMillan, 2021, 2–3.

Loomba, Ania. *Shakespeare, Race, and Colonialism*. Oxford: Oxford University Press, 2002.

McKittrick, Katherine. *Demonic Grounds: Black Women and the Cartographies of Struggle*. Minneapolis: University of Minnesota Press, 2006.

Omi, Michael, and Howard Winant. *Racial Formation in the United States*. London: Routledge, 2014.

Patel, Soham and M. Bilal Nasir, "The Asianist Is Muslim," *Who Is the Asianist: The Politics of Representation in Asian Studies*, edited by Will bridges, Nitasha Tamar Sharma, and Marvin D. Sterling. New York: Columbia University Press, 2022.

Pratt, Mary Louise. *Imperial Eyes: Travel Writing and Transculturation*. London: Routledge, 2007.

Rana, Junaid. *Terrifying Muslims: Race and Labor in the South Asian Diaspora.* Durham: Duke University Press, 2011.

Rana, Junaid, Evelyn Alsultany, Lara Deeb, Carol Fadda, Su'ad Abdul Khabeer, Arshad Ali, Sohail Daulatzai, Zareena Grewal, Juliane Hammer, and Nadine Naber. "Pedagogies of Resistance: Why Anti-Muslim Racism Matters." *Amerasia Journal* 46.1, 2020: 57–62.

Robinson, Benedict S. *Islam and Early Modern English Literature: The Politics of Romance from Spenser to Milton.* New York: Palgrave, 2007.

Rose, Gillian. *Feminism & Geography: The Limits of Geographical Knowledge.* Minneapolis: University of Minnesota Press, 1993.

Rouighi, Ramzi. *Inventing the Berbers: History and Ideology in the Maghrib.* Philadelphia: University of Pennsylvania Press, 2019.

Said, Edward. *Orientalism.* London: Penguin Classics, 2003.

Vitkus, Daniel J. "Early Modern Orientalism: Representations of Islam in Sixteenth and Seventeenth-century Europe." In *Western Views of Islam in Medieval and Early Modern Europe,* edited by David R. Banks and Michael Frassetto, 207–30. New York: Palgrave Macmillan, 1999.

Wann, Louis. "The Oriental in Elizabethan Drama." *Modern Philology* 12.7 (1915): 289–456.

Young, Robert J.C. *White Mythologies: Writing History and the West.* London: Routledge, 2004.

One

Near the end of The Tempest (1611) after the plots and schemes
have been revealed, Prospero pulls back one final curtain to
reveal Ferdinand and Miranda playing chess. Upon seeing her
European audience, which includes her soon-to-be father-
in-law Alonso, Miranda rapturously exclaims "O brave new
world / That has such people in't."[1] Miranda's astonishment
reflects her sheltered upbringing on a deserted island (its
one native inhabitant excepted), her innocence of the ways
of the world, and her naive judgment that relies on physical appearance reflecting quality and character. The incredible people suddenly populating her world usher Miranda
into another, "brave" world, that contains a "superabun-
dance of any valuable quality in men or things" as the word's
early modern usage indicates.[2] The richness and excess of
the moment—the island's ability to endlessly generate—
coupled with her singular use of the phrase "new world,"
suggestively point to a geography that has long been critically
associated with the play, so much so that it has become scholarly dogma. Indeed, the play's proto-imperialist plot coupled
with Prospero's treatment of the island's native inhabitants,
Caliban and Ariel, support colonial and postcolonial interpretations of The Tempest which have successfully argued that
the play mimics and reflects the logics of the enslaving settler
colonial imperial projects that European powers engaged in

DOI: 10.4324/9781003213581-2

from the end of the fifteenth century onward in the western hemisphere.[3]

Insurgent readings by Caribbean and Latin American writers, scholars, activists, and intellectuals of this canonical text's influence upon identity construction, subjectivity, and agency within European racializing imperial regimes reveal the ideological culture work that literary texts perform. They highlight how texts carry certain values and how oppositional readings can disclose the space for questioning and resisting the power relations celebrated in and by such works. Powerful counter-readings and counter-narratives by anti-imperialist artists and intellectuals such as Aimé Césaire, George Lamming, and Roberto Férnandez Retamar promoted a trans-Atlantic imperial frame that explicates the psychological violence of enslavement and empire upon colonized peoples. Their disruption of the tidy narratives emerging from the imperial core, which sanitizes the project of empire in favor of its "civilizing mission," powerfully calls into question the institutional violence that undergirds all such insidious claims.

The political challenges launched by such revolutionary reimaginings of The Tempest were later duplicated within the field of Shakespeare studies. New historical analyses focused their inquiry on the play's geography, arguing for its Atlantic and American context by tracing the play's internal evidence of engagement with English mercantile and colonial voyages to the so-called "New World." In such interpretations, The Tempest's references to "the Bermudas," the violent storm that opens the play which echoes the description of a 1609 hurricane in the Atlantic, Caliban's evocation of his mother's deity "Setebos," Gonzalo's desire to establish a plantation on the island as a utopian social experiment, and the enslavement of Caliban and Ariel by Prospero, all gestured toward trans-Atlantic social, political, and cultural concerns.[4] These readings center this geography as the primary colonial locale of the play's action, concluding, as two prominent critics do, that *The Tempest* "is often considered Shakespeare's American play."[5] Such geographic privileging—particularly from the North American academy which, like much of the USA's hard and soft power, exerts global cultural dominance within the field of Shakespeare studies—has resulted in particularly limited possibilities for the play's setting, untethering it from its stated Mediterranean locale in order to prioritize its Atlantic contexts. Indeed, here, I follow the lead of Jerry Brotton who circumspectly notes that

> In claiming an exclusively American context for the play's production, American new historicist critics overinvest something of their own peculiarly post-colonial identities as American intellectuals within the one text that purports to establish a firm connection between America and the culture which these critics analyse with such intensity: early modern England.[6]

I make this point not to deny the processes of enslavement and dispossession in which English merchants, factors, and settlers were engaged during the period, and which can serve as analogues to *The Tempest*'s action and interests in subjugation of racially and culturally different peoples. I want to suggest, however, that there is an element of American exceptionalism at work in such scholarship, which has shifted the center of gravity of the play's themes and topics westward. Such exceptionalism provincializes our understanding of the play and of the early modern world, in which England's imperial ambitions looked both westward to the Atlantic for territory and eastward into the Mediterranean for trade and traffic. To render the Mediterranean as an afterthought or merely symbolic—or, even worse, a plot point—subordinates that geography's own distinct imperial formations which bear closely upon the play's concern with lineage and the legitimate transmission of power. The geography surrounding the island, somewhere in the Mediterranean between Naples and Tunis but also between Milan and Algiers, has over the centuries been evacuated of critical interest because of Orientalist constructions, which regard its history as important only as it pertains to or touches on Europe. Orientalist representations do not traffic in real engagement with the region; rather, they furnish their audience with tropes and stereotypes that confirm their own assumptions. Thus, the region could be critically ignored as having no cultural and political bearing on *The Tempest*, making it possible to admit to the play's literal geography while casually overriding it to the more preferred environs of the Atlantic world.

THE STAGED MEDITERRANEAN

Deviating from common critical practice, I investigate *The Tempest's* "implicit" and "unmistakable" Mediterranean locale in order to uncover what the particulars of this geography reveal about the play's social and political concerns. In taking this route, I follow the example of scholars such as Andrew Hess, Patricia Parker, Barbara Fuchs, Jerry Brotton, Ania Loomba, and Bernadette Andrea, who have previously argued that the Mediterranean is more than simply an imaginative locale, that the geography was of immediate concern to England's commercial interests, and that it offered near-at-hand examples of cultural contact, exchange, and difference.[7]

The Mediterranean was the preferred region in Shakespeare's own canon and the works of his contemporaries as a contact zone that facilitated encounters with racial and religious Otherness because the geography tethers Europe to Africa to Asia.[8] I argue that the popularity of plays featuring this setting and their common ideological investments, particularly in relation to the plurality of identity found within this space and the various forms of personal or political dangers that resulted from its polyphony and polysemy, demonstrate that it was an important subgenre in the early modern English dramatic canon. The consistency of topics, tropes, topoi, themes, and characters that cohere in and through identity construction and difference in these plays suggests the development of a common stage grammar for this subgenre. Indeed, the vernacular it commonly employed was one of cultural chauvinism and supremacy which was bolstered through European encounters with Mediterranean Otherness. This Otherness often took the form of Islamic difference because the religio-political systems governing the settings of these plays were frequently Muslim, and European characters were in subordinate positions of power wherein they had to navigate the paradox of being both a fish out of water and culturally superior because of their European Christian heritage and identity.

I have termed this subgenre the staged Mediterranean because it offers a skewed simulacrum of the social, political, and cultural forces at work within the real geography of the Mediterranean. I prefer this term over "Turk plays" because it invites an examination into the importance of geography in constructing the relations of power that inhere within these dramas and exhibits how place is tethered to race and religion, exposing how ideas of human difference were being constructed in and through the politics of space and sovereignty.[9] Furthermore, the "Turk plays" designation reproduces early modern discursive forms that limit and bound Muslim identity to one ethnic marker. Thinking about these plays more expansively, through the framework of the staged Mediterranean, allows for the plurality of identities to complicate the social and cultural relations that these texts depict. Staged Mediterranean plays often trade in the idiom of stereotype, especially in their representation of non-Christian, non-European, non-white identity. In these dramas the Mediterranean becomes the space that facilitates experimentation with identity: its fluid waters easing forms of border-crossing, literally into other territories and figuratively into other modes of being. Even as characters flirt with the alluring possibility of "going native," the genre of the staged Mediterranean requires their triumph over non-European, non-Christian, and non-white cultural Otherness. In this way, the staged Mediterranean exploits and capitalizes on the encounters necessitated by the geography of this contact zone, but rather than allowing for "a contact perspective" that challenged forms of cultural dominance and offered new hybrid ways of being, these plays operated with an eye toward controlling the exchanges that the Mediterranean cultivated. Thus, the staged Mediterranean exerts representational and discursive power over this geography in a way that belies its material reality.

As a staged Mediterranean play, The Tempest is a bit of an outlier. While the play very clearly represents encounters with identities that are different from those of its European characters, the dominant power on the island is a European, Christian, white man—making null and void the possibility for experimentation with identity. Even those characters that find themselves in precarious and uneasy positions because of the island's magic and Prospero and Ariel's plots, never seem to lose sight of the power that inheres in their social status and identity. We might grant that Stephano and Trinculo seek to transform their positions because of the new social arena in which they find themselves, yet their comedic episode poses no real danger and their claim to nobility and political power is consistently undermined by their alliance with Caliban. Perhaps this insular quality of Shakespeare's setting, the fact that he does not take advantage of the possibilities of the Mediterranean, demonstrates a thematic discontinuity between the play's ostensible geography and what it chooses to depict. In other words, by eschewing the potentiality that the Mediterranean allows because of the different cultures it brings together, Shakespeare transforms this locale into a place of European sameness and domination, where the real struggle is always and only about European political power and agency. In this view the Mediterranean is simply an afterthought, an exotic backdrop to the play's European concerns. Its waters furnish the instigating event of the plot, yet its cultures have nothing more to contribute.

GEOGRAPHY, RACE, AND RELIGION

Shakespeare makes the effort to locate *The Tempest* within a network of Mediterranean foreign relations through the marriage of the king of Naples's daughter, Claribel, to the unnamed king of Tunis. This event and the origin story of Caliban's mother, Sycorax, show how the Muslim societies of the Mediterranean, conjured through the geographic coordinates of Tunis and Algiers, are vital to the play's primary concerns with legitimate and illegitimate power, dynastic lineage, and cultural purity. While neither the king of Tunis nor Sycorax is explicitly labeled as Muslim, their geographic affiliations inscribe them as such. Arab Muslim expansion in Africa began in the middle of the seventh century. After gaining a foothold in Egypt in 642, Arab Muslim forces captured "the Byzantine capital, Carthage in 697–8," and a few years later, "the Muslim armies reached Morocco and the southern shore of the Mediterranean became part of the Umayyad caliphate."[10] The vastness of the region that came under Muslim control from these conquests ranged from "Atlantic Morocco in the west to the western Egyptian desert in the east, and from the shores of the Mediterranean to the oases of the deep Sahara in the south."[11] From Morocco Muslim forces advanced into Europe, commencing a rule and presence in the region that would last for almost 800 years. By the late Renaissance and early modern period, the monarchs of Portugal and Spain had successfully routed and eradicated Muslims from Iberia and confined Islam to North Africa; meanwhile the eastern border of the Mediterranean, the region known as the Levant, was under the rule of the Ottoman Empire.

For Shakespeare and his contemporaries, therefore, references and inferences to North Africa, or the *Maghreb*, particularly to its major cities and principalities such as Algiers and Tunis, also allude to Islam and Muslim cultures. Geopolitics are religious and racial politics. By this I mean that geographic designations—whether imperial territories, republics, kingdoms, or imagined communities—are implicated within religious, racial, and ethnic categories. For example, Christendom is an ideological geopolitical as well as religio-racial formulation that can be located topographically on a map (itself an ideological representation). As it was imagined in the early modern period, the dominions of Christendom were bound to the landmass of Europe, and thus imbued European cultures with religious and racial identity. The imagined communities and cultures of Islam, by contrast, were situated in Africa and Asia, notwithstanding the multiple advancements of Muslim powers in Europe. By discursively sequestering Islam to the peripheries of Europe, close to its borders in the eastern and southern Mediterranean, European writers could imagine a region free from its religious and racial influence. The idea of Europe was based on its proximity to Islamic cultures, and so both were racialized as white and non-white through religion and through somatic difference rooted in geographic difference.

Contemporary racial classifications along color-coded axes have obfuscated the link between race and geography, particularly in societies like the United States, which is still white supremacist despite the multiplicity of races and cultures within its domains. For example, the US census will ask if one is "White," "Black or African American," "American Indian and Alaska Native," "Asian," "Native Hawaiian or other Pacific Islander," or "Latino/a or Hispanic."[12] While white and Black racialization is noted through the register of skin color, and then explained through geographic ancestral origin (only in the case of Black), all other racial classifications are constructed through geography and reflect older European racial taxonomies that similarly structured human variation or difference. These racializing schemes expose the internal incoherence of racial classification, its simultaneous reliance on skin color as an "accurate" marker of racial difference, and the inadequacy of skin to sufficiently patrol the borders of whiteness. Within a racialized group, ethnicity is reliant on geography, since it signals forms of belonging rooted to a sense of place, community, language, and culture. Race, however, has been used to underpin systems of global theft and exploitation. These systems produce whiteness as dominant and non-whiteness as subordinate by unrooting (in the case of African peoples transported across the Atlantic) and uprooting (in the case of Native peoples worldwide) entire communities. In the early modern period, this form of dispossession from the land and oneself was beginning to be organized and systematized.

Geography was one of the primary ways through which difference was constructed, particularly racial and religious Otherness. Climate theory, for example, explained variations in skin color between people inhabiting different regions, such as locating the origin of blackness in African peoples' proximity to the sun.[13] In "Skin Color and Race," anthropologist Nina G. Jablonski notes that Enlightenment systems of racial classification, like those of Linnaeus (1707–1787) emerged from earlier racializing models that made skin color a reflection of temperament, pointing to

> [Linnaeus'] interpretation of the humoral theory of Hippocrates, Aristotle, and Galen in which particular elements (air, water, fire, and earth) were associated with specific climates, geographies, and humors (blood, phlegm, yellow bile, and black bile). According to this theory, climate and geography produce predominant humors in the body that influence the development of good or bad character and the color of the skin.[14]

By transforming skin color into a mark of character European writers and thinkers were engaged in the process of race-making: they transformed a natural human feature—skin—into a symbol that was freighted with moral and ethical values. Geography, too, was implicated in such racialization, since the locale and climate influenced those qualities found to be beneficial or detrimental to a person's character.

Like race, religious identity or affiliation was also articulated through geographic origin. With the expansion of Islam and its cultures from the Arabian Peninsula westward in the seventh century, the lands that Muslim forces conquered came to acquire meaning within European worldmaking projects and discourses through their alignment with Islam. In the early modern period, most of the southern and eastern basin of the Mediterranean was occupied by the Muslim regimes of the Ottomans and independent Muslim kingdoms like the Saadi dynasty of Morocco. The "Barbary Coast" of the Mediterranean, which included important North African locations such as Morocco, Tunis, and Algiers, was named after the Amazigh people who were (and are) natives of this region and who the Arab conquerors of the seventh century called "Berbers," following "the Greco-Latin understanding that barbarians spoke unintelligible languages."[15] "Berber" was *Barbar* in medieval Arabic, and when transformed into an adjective for the people of this place, *barbarian*, the homophone signaled more than simply geography, particularly as it was deployed in early modern English discourses, such as drama. It marked character and quality, locating "barbarians," beyond the bounds of civilization because of their Muslim religious identity. George Peele's *The Battle of Alcazar* (1594) which depicts the contemporary, real-life events of European interference within an internecine conflict for the Moroccan throne, consistently puns on "barbarian" to indicate both racial and religious identity and to emphasize the cultural difference of "barbarians" from Europeans.[16] Another example of localizing Islam through geography in the early modern period is in the use of "Turk" as a synonym for Muslim. As was common in the early modern English imaginary, Ottoman identity, as rendered through the figure of the "Turk," often stood for Islam and its manifold cultures. By localizing Islam within just one of its many cultures and fixing it within an ethno-racial identity marker such as "Turk," early modern discourses exerted ideological control over the boundaries of Islam, all the while eliding the capaciousness and ethnic diversity of Ottoman imperial identity. Early modern strategies of geographically marking Islam remain with us today through the use of "the Middle East," as a metonym for Muslim-majority countries, as well as the damaging construction, "the Islamic World," both of which flatten the diversity of Muslim peoples, cultures, customs, and regimes into one monolithic—often violent "war mongering," and "war-torn"—block. Despite its deliberately obfuscatory nomenclature, the War on Terror, similarly conjures both Islam and geography through western Islamophobic suturing of terrorism with Islam and Muslims. Conceptualizing Islam within the west has and continues to require spatial thinking that positions the religion outside and on the peripheries of Europe, Christendom, whiteness, and civilization.

MARGINALIZING ISLAM

Despite the centrality of Islam and its cultures to the geography of the Mediterranean, encountering Islam in Shakespeare entails an interpretive practice that looks from the margins in order to see the strategic erasures of Muslim cultures from the representational frame. As bell hooks elucidates in "Choosing the Margin as a Space of Radical Openness," a critical perspective rooted in the margin facilitates an epistemology that harnesses the power of the margin to understand the center.

> Living as we did—on the edge—we developed a particular
> way of seeing reality. We looked both from the outside in
> and from the inside out. We focused our attention on the
> centre as well as on the margin. We understood both. This
> mode of seeing reminded us of the existence of a whole
> universe, a main body made up of both margin and center.
> Our survival depended on an ongoing public awareness of
> the separation between margin and centre and an ongoing
> private acknowledgement that we were a necessary, vital
> part of that whole.[17]

hooks constructs the margin as a critical space that promotes an
orientation toward society wherein its structure as a "whole"
can be fully apprehended. The margin is a literal location, on
the other side of the railroad tracks in hooks's narrative, yet
it is simultaneously a geographically rooted metaphor that
supports the looking relations between the critic and the
object of critique: "to be in the margin is to be part of the
whole but outside the main body."[18] The radical perspective
cultivated through the experience of marginality allows for
it to become a site of resistance and critique, a place from
which, hooks argues, radical intervention within regimes of
dominance is possible.[19] hooks's theorization of the margin as
a site of repression and resistance offers a useful geographic
entry point into the erasures that Shakespeare effects in his
treatment of the Mediterranean in *The Tempest*.

Looking from the margins at what is rendered as peripheral
recuperates the absent presence of Islam within the geography
of the play. Looking from the margins—being attentive to the
codes of the dominant culture, which the marginalized must
learn as a strategy for survival—means recognizing the significance of geographic markers as imbricated racial and religious

markers, so that Algiers is simultaneously an exotic site for the English, who themselves were on the periphery of this geography and an Islamic site. Looking from the margins, allows for an understanding of the shorthand metonymic function of Shakespeare's geographic gestures, so that the king of Tunis does not have to be explicitly called a Muslim to understand that he could *only ever be* a Muslim in the world that Shakespeare had constructed. Looking from the margins exposes the geographic estrangement that Shakespeare employs in the play to repress the Muslim presence from a region where Islamic regimes exerted almost total control.

THE TEMPEST'S AFRICAN WOMEN

Even though *The Tempest* lacks overt references to Islam, the geographic circuits of the play conjure its presence. Its two absent women, Sycorax and Claribel, point to the culture work that the evocation and suppression of Islam perform in the play. The differing circumstances of both women instantiate an encounter with Islam that is left incomplete, because they are relegated to the play's backstory. Their social positions offer opportunities for unrealized cross-cultural, cross-racial, and cross-confessional encounters that point to the power of Muslim regimes within the Mediterranean. However, their marginal and spectral status within the play, never on stage and only seeming to further the patriarchal plotline, allows for the religio-racial questions that their twin plots serve to be sidelined. Looking from the margins at these marginalized women, centers the anxieties generated in staged Mediterranean encounters with the foreign and demands that we question what the repression of Islam accomplishes. Islam is the absent—but powerful—presence in the play against which white European Christian identity consolidates itself but which it simultaneously needs to deny in order to articulate its agency. Sycorax and Claribel are useful in achieving these aims because they signal two strategies of containment that bound the Muslim presence within forms of seemingly inassimilable difference as is the case with Sycorax or through classical narratives that deny contemporary Muslim control of the geography as we find with Claribel.

The "damned witch" Sycorax is *The Tempest's* avatar for the monstrous Islamic feminine. In addition to practicing "mischiefs manifold and sorceries terrible Sycorax is described in Prospero's screed as physically repulsive, "a foul witch," bent into a "hoop," from old age, and as bestial, "littering," her son, who because he is "hag-born," was "not honored with / A human shape."[20,21] The excessive gendered violence of Prospero's appraisal of Sycorax's moral and behavioral failings can be attributed to his anger at Ariel for reminding him that he had promised the spirit its liberty, yet the urgency of his frenzied claims about the difference between Sycorax as Ariel's master/owner and himself attest to another kind of anxiety: the need to draw a distinction between himself and Sycorax. The difference Prospero seeks to establish between them is ontological and epistemological: her Otherness is gendered, racial, and religious; and through the intersection of those qualities she becomes inhuman. Feminist film critic Barbara Creed developed the term "monstrous-feminine" to describe the function of women's monstrosity in horror films. Rather than just a female version of a male monster, Creed's "monstrous-feminine" investigates "what it is about woman that is shocking, terrifying, horrific, abject," emphasizing the gendered horror that women elicit in such narratives, which frequently yoke their monstrosity to sexuality.[22] Although not a horror text, The Tempest is invested in monstrosity; for example, the word "monster" appears 38 times in the play, the most out of any of Shakespeare's plays—the runner-up is Othello, where it appears six times.[23] The word is applied exclusively to Caliban by the fools Stephano and Trinculo, and implies his questionably human status, not only in their eyes, but also according to the higher status white European characters on the island. Caliban's monstrosity, however, is not unique to him: it is an inheritance from his mother, whose own religio-racial difference and deviant sexuality rendered her monstrous.

Sycorax's religious affiliation, like all references to Islam in Shakespeare's plays, is expressed through the geographic register. During his outburst at Ariel, Prospero reminds him that she had been "banished" from "Argier," because of her witchcraft, her pregnancy saving her life.[24] Sycorax's homeland, Algiers, had been an Ottoman regency—gifted to Sultan Süleyman in 1529—for almost 80 years by the time of Shakespeare's composition of The Tempest.[25] Even before its official incorporation into the Ottoman Empire, Algiers was largely a Muslim-majority locale and a contested geography between European Christian forces and Ottoman and North African Muslim ones. As the place from where she was exiled and presumably her own native land, Algiers endows Sycorax's character with geographic, religious, and cultural meaning. It was one of the main Ottoman-controlled trading posts in the early modern Mediterranean; moreover, it served as a base for Barbary pirates and corsairs. The danger of this geography was in its capacity to lure European and English people into "turning Turk" voluntarily or being forced into enslavement. The danger in The Tempest, however, is in the magical and deviant power of a North African Muslim woman.[26] Her geographic origin further secures her difference from Prospero and his kin by aligning her with an Otherness that seems incompatible with the social and cultural mores espoused by Prospero. However, this early scene, which details Sycorax's life, death, and supernatural career also serves to establish similitude between these two magical figures. Both wield incredible power over the spirits of the island, both are exiles, and both have a child. Thus, gender, race, religion, and geography come to fabricate difference in order to obscure sameness.

Rather than treating Algiers as a topical yet passing reference in *The Tempest*, I advance that the locale is vital to apprehending the Islamic difference that the play seeks to exclude from the normative, hegemonic European identity it upholds. The Muslim Mediterranean provides Shakespeare with an Other that facilitates the construction and maintenance of white, Christian Europeanness. While England may have been on the frontiers of the known world of the Middle Sea, knowledge about the Mediterranean and its social, political, religious, and cultural structures was not so distant. Several books on the topic would have been available to English readers including Thomas Washington's translation of Nicolas de Nicolay's *Navigations, Peregrinations, and Voyages Made into Turkey* (1585) from French, and John Pory's English translation of Leo Africanus's *A Geographical History of Africa* (1600) from Italian. These texts were widely printed in the early modern period, and both offered first-hand accounts of travel into Muslim geographies, providing ethnographic studies of the people and places they encountered, and marking cultural, racial, and religious differences. These texts performed important culture work, translating difference for their readers while simultaneously domesticating

Otherness by containing it within the material boundaries of the book and the ideological boundaries of European discourse. Nicolay's *Navigations* chronicles his 1551 diplomatic journey from France to Istanbul, that took him through Ottoman-controlled North Africa, including Algiers, which he observed "is very merchantlike, for that she is situated upon the Sea, and for this cause marvelously peopled, for her bigness: she is inhabited of Turks, Moors, and Jewes in great number."[27] Nicolay was a well-born French subject, part of an ambassadorial mission from King Henry II to the court of Sultan Süleyman, had seen much in his capacity as a royal geographer, and recognized the commercial importance and vitality of this Mediterranean locale.[28] The remarks also confirm the plurality of identity found within such geographies, as well as the distinction that Nicolay draws between "Turks" and "Moors," denoting difference instead of collapsing Muslim identities under a single ethnic marker. Commenting on the kinds of "Turks" he finds in Algiers, Nicolay notes:

> The most part of the Turks of Algier, whether they be of the king's household or the Gallies, are Christians reneged, or Mahumetised, of all Nations, but most of them Spaniards, Italians, and of Provence, of the Islands and Coasts of the Sea Mediterranean, given all to whoredome, sodometrie, theft, and all other most detestable vices, living only off rovings, spoils, & pilling at the Seas, and the Island, being about them: and with their practice art bring daily to Algier a number of poor Christians, which they sell unto the Moors, and other merchants of Barbary for slaves, who afterward transport them and sell them where they think good, or else beating them miserably with slaves, do imply and constrain

them to work in the fields, and in all other vile and ancient occupations and servitude almost intolerable.[29]

Explicating the identity of the "Turks" he encounters, Nicolay emphasizes that they are Christian converts to Islam, renegade Christians who have abandoned their faith to pursue the material wealth and sexual license allegedly permitted by Islam. Of note is that Islam offers only earthly gain and pleasure, no form of spirituality or salvation. His inventory of vices to which these "Turks" are inclined begins with their venal disposition and is swiftly followed by the threat they pose to their former Christian brethren, the most dangerous and immediate threat being that of captivity and enslavement. Nicolay's catalogue makes the seductions of conversion to Islam, or "turning Turk," in the common parlance of early modern discourse, explicit while simultaneously emphasizing the existential danger that such conversions pose to Christian identity in the Mediterranean.

From the debauchery of Algiers's "Turks," Nicolay's narrative shifts to a description of the city's women, highlighting their clothing or lack thereof to similarly construct them through registers of sexual deviance. Nicolay observes that,

all along the river and the shore the Moorish women and maiden slaves of Algier do go to wash their linen, being commonly whole naked, saving that they wear a piece of cotton cloth of some strange color to cover their secret parts, (which notwithstanding for a little piece of money they will willingly uncover). They wear also for an ornament about their neck, arms, and legs, great collars or bracelets of latten, set with certain false stones. But as for the wives of the Turks or Moors, they are not seen to go uncovered,

Figure 1.1 A "Moorish" woman, from Nicolay, *Navigations* "A Mayden Moorisque." LUNA: Folger Digital Image Collection, Folger Shakespeare Library.

for they wear a great Bernuche made of a blanket of white, black, or violet color, which covers their whole body and the head. And to the end you should more easily comprehend the manner of all their apparel, I have thought good in the end of this present Chapter lively to set forth unto you, a woman as she goes in the street, and a maiden Moore being a slave.[30]

Clothing, covering, and veiling become important signs of female chastity and virtue in this episode. Nicolay makes no effort to distinguish between the free or enslaved women at the river when he coolly notes that they are, "commonly whole naked, saving that they wear a piece of cotton cloth of some strange color to cover their secrete parts, (which notwithstanding for a little piece of money they will willingly uncover)." He establishes a correlation between the amount of clothing the women wear and their willingness to uncover themselves (for money). His parenthetical—a neat aside— condemns all of the women as sex-workers because it seems they all "will willingly" expose themselves. Nicolay contrasts the overt sexuality of the "Moorish" women at the river with that of "the wives of the Turks and Moors," whose physical beings are denied to him because of their extreme veiling practice. Their coverings point to their status as wives and implicitly signal their modesty because their veils shield their bodies from the gaze of outsiders, unlike the bare bodies of the "Moorish" women by the river. The *Navigations* offers its readers several woodcut images depicting the people of the geographies through which Nicolay travels, corroborating the truth of his narrative and impressions while also visually capturing the natives, bringing them home to Europe to be feasted upon by the hungry gaze of his audience. The woman of

Algiers that he *can* depict is one whose social position allows her to pose for him. At the same time, the underlying logic of the woodcuts is to taxonomize Otherness, so she also stands in for all the women of Algiers.[31] Thus, the *Navigations* presents Algiers as a site that cultivates and encourages forms of deviance both religious and sexual, and where, even though Islam is rarely mentioned, it is understood through ethnic identity markers such as "Turk" and "Moor."

While Nicolay's *Navigations* offers an ethnographic account of travel through the Muslim Mediterranean, Leo Africanus's *A Geographical History of Africa*, provided early modern European audiences with a detailed account of the geographies and peoples of Africa from the perspective of a cultural insider. Before he acquired the Christian name, "Giovan Lioni Africano," and became widely known throughout Europe as "Iean Leon, African," "Ioannes Leo Africanus," and "Iohn Leo," he was a Muslim "North African traveler and diplomat from Fez named al-Hasan al-Wazzan."[32] Captured by Spanish pirates in the eastern Mediterranean, al-Wazzan was taken to the court of Pope Leo X and after 15 months in captivity he was baptized in a grand ceremony at St. Peter's.[33] While European writers had a variety of names for him, al-Wazzan gave himself the Arabic name Yuhanna al-Asad—Yuhanna the Lion.[34] As Natalie Zemon Davis points out the name "suggests the entanglement of values, perspectives, and personae in his life in Italy in the next seven years."[35] Changing names and shifting identities were part and parcel of life in the Mediterranean, where cultural and confessional borders were sometimes voluntarily—and at other times forcibly— crossed. Part of the appeal and notoriety of Leo Africanus's *A Geographical History* was that it is written by a "More," ("Moor") who converted to Christianity. As Pory exhorts,

But, not to forget His conversion to Christianity, amidst all these his busy and dangerous travels, it pleased the divine providence, for the discovery and manifestation of God's wonderful works, and of his dreadful and just judgements performed in Africa (which before the time of John Leo, were either utterly concealed, or unperfectly and fabulously reported both by ancient and late writers) to deliver this author of ours, and this present Geographical History, into the hands of certain Italian Pirates, about the isle of Djerba, situate in the gulf of Capes, between the cities of Tunis and Tripolis in Barbary. Being thus taken, the Pirates presented him and his Book unto Pope Leo the tenth: who esteeming of him as of a most rich and invaluable prize, greatly rejoiced at his arrival, and gave him most kind entertainment and liberal maintenance, till such time as he had won him to be baptized in the name of Christ, and to be called John Leo, after the Pope's own name.[36]

In short, al-Wazzan's capture, bondage, and eventual liberty are framed in Pory's narrative as divine intervention wherein being beset by pirates and alienated from his homeland, language, culture, and religion are things worthy of praise because they brought him into the fold of Christianity. For Pory, the Christian pirates "discover" rather than abduct al-Wazzan. Their actions, or non-actions, present a contrast to those of the renegade Christian pirates or "Turks" in Nicolay's account, who are condemned for the same because they are delivering Christians into the hands of non-Christians. Moreover, by the time Pory's translation was printed, John Leo or Yuhanna al-Assad had returned to Islamicate North Africa to resume his life as al-Hasan al-Wazzan, a Muslim. His nine-year sojourn in Christendom and his Christian identity was a thing of his past.[37] Whether Pory was ignorant of or deliberately ignored this historical coda is unclear. For clarity, I use Leo Africanus, when referring to the writer of the *A Geographical History* because that is the name by which he became known in England and Europe; however, when discussing his life before and after his conversion I use al-Wazzan.

Leo Africanus's *A Geographical History* has long been put into dialogue with Shakespeare, particularly as an analogue or blueprint for *Othello*, but al-Wazzan's Mediterranean itinerary also has something to offer investigations of *The Tempest*.[38] Not only does his journey mimic Prospero's—a separation from his homeland and then a return—but also *A Geographical History* provides an intimate and knowledgeable perspective on the peoples, cultures, and geographies which are explicitly referenced in the play. Africanus's "eyewitness" account and narrative, which "largely, particularly, and methodically deciphered the countries of Barbary, Numidia, Libya, The land of Negros, and the hither part of Egypt, as (I take it) never any writer either before or since his time hath done," was the authority on Africa for early modern Europeans, translated into multiple languages including Latin, Italian, French, Spanish, and English.[39] While the book attempts to provide an account of the entire continent, its main focus and the specialty of its author lies in the geography of "Barbary," of the locales of the Muslim Mediterranean. Thus, Africanus's narrative opens up Shakespeare's geographic referents in *The Tempest*, by providing ethnographic, cultural, religious, and racial context. His commentaries on these places, peoples, and customs offer a powerful subtext and history only hinted at in Shakespeare. For instance, Africanus spends considerable energy in *A Geographical History* chronicling the practice of witchcraft in diverse regions of Africa. Writing about the many supernatural practitioners of Fez, including "fortunetellers," "diviners," "conjurers," and "enchanters," Africanus rehearses a lengthy description and tirade on "women-witches":

> which are affirmed to have familiarity with devils: some devils they call red, some white, and some black devils: and when they will tell any man's fortune, they perfume themselves with certain odors, saying, that then they possess themselves with that devil which they called for: afterward changing their voice, they feign the devil to speak within them: then they which come to enquire, ought with great fear & trembling aske these vile & abominable witches such questions as they mean to propound, and lastly offering some fee unto the devil, they depart. But the wiser and honester sort of people call these women Sahaoat, which in Latin signifies Fricatrices, because they have a damnable custom to commit unlawful venery among themselves, which I cannot express in any modester terms. If faire women come unto them at any time, these abominable witches will burn in lust towards them no otherwise than lusty yoonkers do towards young maids, and will in the devils behalf demand for a reward, that they may lie with them: and so by this means it often falls out, that thinking thereby to fulfill the devils command they lie with the witches. Yea some there are, which being allured with the delight of this abominable vice, will desire the company of these witches, and feigning themselves to be sick, will either call one of the witches home to them, or will send their husbands for the same purpose: and so the witches perceiving how the matter stands, will say that the woman is possessed with a devil, and that she can no way be cured, unless she be admitted into their society. With these words

her silly husband being persuaded, doth not only permit her so to do, but makes also a sumptuous banquet unto the damned crew of witches: which being done, they use to dance very strangely at the noise of drums: and so the poor man commits his false wife to their filthy disposition. Howbeit some there are that will soon conjure the devil with a good cudgel out of their wives: others feigning themselves to be possessed with a devil, will deceive the said witches, as their wives have been deceived by them.[40]

I have quoted Africanus at length here because his invective forms the basis for the kind of vitriol directed at Sycorax by Prospero and the kind Caliban has learned to direct at himself, also presumably learned at Prospero's knee. For Africanus, these women are objectionable on several grounds, not the least of which is their association with the devil, a familiarity that then underwrites their lewd and immoral behavior. While the devil is central in Africanus's initial construction of these "witch-women," their illicit sexuality renders them wholly monstrous. The account emphasizes the women's deception in using the devil to lure other women into their orbit in order to gratify their sexual appetites. Same-sex desire, for Africanus, is demonic and unnatural in its capacity to usurp male, sexual and patriarchal power. In addition to being sexually displaced, the husbands become panders in the narrative, delivering their wives into the monstrous clutches of the witches. Near the end of the section, however, Africanus reasserts masculine agency by pointing to some men who use violence to reaffirm their power or to turn the proverbial table on the witches by pretending that they are also possessed by the devil, presumably to lure the witches into performing the same cure on them as they have on their wives.

The episode highlights these women's sexual agency, which falls outside of patriarchal control. Their alliance with the devil cements their socially outcast status, allowing their sexual agency to be fashioned as monstrous precisely because it trespasses the rigid chastity mandated by patriarchy. Through her pregnancy, Sycorax, like Africanus's "women-witches," exhibits an improper sexuality. While Prospero claims that Caliban was "got by the devil" upon Sycorax, Caliban's social and cultural inheritance is through his mother's lineage.[41] He traces his right to the island via Sycorax, "This island's mine, by Sycorax my mother;" routinely swears by her "All the charms / Of Sycorax, toads, beetles, bats, light on you!."[42] Like the women who peddle the occult in Fez, Sycorax's power lies in her agency over herself, her ability to usurp the male privilege and establish her own lineage. Her danger and unruliness, which threaten the European worldmaking Prospero attempts, reside in her geographic difference. Her African and Muslim origin fixes her demonic energies within non-European and non-Christian spheres.[43]

Travel from and to Africa aligns Sycorax with the other woman who is mentioned but never seen in *The Tempest*, Claribel. The marriage between Claribel and the king of Tunis, provides the instantiating event for the action of the play, with the bridal party waylaid by Prospero's tempest on the journey back to Naples. After being stranded on the island, several members of Alonso's court bemoan the marriage "of the King's fair / daughter Claribel to the King of Tunis."[44] Indeed, one courtier notes that "Tunis was never graced before with such a paragon to their queen;" to which Gonzalo remarks "not since widow Dido's time," and emphasizes his comparison by announcing "This Tunis, sir, was, Carthage."[45]

The comic exchange obscures the ideological work being performed in these lines. The shift from the contemporary interracial and cross-confessional marriage between Claribel and the king of Tunis to the classical story of Dido serves a dual function. Firstly, it transforms Claribel into an African queen—which she is by marriage—but is now made a monarch in her own right, nullifying the necessary role of her African king. Secondly, and more perniciously, by reverting Tunis to Carthage, the play obscures Tunis's contemporary religious and cultural identity, thereby erasing Islam from the representational frame. Indeed, the success of such measures is witnessed by critical claims that the king of Tunis's religious identity is uncertain because he is not explicitly identified as Muslim.[46]

However, as I have been advancing in *Shakespeare through Islamic Worlds* geography is a symbolically loaded shorthand. The classical referent is also an important signifier for early modern geopolitics, as Jerry Brotton points out: it was deployed in order to discursively organize the region inside a familiar schema, by offering a tidy analogue for the different imperial systems occupying and operating within this zone.[47] For instance, Charles V had tapestries commissioned that memorialized his wars against the Ottoman Empire using "the invocation of classical Carthage in the midst of the capture of present-day Tunis" to reinforce and naturalize European possession of the Mediterranean.[48] Brotton further observes that the analogy "located Charles's victory within the larger dimensions of Roman imperialism to which, as the officially titled 'Holy Roman Emperor,' Charles hoped to emulate."[49] Early modern discourses were quite deliberate in mobilizing Mediterranean history to craft not only European self-image but also to frame contemporary geopolitics. *The Tempest* may be harnessing these strategies with its own classical referent, transforming Tunis's current political regime into one more familiar, one that was already seen as a cultural inheritance of Europe. In doing so, however, the play "sanitizes" Islam and Muslims from its geography.[50]

Despite Gonzalo's attempt to turn Tunis into Carthage, Leo Africanus's *A Geographical History* reminds its readers that "upon the decay of Carthage Tunis began to increase both in buildings and inhabitants."[51] Tunis not only represents the present, contemporary moment, but also it is fecund and alive, increasing in size and people, unlike dead and decomposed Carthage. Rather than harkening to its classical glory, Africanus points to its present power, especially that of its Muslim ruler who "was saluted king of all Africa, because indeed there was no prince of Africa at the same time comparable unto him."[52] Gonzalo's reversal leeches power from Tunis and its monarch and imbues it to the Neapolitan Claribel, a stratagem that further erases Muslims from the geography they inhabit in order to empower Europeans within this space. Gonzalo's attempts at making the marriage palatable through his references to Dido are ultimately unsuccessful because Alonso believes the shipwreck has cost him his son and heir, and with his daughter now "so far from Italy removed," he regrets the match.[53] Rubbing salt in his brother's wound, Sebastian berates him:

Sir you may thank yourself for this great loss,
That would not bless our Europe with your daughter,
But rather lose her to an African,
Where she at least is banished from your eye
Who hath cause to wet the grief on't

...

You were kneeled to and importuned otherwise
By all of us, and the fair soul herself

Weighted between loathness and obedience at
Which end o'the beam should bow.[54]

Sebastian's jealousy over his brother's position surely
motivates his callous disregard for Alonso's grief; however,
his words expose the underlying anxieties of this exog-
amous, inter-religious union. By deploying geographic
markers as well as color-coded discourse, he hints at the racial
thinking underpinning the opposition to the marriage and
the perceived cultural gulf it attempts to bridge. Instead of
contracting a marriage for Claribel in "our Europe," Alonso
disposed of her "to an African." Sebastian's rhetorical gesture
also obscures the proximity of Europe and Africa especially in
the Mediterranean, where the distance from Naples to Tunis
is only 354 miles, in contrast to the 1314 miles between
London and Naples.

Europe and Africa operate here as geographic shorthand
to connote differences in religion, race, and culture. The king
of Tunis's rank does not matter to Sebastian because all he
sees is the "African," who is utterly Other to and incompatible with "our Europe." Indeed, the use of "our" constructs
a community based around shared cultures, customs, values,
mores, and, critically, religion and race. It does not need to
be said because it is already implicit in both "African" and
"Tunis," that the king is somatically dark and Muslim. In fact,
the use of "fair soul" and "loathness" regarding Claribel's
own unease regarding her marriage emphasize this point. As
Kim F. Hall has incisively demonstrated, "fair" was a loaded
word that described a light complexion and performed ideological work beyond simply identifying a woman's beauty.
Hall argues that fair began to acquire racialized significance
"just at the moment of intensified English in colonial travel

and African trade."[55] She further contends that the word "carries specifically gendered judgments," and "has moral, sexual, and ethical implications," in addition to "economic" ones, signaling the higher value ascribed to it.[56] Fair, then, has a vast semantic network undergirding its use, and in the context of *The Tempest*, Claribel's fairness bespeaks both her race and her value. She is the white prize bestowed upon "an African." For her part, Claribel feels "loathness" toward the marriage suggesting her disinclination, yet the word also means "harmfulness," "unpleasantness," and "enmity," indicating the social and cultural jeopardy in which this marriage might place her.[57] Her marriage to a king raises her social position, but his African origin endangers her white European social status, which is prioritized in Sebastian's rehearsal. Despite facilitating a dynastic alliance, the marriage makes Claribel an outcast from "our Europe." In this way, she comes to resemble Sycorax: an exiled woman at the mercy of "an African's" sexual appetite.

Women crossing confessional boundaries is a common trope in early modern English drama. Shakespeare's own corpus features Jessica in *The Merchant of Venice* abjuring her Jewish faith in order to marry the Christian Lorenzo. These confessional border-crossings usually operate unidirectionally, away from irreligious non-Christian belief toward the universal truth of Christianity. In *The Tempest*, Shakespeare comes close to depicting the opposite, the "turning Turk," of a Christian woman through her marriage to a Muslim king. The events of Claribel's marriage, however, happen safely off-stage. They are so obscene that they can only be mentioned as accomplished fact and then repressed through reframing in the classical past and geographic coordinates. The elision of Islam in this fashion successfully evacuates the Muslim presence from the Mediterranean. It also hides the reality of the daily conversions occurring in this geography, particularly the movement of Christian women into the households of Muslim men either as enslaved concubines or wives. It was common practice for Ottoman sultans to fill their harems with kidnapped and enslaved women from Christian territories in the Mediterranean and Europe. The Tempest is silent on this threat of Mediterranean life, but other early modern English plays such as Thomas Heywood's The Fair Maid of the West (1597) and Philip Massinger's The Renegado (1624) dramatize this danger, emphasizing the imperiled social position of white women in this geography and their apparent desirability to Muslim potentates. The Tempest leaves this fear unvocalized and gives the union patriarchal sanction, while also undermining Alonso's authority through the objections raised by Sebastian and the absent Claribel. Her narrative serves as a cautionary tale of foreign, Muslim alliance because once she is married, she is for all intents and purposes lost to "our Europe," her claim to Naples tenuous not because of the literal distance between Naples and Tunis but because of the cultural, racial, and religious expanse now separating her from her homeland. Marriage to "an African" has made her non-European and non-Christian, to the extent that she is no longer a viable heir for Naples.

Emphasizing the Mediterranean as an important cultural geography in The Tempest exposes the play's ideological investments in patriarchal authority and European dynastic futurity and uncovers how contact with the Muslim Other threatens these aims. Even as the play depicts Christian encroachment within the Mediterranean through Prospero's occupation of the island, in reality, Muslim regimes controlled much of this geography. My aim, throughout this chapter, however, has not been to uncritically advance the idea of a Muslim presence. It was a historical fact. Rather, I hope to convey the significance of Shakespeare's erasure of Islam and Muslims and his use of coded language to conjure and then banish them. These moves signal the play's cultural and imaginative commitment to creating a Mediterranean free from the kinds of religious and racial differences that were characteristic of and natural to the locale.

The Tempest demonstrates how the Mediterranean can be incorporated into European imperial racial projects, so that it, the difference inherent in it, the difference represented by Caliban can remain a "thing of darkness," acknowledged but ultimately left behind in favor of prosperity in a religiously pure and racially homogenous Europe. The idea of such a Mediterranean, where movement is the purview of European characters and the natives of the island are confined to the "hard rock" designed to imprison them, is the stuff of fantasy.[58] It belies the fluidity of this arena, which was not only cleaved by forms of imperial competition—between various European powers, Muslim regimes, such as the Saadi dynasty of Morocco and the Ottomans, and African polities—but also connected by the flow of people and goods. The Mediterranean has always been multicultural, and it was so in Shakespeare's time. *The Tempest*, however, accepts but limits that fact. I focus my analysis of the play on Sycorax and Claribel because they, too, occupy the margins and highlight the Muslim cultures that are deliberately made peripheral to the play's action. Thinking through difference and through the margins, however, exposes religious, racial, and cultural chauvinism at the play's center. Even as Islam and Muslims are relegated to the sidelines of Shakespeare's play, they manage to influence its action because the white, patriarchal, European, and Christian power so forcefully articulated at play's end, only comes into being through the difference contained at the center of the island and its Muslim Mediterranean borders.

NOTES

1 William Shakespeare, *The Tempest: A Case Study in Critical Controversy*, ed. Gerald Graff and James Phelan (Boston: Bedford/St. Martin's, 2009), 5.1.183–84.

2 *Oxford English Dictionary*, s.v. "brave (adj., n., and int.)," accessed October 11, 2022.

3 See, for example, Aimé Césaire, *A Tempest: Based on Shakespeare's The Tempest, Adaptation for a Black Theatre*, trans. Richard Miller (New York: TCG Translations, 2002); George Lamming, *The Pleasures of Exile* (Ann Arbor, MI: University of Michigan Press, 1992); Roberto Fernández Retamar, *Caliban and Other Essays*, trans. Edward Baker (Minneapolis: University of Minnesota Press, 1989).

4 See, for example, Paul Brown, "'This Thing of Darkness I Acknowledge Mine': *The Tempest* and the Discourse of Colonialism," *Political Shakespeare: Essays in Cultural Materialism*, ed. Jonathan Dollimore and Alan Sinfeld (Manchester: Manchester University Press, 1994), 48–71; Stephen Greenblatt, *Learning to Curse: Essays in Early Modern Culture* (London: Routledge, 2015).

5 Virginia Mason Vaughan and Alden T. Vaughan. "*The Tempest* and Early Modern Conceptions of Race," *The Cambridge Companion to Shakespeare and Race*, ed. Ayanna Thompson (Cambridge: Cambridge University Press, 2021), 139.

6 Jerry Brotton. "'This Tunis, Sir, Was Carthage': Contesting Colonialism in *The Tempest*," *Post-Colonial Shakespeares*, ed. Ania Loomba and Martin Orkin (London: Routledge, 1998), 27–28.

7 Andrew C. Hess, "The Mediterranean and Shakespeare's Geopolitical Imagination," *The Tempest and Its Travels*, ed. Peter Hulme and William H. Sherman (Chicago: University of Chicago Press, 2000), 121–130; Jerry Brotton, "Carthage and Tunis, The Tempest and Tapestries," *The Tempest and Its Travels*, ed. Hulme and Sherman, 132; Barbara Fuchs, "Conquering Islands: Contextualizing *The Tempest*," *Shakespeare Quarterly*, 48.1 (1997), 45–62. Patricia Parker, "Barbers and Barbary: Early Modern Cultural Semantics," *Renaissance Drama*, 33 (2004), 201–44.

8 Jonathan Burton, *Traffic and Turning: Islam and English Drama, 1579–1624* (Newark, DE: University of Delaware Press, 2005), 11.

9 In his introduction to *Three Turk Plays*, Daniel Vitkus seems to coin this term and define it in relation to the popularity of Ottoman material on the English stage noting that the subgenre exposes ambivalent English reactions to Islam and the Ottoman Empire. Daniel Vitkus, *Three Turk Plays: From Early Modern England*. (New York: Columbia University Press, 2000) 3.

10 Corisande Fenwick, *Early Islamic North Africa: A New Perspective* (London: Bloomsbury, 2020), 1.

11 Fenwick, *Early Islamic North Africa*, 3.

12 "About the Topic of Race," United States Census Bureau, March 1, 2022. www.census.gov/topics/population/race/about.html

13 Kim F. Hall, *Things of Darkness: Economies of Race and Gender in Early Modern England* (Ithaca: Cornell University Press, 1995), 92–98.

14 Nina G. Jablonski, "Skin Color and Race," *The American Journal of Physical Anthropology*, 175.2 (2021), 439.

15 Ramzi Rouighi, *Inventing the Berbers: History and Ideology in the Maghrib* (Philadelphia: University of Pennsylvania Press, 2019), 18.

16 See Ambereen Dadabhoy, "Barbarian Moors," *The Cambridge Companion to Shakespeare and Race*, ed. Ayanna Thompson (Cambridge, Cambridge University Press, 2021), 30–46.

17 bell hooks, "Choosing the Margin as a Space of Radical Openness," *Framework: The Journal of Cinema and Media*, 36 (1989), 21.

18 hooks, "Choosing the Margin," 20.

19 hooks, "Choosing the Margin," 21–23. Being a subject from the margins has helped me create and cultivate a critical orientation attuned to the erasures of the center, or dominant culture, of which Shakespeare's works are in the process of creating. For an analysis of Black feminist marginality in the creation of knowledge, particularly in Black women's theorization of spatial relations see Katherine McKittrick, *Demonic Grounds: Black Women and Cartographies of Struggle* (Minneapolis: University of Minnesota Press, 2006).

20 For the monstrous feminine, see Barbara Creed, *The Monstrous-Feminine: Film, Feminism, Psychoanalysis* (London: Routledge, 2015).

21 Shakespeare, *Tempest*, 1.2.264–65; 283; 322; 258) 259 284–85.

22 Creed, *The Monstrous-Feminine*, 3–5.

23 *Open Source Shakespeare: Concordance*, s.v. "Monster (n.)," accessed October 14, 2022, www.opensourceshakespeare.org/concordance/o/?i=764 674&pleasewait=1&msg=sr

24 Shakespeare, *Tempest*, 1.2.266.

25 Tal Shuval, "The Ottoman Algerian Elite and Its Ideology," *International Journal of Middle East Studies*, 32.3 (2000), 325.

26 Ania Loomba, *Shakespeare, Race, and Colonialism* (Oxford: Oxford University Press, 2002), 166.

27 Nicolas de Nicolay, *The Nauigations, Peregrinations and Voyages, Made into Turkie by Nicholas Nicholay Daulphinois, Lord of Arfeuile, Chamberlaine and Geographer Ordinarie to the King of Fraunce* [...] *Translated Out of the French by T.Washington theYounger* (London, 1585), 7. Accessed via Early English Books Online.

28 David Brafman, "Facing East: The Western View of Islam in Nicolas de Nicolay's 'Travels in Turkey'." *Getty Research Journal*, 1 (2009), 153–60.

29 Nicolay, *The Nauigations*, 8.

30 Nicolay, *The Nauigations*, 9.

31 For more on Nicolay and the woodcuts of Muslim women in *The Nauigations* see, Roland Betancourt and Ambereen Dadabhoy "Geographies of Race: Constructions of Constantinople/Istanbul in the Western European Imaginary," Eds. Noémie Ndiaye and Lia Markey. *Seeing Race Before Race:Visual Culture and the Racial Matrix in the Premodern World* (Tempe: ACMRS Press, 2023). https://asu.pressbooks.pub/see ing-race-before-race/chapter/geographies-of-race-constructions-of-constantinople-istanbul-in-the-western-european-imaginary/

32 Natalie Zemon Davis, *Trickster Travels: A Sixteenth-Century Muslim between Worlds* (NewYork: Hill and Wang, 2006), 3–4.

33 Davis, *Trickster Travels*, 62–64.

34 Davis, *Trickster Travels*, 65.

35 Davis, *Trickster Travels*, 65.

36 Leo Africanus, *A Geographical Historie of Africa, Written in Arabicke and Italian by Iohn Leo a More, Borne in Granada, and BroughtVp in Barbarie.* [...] *Translated and Collected by Iohn Pory, Lately of Goneuill and Caius College in Cambridge.* London: 1600.

37 Davis, *Trickster Travels*, 249–53.

38 Emily C. Bartels, "Making More of the Moor: Aaron, Othello, and Renaissance Refashionings of Race," *Shakespeare Quarterly*, 41.4

(1990): 433–54; Andrew Hadfield, "Race in *Othello*: The *History and Description of Africa* and the Black Legend," *Notes and Queries*, 45.3 (1998): 336–39; Daniel J. Vitkus, "Turning Turk in *Othello*: The Conversion and Damnation of the Moor," *Shakespeare Quarterly*, 48.2 (1997): 145–76; Jonathan Burton, "'A Most Wily Bird': Leo Africanus, Othello and the Trafficking in Difference," *Post-Colonial Shakespeares*, ed. Ania Loomba and Martin Orkin (London: Routledge, 2003), 55–75. In *Shakespeare, Race and Colonialism*, Ania Loomba points to Africanus's description of Tunis (166).

39 John Pory, "To the Reader," in Africanus, *Geographical Historie*, n.p.

40 Africanus, *Geographical Historie*, 148–49.

41 39 1.2.322.

42 1.2.334; 342–43

43 Sylvia Wynter, "Afterword: Beyond Miranda's Meanings: Un/silencing the 'Demonic Ground' Of Caliban's Woman," *Out of the Kumbla: Caribbean Women and Literature*, ed. Carole Boyce Davies and Elaine Savory Fido (Trenton, NJ: Africa World Press, 1990), 355–66.

44 2.1.68–69.

45 2.1.68–69.

46 Marjorie Raley, "Claribel's Husband," *Race, Ethnicity, and Power in the Renaissance*, ed. Joyce Green MacDonald (Madison, NJ: Fairleigh Dickinson University Press, 1997), 95–119.

47 Brotton, "This Tunis," 33.

48 Brotton, "This Tunis," 34. For more on these tapestries see Brotton, "Carthage and Tunis."

49 Brotton, "This Tunis," 34.

50 Brotton, "This Tunis," 36.

51 Africanus, 246.

52 Africanus, *Geographical Historie*, 247. Loomba also focuses on this moment; see *Shakespeare, Race, and Colonialism*, 166.

53 51 2.1.107.

54 2.1.120–28.

55 Hall, *Things of Darkness*, 3.

56 Hall, *Things of Darkness*, 69–70.

57 *Oxford English Dictionary*, s.v. "loathness (n.)," accessed October 19, 2022.

58 1.2.346.

REFERENCES

Africanus, Leo. *A Geographical Historie of Africa, Written in Arabicke and Italian by Iohn Leo a More, Borne in Granada, and Brought Vp in Barbarie. Wherein He Hath at Large Described, Not Onely the Qualities, Situations, and True Distances of the Regions, Cities, Townes, Mountaines, Riuers, and Other Places Throughout all the North and Principall Partes of Africa; but also the Descents and Families of their Kings ... Gathered Partly Out of His Owne Diligent Obseruations, and Partly Out of the Ancient Records and Chronicles of the Arabians and Mores. before which, Out of the Best Ancient and Moderne Writers, is Prefixed a Generall Description of Africa, and also a Particular Treatise of all the Maine Lands and Isles Vndescribed by Iohn Leo. ... Translated and Collected by Iohn Pory, Lately of Goneuill and Caius College in Cambridge.* London, 1600. Accessed via Early English Books Online.

Andrea, Bernadette. *Women and Islam in Early Modern English Literature.* Cambridge: Cambridge University Press, 2008.

Bartels, Emily C. "Making More of the Moor: Aaron, Othello, and Renaissance Refashionings of Race." *Shakespeare Quarterly* 41.4 (1990): 433–54.

Brafman, David. "Facing East: The Western View of 'Travels in Turkey'." *Getty Research Journal* 1 (2009): 153–60.

Brotton, Jerry. "'This Tunis, Sir, Was Carthage': Contesting Colonialism in *The Tempest.*" In *Post-Colonial Shakespeares*, edited by Ania Loomba and Martin Orkin, 23–42. London: Routledge, 1998.

——— "Carthage and Tunis, The Tempest and Tapestries," *The Tempest and Its Travels*, edited by Peter Hulme and William H. Sherman, 121–30. Chicago: University of Chicago Press, 2000.

Brown, Paul. "'This Thing of Darkness I Acknowledge Mine': *The Tempest* and the Discourse of Colonialism." In *Political Shakespeare: Essays in Cultural Materialism*, edited by Jonathan Dollimore and Alan Sinfeld, 48–71. Manchester: Manchester University Press, 1994.

Burton, Jonathan. "'A Most Wily Bird': Leo Africanus, Othello and the Trafficking in Difference." In *Post-Colonial Shakespeares*, edited by Ania Loomba and Martin Orkin, 55–75. London: Routledge, 2003.

———. *Traffic and Turning: Islam and English Drama, 1579–1624.* Newark: University of Delaware Press, 2005.

Césaire, Aimé. *A Tempest: Based on Shakespeare's* The Tempest, *Adaptation for a Black Theatre.* Translated by Richard Miller. New York: TCG Translations, 2002.

Creed, Barbara. *The Monstrous-Feminine: Film, Feminism, Psychoanalysis*. London: Routledge, 2015.

Dadabhoy, Ambereen. "Barbarian Moors: Documenting Racial Formation in Early Modern England." In *The Cambridge Companion to Shakespeare and Race*, edited by Ayanna Thompson, 30–46. Cambridge: Cambridge University Press, 2021.

Davis, Natalie Zemon. *Trickster Travels: A Sixteenth-Century Muslim between Worlds*. New York: Hill and Wang, 2006.

Fenwick, Corisande. *Early Islamic North Africa: A New Perspective*. London: Bloomsbury, 2020.

Fuchs, Barbara. "Conquering Islands: Contextualizing The Tempest," *Shakespeare Quarterly* 48.1 (1997): 45–62.

Greenblatt, Stephen. *Learning to Curse: Essays in Early Modern Culture*. London: Routledge, 2015.

Hadfield, Andrew. "Race in Othello: The History and Description of Africa and the Black Legend." *Notes and Queries* 45.3 (1998): 336–39.

Hall, Kim F. *Things of Darkness: Economies of Race and Gender in Early Modern England*. Ithaca, NY: Cornell University Press, 1995.

Hess, Andrew C. "The Mediterranean and Shakespeare's Geopolitical Imagination." *The Tempest and Its Travels*, edited by Peter Hulme and William H. Sherman, 121–30. Chicago: University of Chicago Press, 2000.

hooks, bell. "Choosing the Margin as a Space of Radical Openness." *Framework: The Journal of Cinema and Media* 36 (1989): 15–23.

Jablonski, Nina G. "Skin Color and Race." *The American Journal of Physical Anthropology* 175.2: Special Issue: Race reconciled II: Interpreting and communicating biological variation and race in 2021: 437–47. https://doi.org/10.1002/ajpa.24200

Lamming, George. *The Pleasures of Exile*. Ann Arbor, MI: University of Michigan Press, 1992.

Loomba, Ania. *Shakespeare, Race, and Colonialism*. Oxford: Oxford University Press, 2002.

Nicolay, Nicolas de. *The Nauigations, Peregrinations and Voyages, made into Turkie by Nicholas Nicholay Daulphinois, Lord of Arfeuile, Chamberlaine and Geographer Ordinarie to the King of Fraunce Conteining Sundry Singularities which the Author Hath there Seene and Obserued: Deuided into Foure Bookes, with Threescore Figures, Naturally Set Forth as Well of Men as Women, According to the*

Diuersitie of Nations, their Port, Intreatie, Apparrell, Lawes, Religion and Maner of Liuing, Aswel in Time of Warre as Peace: With Diuers Faire and Memorable Histories, Happened in our Time. Translated Out of the French by T. Washington the Younger. London, 1585. Accessed via Early English Books Online.

Retamar, Roberto Fernández. Caliban and Other Essays. Translated by Edward Baker. Minneapolis: University of Minnesota Press, 1989.

Rouighi, Ramzi. Inventing the Berbers: History and Ideology in the Maghrib. Philadelphia: University of Pennsylvania Press, 2019.

Shakespeare, William. The Tempest: A Case Study in Critical Controversy, edited by Gerald Graff and James Phelan. Boston: Bedford/St. Martin's, 2009.

Shuval, Tal. "The Ottoman Algerian Elite and Its Ideology." International Journal of Middle East Studies 32.3 (2000): 323–44. doi:10.1017/ S0020743800021127.

United States Census Bureau, "About the Topic of Race," March 1, 2022. www. census.gov/topics/population/race/about.html

Vaughan, Virginia Mason, and Alden T. Vaughan. "The Tempest and Early Modern Conceptions of Race." In The Cambridge Companion to Shakespeare and Race, edited by Ayanna Thompson, 139–57. Cambridge: Cambridge University Press, 2021.

Vitkus, Daniel J. "Turning Turk in Othello: The Conversion and Damnation of the Moor." Shakespeare Quarterly 48.2 (1997): 145–76.

Wynter, Sylvia. "Afterword: Beyond Miranda's Meanings: Un/silencing the 'Demonic Ground' Of Caliban's Woman." In Out of the Kumbla: Caribbean Women and Literature, edited by Carole Boyce Davies and Elaine Savory Fido, 355–66. Trenton, NJ: Africa World Press, 1990.

Turning to the "Turk" in Shakespeare's History Plays
Two

In 1599 Thomas Dallam set off on a dangerous voyage through the Mediterranean Sea to Istanbul, the capital of the Ottoman Empire that culminated in an audience with the Ottoman sultan, Mehemet III. Dallam was part of a diplomatic voyage on behalf of his monarch Queen Elizabeth I, to negotiate favorable commercial terms with the Sublime Porte, as the Ottoman capital was often called, which would allow the English to circumvent the Venetian and French trading monopolies in Mediterranean's lucrative markets. Dallam was not, however, a diplomat; on the contrary, he was a young organ maker from Lancashire, who found himself in the heart of an empire that controlled much of Asia, North Africa, and Europe. Dallam's role in the embassy was based on his skilled craftsmanship: he had won the royal contract to make and deliver "an elaborate and complicated organ which, [when] played by hand or regulated intervals by clock-work, would give forth melodies while artificial birds chirped and clapped their wings and wooden angels set trumpets to their lips," which was being gifted by the queen to the sultan.[1] The marvelous instrument gained Dallam an audience with the sultan and an invitation to convert to Islam—with the promise of two wives—and remain in Istanbul. Dallam's diary, preserved in a manuscript, was first published by the Hakluyt Society in 1893 along with the diary of the English Chaplain Dr. Covel,

DOI: 10.4324/9781003213581-3

in order to provide readers with "the experiences of men who resided in Constantinople during the earlier days of the Levant company."[2] Both narratives exhibit, for the volume's editor, James Theodore Bent, the struggle of the English nation "to gain for itself those rights—or capitulations, as they are called—which formed the basis of the prosperity of the Company during the ensuing century and a half."[3] The early difficulties of the English to gain a foothold in Mediterranean trade, support the hindsight narrative of English resilience and power that Bent's project promotes. The stories of English lives imperiled within the foreign and hostile geography of the Muslim Mediterranean and the Ottoman Empire itself offer proof of the strength and legitimacy of the British Empire, which was based on the fearlessness of enterprising English merchants, determined to set up trading companies in distant and foreign locales. Even as Bent attempts to enfold Dallam's narrative into the larger project of late Victorian British imperialism, the *Diary* disrupts such aims through Dallam's uneasiness with the integrity of his own venture, especially because it involved an alliance with the dangerous Islamic Other.

Throughout the *Diary*, Dallam recounts his own marginalized position within the diplomatic embassy and the marginalization of the English in the geography of the Muslim Mediterranean. In 1599 the English had yet to feel confident in the trade agreements that would allow them access to the markets long monopolized by the Venetians and French, or to feel safe operating their factories in Ottoman-controlled territories. For instance, the *Diary* records the English ambassador in Istanbul's delicate relationship with the Venetian bailo ('baylie'), which may have indicated his desire to maintain civil relations with the Venetian diplomat.[4] Venice had established commercial relations with Constantinople in the thirteenth century, and after the Ottoman conquest of the city in 1453, the republic continued to maintain a diplomatic and mercantile presence in Istanbul.[5] While it was precisely this power that the English sought to circumvent with their own treaties and capitulations with the Sublime Porte, their upstart position within this space meant that they also had to depend upon the experience of others more familiar with the geography and the culture. From power-hungry bureaucrats eager for bribes at various ports of entry to crewmembers dying suddenly during the journey, the *Diary* presents a narrative of danger, both quotidian and fatal for those foreign to this region.[6] While the personal threat to Dallam's life and religion is most obvious when he is inside the Ottoman imperial saryı—which Dallam Anglicizes as *surralia* while the common term among other European writers of the period is *seraglio*—those threats are also evident throughout the narrative.

One incident highlights the precarious position of Dallam's party: upon reaching Istanbul, the captain of the ship offered an official salute to the sultan by setting off a mighty round of the *Hector's* guns, and "discharged eight score great shot and betwixt every great shot a volley of small shot; it was done with very good decorum and true time, and it might well deserve commendations."[7] According to Dallam this triumphant volley astounds its Ottoman audience who found it "very strange and wonderful," yet he remains concerned as to the appropriateness of the action, since it is an act of obeisance to a non-Christian and non-European potentate. His unease manifests as fear, which is quickly confirmed by the inexplicable death of one of his crewmembers:

> but one thing I noted, which persuaded my simple conceit
> that this great triumph and charge was very evil bestowed,

being done unto an infidel. There was one man sick in the ship, who was the ship's carpenter, and with the report of the first great piece that was discharged he died.[8]

Despite noting that his fellow crewmember was already ill, Dallam attributes the cause of the death to the honor bestowed upon the Ottoman sultan. Writing about Dallam's *Diary* as an Orientalist text, Eric de Barros incisively points to the swift and unforeseen deaths that befall Dallam's shipmates as examples of the lethal danger that the Orient poses, which is represented as "punishment" to the English for "crossing" into Ottoman imperial dominions.[9] De Barros argues that Dallam's sparse remarks on the deaths demonstrate the geography's menace: "it is as if [Dallam] is suggesting that a barely or simply mentioned death—in effect, the exclusion of the body and soul from a religious narrative of redemption and salvation—is a consequence of boundary violating travel."[10] The imagined boundary between Christendom and Islam, between Europe and Asia, is one the Ottomans are constantly crossing in the way they incorporate religious difference into their imperial body politic and in the territories they control. In Dallam's narrative, these spheres must be kept separate and their boundaries firmly policed and reinforced. Thus, the narrative yokes the death of the crewmember to an "evil" action intended to offer homage to an "infidel" ruler. By refracting the gun salute through the lens of religious difference, Dallam displays common early modern cultural prejudices that demonized Muslims and delegitimized Islam as a religion. In its early modern usage, "infidel" meant "unbeliever" in the "true religion" and was usually applied to "an adherent of a religion opposed to Christianity."[11] Religious bigotry arises in a moment where the English are so very clearly at a disadvantage, and it allows Dallam to rhetorically empower both himself and the crew through their right and proper Christian faith.

Regardless of his misgivings, Dallam still manages to perform the duties for which he was brought on the embassy to Istanbul. He spends the month of November 1599 assembling the organ in Topkapı Sarayı, and here, too, he finds the specter of death following him. Even though he is very well taken care of at the palace—eating grapes every day after having meat—Dallam writes that the location where he was to assemble the organ was both a house of pleasure and death.[12] Dallam's matter-of-fact accounting that "in this little house, that emperor [Sultan Mehmet III] that reigned when I was there, had nineteen brothers put to death in it, and it was built for no other use but for the strangling of every emperor's brethren" is followed by a detailed description of the riches in the rooms, including the silken carpets and elaborate mirrors, as though to say more about such violence would invite some of that danger upon himself.[13] In fact, much of Dallam's narrative while in the sarayı is peppered with fear of his imminent death because of some breach in conduct or propriety. At the same time, however, he is dazzled by the immense wealth and beauty of the palace and by extension the sultan and the Ottoman Empire itself.

Dallam's *Diary* exhibits the twin emotions that characterize early modern (travel) writing about the Ottoman Empire: fear and desire. Nowhere is this more apparent than in his meeting with the sultan to demonstrate the workings of his organ. Having already witnessed its many moving parts, including a bushel of blackbirds and thrushes that sang and moved their wings, trumpets, songs, and chimes, the sultan wished to hear the organ played. Dallam notes that the sultan sat in "wonder" at the spectacle of the organ—a direct compliment to his own craftsmanship—and he, in turn, is awestruck by the imperial court: "he sat in great state, yet the sight of him was nothing in comparison of the train that stood behind him, the sight whereof did make me almost to think that I was in another world."[14] Dallam is transported by the magnificence of the sultan's retinue, which numbers approximately 400 in his estimation, who wear cloth of gold and tissue and great pieces of silver adorning the belts on their waists. He is only recalled from his own astonishment by the Kapı Agha—the chief official in charge of the sultan's domestic space—bidding him to play the organ. Unfortunately for Dallam, the seating arrangements force him to "turn [his] back right toward [the sultan] and touch his knee with my breeches," both of which, he has been warned by the ambassador, are punishable by immediate execution.[15] As he plays, the sultan's view is blocked, and "in his rising from his chair, he gave me a thrust forwards, which he could not otherwise do, he sat so near me; but I thought he had been drawing his sword to cut my head." Dallam's mortal fear of physical contact with the sultan may strike modern readers as comedic in the vein of an upstairs/downstairs encounter, but it was not unwarranted. The strict protocols governing the behavior of foreigners within Ottoman dominions, and most especially in the presence of the sultan, were well-known. However, Dallam's fear also encodes the danger of contact with the Muslim Other that could literally lead to his own violent death, like those of the sultan's nineteen brothers and the random deaths of his fellow, anonymous crewmembers.

The lethal potential of the geography of the Ottoman palace offers a microcosm of the dangers that the Ottoman Empire posed to Englishmen who enter its sphere of power and influence. The possibility of cultural (and religious) conversion is even presented in the form of two Englishmen "turned Turk" who serve as dragomen or interpreters for the sultan. One is a "Cornishman," and the other is from Lancashire and given the name, "Finche."[16] About the anonymous Cornishman, Dallam is virtually silent, perhaps owing to an incident when Dallam unwittingly found himself in an area where "the Grand Senior and his Concubines," were about to promenade.[17] The Cornishman's negligence saw him fired from the ambassador's service, but allowed Dallam to observe not only the sultan and his odalisques at play, but also the African eunuchs who guarded the harem. Like the earlier encounter with the sultan, this scene is darkly comic:

> Now, as I was running for my life, I did see a little of a brave show, which was the Grand Senior himself on horseback, many of his concubines, some riding and some on foot, and brave fellows in their kind, that were gelded men, and keepers of the concubines, negroes that were as black as jet, but very brave; by their sides great scimitars, the scabbards seemed to be all gold.[18]

Dallam has once again had a forbidden encounter, which should have left him dead, yet he manages to escape. His reward is also the reader's reward: access to the private and domestic sphere of the Ottoman Empire—which was denied to Ottoman subjects—to sights such as the concubines of the harem guarded by scimitar-wielding African eunuchs, and indeed the sultan himself. Dallam exhibits more feelings toward his second dragoman, Finche, who he not only names, but further notes that he was "in religion a perfect Turk, but he was our trusty friend."[19] He makes no mention of friendship with the "Cornishman"; however, the "Englishman, born in Chorley, Lancashire" is a "trusty friend," because he ensures that Dallam does not fall prey to mercenary native "Turks." Even though "turning Turk," in the common idiom of the day, meant betrayal against religion and nation, Finche's religious conversion is overlooked in the face of his act of national solidarity. Moreover, Dallam offers no commentary on the conversion of his fellow countrymen, nor is he struck by the paradox of Finche being both a "Turk" and an Englishman or "Cornishman." While these identity markers indicate ethnicity, in Dallam's narrative and in early modern English discourse more broadly, "Turk" is always a synonym for Muslim, thus easily solving the apparent contradiction of an English or Cornish "Turk." The appeal to a form of Englishness at the core of the converted Muslim or "turned Turk" also suggests a fixed or stable national, English identity that remains unchanged in the face of the many other transformations effected within the fluid geography of the Mediterranean. At the same time, the presence of English and European "Turks" bespeaks the allure of Islam and the Ottoman Empire, which crucially is always rendered as a material desire rather than an articulation or conviction of faith. "Turning Turk" is a legitimate fear that peppers Dallam's *Diary*, and a potential consequence of continued English ventures in the Muslim Mediterranean and with the Ottoman Empire.

IMPERIAL INTIMACIES

Dallam's experiences in the Ottoman Empire and within the intimate spaces of the imperial palace are nested within larger geopolitical maneuverings by the English crown at the end of the sixteenth century. They relate the thrills and chills of one man's journey into a space of radical difference and alterity, yet they simultaneously speak to the anxieties and desires that animate affairs of state. The diplomatic mission that Dallam accompanies is only part of the story of England's negotiations with the Ottoman Empire during the reign of Queen Elizabeth I. In 1578, the queen sent William Harborne to Istanbul on a clandestine mission to open a channel of communication with the Ottoman sultan and obtain certain commercial capitulations on her behalf.[20] Several reasons may have contributed to Elizabeth's decision to pursue a political alliance with Murad III, who then occupied the imperial seat. In 1570, the queen had been excommunicated by Pope Pius V, who declared her a heretic and released all Catholics under her rule from loyalty to her. Identifying the Papal Bull as the impetus for England's increased alliance with Istanbul, Lisa Jardine notes that

> the papal intention was further to isolate England from the rest of Catholic Europe—although in fact its immediate effect was to generate an upsurge of English patriotism and loyalty. An unlooked-for consequence of the Bull, however, was that it freed English merchants from the Catholic Church's embargo on (and heavily punitive fines for) trading in the infidel oriental marketplace.[21]

Not only did the excommunication backfire on the Pope, but also it spurred the crown to look to other markets to secure its independence from Rome and Spain. While trade with Muslims may have been prohibited by the Catholic Church, Elizabeth was not the first European monarch to establish a commercial or diplomatic alliance with an Ottoman sultan. Several decades earlier, Francis I approached Sultan Süleyman the Magnificent for military aid against the growing power of the Habsburgs.[22] The ensuing Franco–Ottoman alliance formalized commercial and military ties with the installation of a French ambassador in Istanbul in 1535.[23] As Pascale Barthe points out about this strategic relationship, "circumventing if not entirely replacing the Venetians at the Sublime Porte, the French quickly established themselves as the Ottomans' privileged Christian interlocutors long before the English and the Dutch."[24] This politically expedient alliance, like that sought by Queen Elizabeth in 1570, undermines the ideological and discursive fiction that is Christendom, the idea of a unified Christian Europe ideologically and militarily opposed to the non-Christian Ottoman and Muslim societies at its borders. Indeed, Elizabeth I's excommunication testifies to the fractures within Christendom and Europe that made political intimacy with the other powers inhabiting Europe necessary regardless of religious affiliation.

Queen Elizabeth's letters to the sultan demonstrate the English crown's willingness to cross religious boundaries in order to establish diplomatic and commercial relations. Writing about the isolation of Elizabethan England, Matthew Dimmock notes that the Papal Bull coupled with Spanish aggression resulted in the English "being squeezed out of their traditional Northern European markets for both exports and imports," and that "the Spanish clearly felt that this strategy of embargo would ultimately bring them victory."[25] Finding themselves between a rock and a hard place, it made both political and commercial sense for the English to seek succor from an imperial power that could rival the Pope as well as the Holy Roman Emperor. However, both official and unofficial traffic in the Mediterranean and with the Ottoman Empire resulted in criticism abroad. As Dimmock

SOLYMAN.

Figure 2.1 Ottoman Sultan Sülyeman, from Knolles *General History of the Turks* "Solyman." LUNA: Folger Digital Image Collection, Folger Shakespeare Library.

notes, Catholic polemics identified England's diplomatic treaties with Muslim potentates in Morocco and the Ottoman Empire as a scandalous betrayal of Christian fraternity.[26] Even as the queen "took to repeatedly denying that the English had anything more than a simple trading relationship with the Ottomans," her chief spy, Francis Walsingham was using the official English agent in Istanbul, William Harborne, to convince the sultan to attack their mutual enemy, Spain. He suggested they make a "show of arming to the sea for the King of Spain's dominions, hold the King of Spain in suspense, by means whereof he shall be the less bold to send forth his best forces into these parts."[27] As Lisa Jardine argues, these machinations demonstrated how "the English government was able to exploit the strong commercial base established by the English merchants (under the agency of Harborne) in Constantinople [sic] to significant effect, in relation to the European political arena."[28]

Indeed, the queen capitalized on the supposed shared religious values between Protestantism and Islam—their mutual abjuration of idols—to reinforce the alliance as one in service of right and true religion. In a letter to Murad III, Elizabeth underscores this point by referring to herself as "the most invincible and most mighty defender of the Christian faith against all kinds of idolatries."[29] The tactic was useful, as Jerry Brotton suggests in *The Sultan and the Queen* because it was similarly employed by Harborne to persuade the sultan into entering into "a military coalition" that would accomplish "the destruction of idol-worshippers."[30] The articulation of religious commonality with Muslims illustrates the way Christian states were able to justify their political and commercial exchanges across confessional lines. The boundary between Islam and Christendom became far more permeable in the face of England's religious and political marginalization within Europe. Subscribing to the axiom that "the enemy of my enemy is my friend," the queen and her agents treated Muslim regimes as coveted allies whose incredible military powers could potentially be marshaled against England's foes. All the while, Protestant polemicists in England and on the Continent aligned the "Turk" with Catholicism. As Daniel Vitkus explains, "English Protestant texts associated both the Pope and the Ottoman sultan with Satan or the Antichrist."[31] Despite the amity cultivated by Elizabeth I's diplomatic and commercial overtures to the sultan, English clergymen like

John Foxe called both Islam and the Ottoman Empire the scourge of God, decrying the "the ruin & subversion of so many Christian Churches, with the horrible murders and captivity of infinite Christians."[32] The disparity between the queen's private negotiations with the Sublime Porte and the public denunciation of the "Turk" highlights the differences between the "realpolitik" of affairs of state and the prejudice of religious polemic.[33]

The varying points of view toward this non-Christian and (non) European Other underscore the shifting, contingent, and politically and culturally expedient approach to the "Turk" that was common in early modern English culture. In some ways, these divergent perspectives may suggest that early modern English sentiments about Islam, Muslims, and the Ottoman Empire are not Orientalist because they display a distinct polyphony of perspectives rather than a stable hegemonic discourse. In fact, the queen's cordial epistolary relationship not only with Murad III, but also with his mother, the Valide Sultan Safiye, supports this interpretation of the Anglo-Ottoman alliance with written evidence of mutual recognition and the desire for amicable relations between the two polities that transcends religious divides. Bernadette Andrea has shown how the Queen's direct correspondence with the Valide Sultan—one woman to another—allowed the English unprecedented access to the sultan through his mother.[34] Andrea further contends that the letters between Elizabeth and Safiye display the political power and agency that these women rulers and political figures were able to carve out in a traditionally masculine and patriarchal domain. She argues that "womanliness, exercised by women as agents rather than imposed on them as objects of exchange, thus becomes the means to establish political and economic bonds across cultures."[35] Not only do these letters confirm the English desire to establish friendly political terms with the Ottoman Empire, they simultaneously expose the power of elite Ottoman women, particularly the mothers of the sultan, over affairs of the empire. They uncover the way these women articulated their political agency and their astute mobilization of gender to achieve their goals. These letters further expose the intimacies that were being cultivated across religious lines and explicitly reveal the asymmetrical relationship between the English and the Ottomans.

As Gerald MacLean and Nabil Matar remark, relations between the English crown and Muslim regimes were "complex, dynamic, and subject to regular sea changes;" so much so that "it remains notable that at no time during this period did religious difference constitute an insurmountable obstacle to trade, politics, or diplomatic negotiation."[36] The archival evidence of direct correspondence between the monarchs, along with commercial and diplomatic compacts, illustrates the ambiguous, ambivalent, and shifting rhetorical position of the Ottoman Empire in relation to England, from Christendom's existential threat to an uneasy ally against the Catholic Church. The nuances that scholars such as Brotton, MacLean, Matar, and Andrea have traced within England's relationship with the Ottoman Empire demonstrate the ideological fluidity that characterizes early modern English attitudes toward Islamic cultures.[37]

"TURKS" ON THE STAGE

While politics may make strange bedfellows, that association does not always translate into wider cultural acceptance. Even the agents in charge of establishing and sustaining this relationship, like Dallam and Harborne, had reservations about dealing with the "Turk." Indeed, Brotton reveals that Harborne prayed "that her Majesty in her just defense might never need this heathen tyrant his assistance" and was relieved when the military alliance never materialized.[38] Harborne's anxiety "about trafficking with the 'infidel'" points to the ambivalence underwriting these cross-cultural and confessional exchanges.[39] In reality, the power differential between the English and the Ottomans required that the former overlook religious difference in order to facilitate an alliance with the latter. In English popular culture, however, the precarity of the English in these tense Mediterranean negotiations is transformed into the reverse. Their powerlessness is turned into power in their relations with the "Turk" in public discursive arenas such as the English stage. At the same time that the Queen engaged in these negotiations with the Ottoman Empire, beginning as early as 1579, the English stage proliferated with images of the "Turk."[40] Louis Wann records that the anonymous play *The Blacksmith's Daughter* was "referred to in [Stephen] Gosson's *School of Abuse* (1579) as 'containing the treachery of Turks, the honorable bounty of a noble mind, the shining of virtue in distress.'"[41] Wann's important archival work shows that between 1579 and 1642, 47 plays contained "Oriental" characters, settings, or subject matter.[42] Out of those, "Turks" appeared in 31 plays.[43]

Wann attributes the popularity of the "Turk" to the choice to set many of these plays in the Ottoman Empire, noting that "they occur oftener than the Westerners themselves—a fact more striking than appears at first sight; [...] Clearly the interest in the Turks was stronger than in any other Oriental race."[44] Wann's Eurocentric terminology, which adopts "Oriental" as a neutral descriptor for Islamicate peoples and cultures, may be excused because he was writing in 1915, but it should also be noted that such language continues the project of Othering in which the plays were engaged. As astute readers of Said, we recognize the frame of Orientalism under which Wann's study operates, which classifies and taxonomizes the Orient in order to make cultural evaluations through western value systems. Nonetheless, the archival work offered here provides us with important information about English dramatic interest in Muslim cultures and the vast range of plays devoted to this theme. The popularity of the "Turk" on the stage can be traced to the geographic proximity of the Ottoman Empire to Europe, the widespread European Christian concerns—broadcast weekly in sermons—with Ottoman incursions into southeastern Europe and the Mediterranean, and the increased English trade in geographies under Ottoman dominion. English cultural and religious anxieties and debates about the Ottoman Empire found easy expression on the stage, as Wann establishes.

The popularity of the "Turk" does not, however, equate to a positive construction of Ottoman identity in English drama. Indeed, throughout this book I have put "Turk" in quotation marks because "Turk" was almost exclusively an early modern English and European discursive construction. I similarly use quotation marks around the term "Moor" to mark it as a Eurocentric construction that seeks to Otherize African and Muslim people in Europe. As F. Aslı Ergul contends, Ottomanness was more than its ethnic origins and Islamic religious affiliation: "the cosmopolitan social construction of the Ottoman Empire—Islamic tradition, Turkish heritage, the background of Byzantium and also numerous ethnic and religious cultures—was a synthesis."[45] The Ottoman Empire routinely incorporated its Others—Greeks, Europeans, Africans—into its body politic, creating a hybrid culture around and through such absorptions as well as its Asian and Muslim cultural inheritance. Thus, recognizing these self-naming practices and understanding the diverse culture that comprised the Ottoman polity, is both accurate and ethical, as is referring to its subjects as Ottomans. Returning to my theme, the theatrical representation of the "Turk" functioned as yet another tidy shorthand to convey certain stereotypes about Islam and Muslim identity, such as rapacious sensuality, extreme violence, luxuriant wealth, and religious misbelief. Consequently, the "Turk" of the early modern English stage is very much a discursive, Orientalist construct, loosely tethered to Ottoman identity, but containing the fears and desires of the culture fabricating him for its own ideological purposes. Despite gaining popularity on the stage during a moment of deliberate English cordiality with the Ottoman Empire, the stage "Turk" is most often demonized, as in other forms of public discourse.

Even as Queen Elizabeth was formalizing trade agreements with the Ottoman Empire and Thomas Dallam's organ was being installed in Topkaı Sarayı, William Shakespeare was writing his history plays. While not composed or performed in chronological order, the sequence of eight plays chronicles the internecine battle for the English crown starting with Henry Bolingbroke's rebellion (1399) which resulted in the deposition of King Richard II, and culminating in the Battle of Bosworth Field (1485), wherein Henry Tudor, Earl of Richmond, defeated Richard III, and took the English throne. By the 1590s it was clear that the queen would not marry and produce an heir, prompting questions about political power and dynastic lineage to haunt these plays depicting the civil wars just two or three generations removed from Shakespeare's own time. One way to look at Shakespeare's history plays, then, is through the contemporary political anxieties of late Elizabethan England, which include English engagement, dialogue, and traffic with the Ottoman Empire. While no "Turk" physically appears onstage, the many references that point to Islam, Muslims, and the Ottoman Empire offer meaningful subtexts through which to read and understand the concerns animating Shakespeare's history plays. Jerry Brotton has aptly suggested that Shakespeare is "haunted" by "the specter of the Turk" and that "the Turk, in his figurative presence and physical absence is, in a clinical sense, *ambivalent*: it is both dreaded and anticipated."[46] The ambivalence of the "Turk" in Shakespeare's history plays is also liminal, by which I mean the "Turk" represents a threshold of conduct and behavior, through which the morality and virtue of England and the English is judged and measured. The shadowy presence of the "Turk" in these plays signals something more than ambivalence, skewing instead toward a form of "imperial envy" for the power and glory of the Ottoman Empire, against which the English are a tiny nation on the periphery of the known world of the Mediterranean. As Gerald MacLean has theorized, "imperial envy," in this context "usefully describes the evolving dynamic of early modern English responses to encounters with the Ottoman Empire at a time when the English were seeking to find a place for themselves in the larger world beyond their insular realm."[47] MacLean's provocation suggests that the Ottoman Empire served as a model through which the English could imagine their own nascent and emerging imperial enterprise. He, thus, exposes the multifaceted ways in which the Ottoman Empire functioned in the English imaginary, not simply as a foreign Other encroaching upon European and Christian lands, but also as an exemplary empire of the age, one whose power and might was to be envied and emulated. My own use of ambivalence and imperial envy in conceptualizing Shakespeare's mobilization of the "Turk" in his history plays adopts the work of Brotton and MacLean and further argues that these two approaches are complicated by the ways in which Islam and the "Turk" are racialized in these plays. That process of racialization relies upon representing both Islam and the "Turk" as religiously, culturally, and politically illegitimate. Consequently, even as the "Turk" may be the object of English imperial envy, the plays exhibit discursive strategies of deliberate Othering that render the Ottoman Empire as incommensurate and incompatible with English values.

Shakespeare's "Turks" only materialize in his plays as shadows or references. A cursory search of the word "Turk" in a Shakespeare concordance reveals that the word (including offshoots like "Turkish") appears "17 times in 37 speeches within 18 works."[48] Looking at the number of times and the context in which a word appears in the Shakespearean corpus demonstrates the semantic and ideological uses of the term and its relationship to the larger thematic concerns of a particular play. It makes sense that in an English history play the "Turk" is not onstage; these plays are, after all, about the volatile political upheavals and rebellions in medieval England. What place is there in that story for the Ottoman Empire? Nonetheless, the "Turk" is a spectral presence: Jerry Brotton notes that out of the many allusions to the "Turk" in Shakespeare's canon "more than a third of these references are the history plays," revealing the playwright's fascination with this figure, especially in the context of his own local history and political moment.[49] Moreover, Mark Hutchings argues that Shakespeare's attraction to the "Turk" has as much to do with the theatrical tradition in which he worked as it did with the political and popular discourses about the Ottoman Empire. He notes that "Shakespeare worked the Turk motif into many of the plays he composed in the last decade of Elizabeth's reign. This statistic alone further testifies to the popularity of the motif," proving that Shakespeare "drew on and refracted the established playhouse presence of this material."[50] Citing plays such as Thomas Kyd's *The Spanish Tragedy* (1587) and Christopher Marlowe's *Tamburlaine the Great*, parts I and II, (1590) among other "Turk" plays, Hutchings advocates for the stage tradition developed in repertory companies as an important source for Shakespeare's treatment of the subject matter. In other words, Hutchings alleges that the "Turk" was already familiar on the English stage and so audiences had been trained to expect certain behavior from this stock figure. It is doubly curious, then, that the material presence of the "Turk" is excluded from Shakespeare's corpus of plays, given the discursive presence of the Ottoman Empire in the culture at large and the popularity of the "Turk" on the stage.

SHAKESPEARE'S "TURKS"

Shakespeare did not compose his history plays in chronological order. In fact, he started with the most recent past, the tumultuous reign of King Henry VI—taking three plays to depict the civil unrest leading to his demise—and the overlapping rise and fall of King Richard III, whose death ushered in the Tudor dynasty and eventually the reign of Shakespeare's own monarch, Elizabeth I. A couple of years after finishing this first tetralogy, Shakespeare began his second sequence of four plays: this time, rehearsing the violent and bloody events that preceded his first series. The second tetralogy, which includes *Richard II* (1597), *Henry IV part 1* (1598), *Henry IV part 2* (1599), *and Henry V* (1599), is Shakespeare's deep dive

into the causes for the later civil conflict and a meditation on
the abuse of power by the privileged noble class. These plays
ruminate on the reciprocal duties and obligations owed to
monarchs and subjects, while they depict routine violations
of those duties and the deadly consequences that follow,
and the action culminates in a deliberate war of aggression
against the French, spearheaded by King Henry V. Although
Henry V concludes triumphantly, Shakespeare's audience
already knew from their own recent history that civil war
in England would shortly follow. It may seem difficult and
even absurd to imagine what place the "Turk" has in this particular narrative about English politics; however, Shakespeare
uses precisely that figure to limn the moral and virtuous character of English power and kingship. While the trope of the
"Turk" appears in several of the history plays, I focus here on
four important moments that crystallize the rhetorical and
ideological function of this figure within this genre. These
moments uncover the political utility of opposition to Islam
and the Ottoman Empire and expose the powerful position of
both within the early modern English imaginary. They further
underscore the ways in which the Otherness of Islam and
the Ottoman Empire was racialized in order to justify naked
and ruthless English political ambition. In addition, these
moments contain forms of early modern Orientalism, with
their emphasis on cultural incommensurability and alterity.

Two references to Islam, Muslims, and the "Turk" occur
near the end of *Richard II*, which emblematize how the religion and its believers are often depicted in early modern
European discourses, as racialized enemies of Christianity
and therefore appropriate antagonists. In the first instance,
the newly crowned Henry IV attempts to unravel the mystery
behind the murder of his uncle the Duke of Gloucester and

plans to recall the exiled Mowbray back to England. He learns from the Bishop of Carlisle that Mowbray has died,

> Many a time hath banished Norfolk fought
> For Jesu Christ in glorious Christian field,
> Streaming the ensign of the Christian Cross
> Against black pagans, Turks, and Saracens;
> And, toiled with works of war, retired himself
> To Italy, and there at Venice gave
> His body to that pleasant country's earth
> And his pure soul unto his captain, Christ,
> Under whose colors he had fought so long.[51]

Carlisle's elegy for Mowbray celebrates his actions while in exile, which include his militant Christianity: fighting for the faith against nonbelievers, represented here by Muslims. For Carlisle and for the underlying, common ideology of the play, war in the service of Christ is always a noble act, which "purifies the soul" in preparation for union with Christ. It is rendered particularly valiant here through the specific enemies of Christ that Mowbray fought: "black pagans, Turks, and Saracens." Carlisle's list yokes these different racial and ethnic identities to Islam through their apparent misbelief, which also makes them fit for white European Christian aggression. Carlisle's "Turks" and "Saracens" are easily legible within medieval and early modern naming conventions that identified Muslims through such markers. As discussed earlier in this chapter, the dominance of the Ottoman Empire in early modern European culture is reflected in the use of "Turks" as shorthand for all Muslims. Such positioning was aided by the fact that the Ottomans controlled, at the time of

Shakespeare's writing, the holy cities of Mecca and Medina as well as the Holy Land, which had come under Ottoman rule in 1516. "Saracens" recalls the medieval western Latin term for Muslims. It is, as Geraldine Heng has argued a "lie," which subsumes the many differing regional cultures of Islam under one banner.[52] Heng notes that this "lie" originated from St. Jerome,

> who suggested that Arabs took for themselves the name of Saracens in order to falsely claim a genealogy from Sara, the legitimate wife of Abraham, "to conceal the opprobrium of their origin; because their true mother, Hagar, was a slave."[53]

The "lie," of course is a fabrication of the Latin West that reveals more about the namers than it does the named. Not only does the genesis of the term reify the importance of rank, free and enslaved, wife and concubine, but also it establishes that religious inheritance can only be claimed via forms of patriarchal legitimacy. "Saracen," by its very nature, represented all forms of illegitimacy, that of descent as well as of religion. It became a convenient label for Europeans who struggled with the success of Islam as its influence reached beyond the Arabian Peninsula and into the so-called west.

In early modern discourses, Islam was frequently constructed as pagan, and, therefore, not a legitimate religion or theology. Portraying Islam in this way was strategic, an attempt to counter both Muslim expansion into Christian and European territories and Islam's claims to be the final articulation of the monotheistic Abrahamic tradition. As Daniel Vitkus notes,

> The Islamic claim to supersede a flawed and incomplete
> Christianity was an unthinkable phenomenon, and so it
> was denied in various ways, including, in both learned and
> popular treatments, a definition of Islam as a "pagan"
> misbelief akin to other forms of idolatrous paganism that
> Western Europeans associated with the Middle East.[54]

To contain the geographic threat of Muslim regimes and the theological challenge posed by Islam, early modern discourses religious, cultural, and popular sought to upend Islam's founding creed, that of "no God but God." Attributing paganism and polytheism to Islam countered its genesis and history. According to Muslim tradition, the Prophet Muhammad received the message of Allah (God) from the angel Gabriel while he was in meditative seclusion in the mountains surrounding the city of Mecca. At the time of these revelations (610 C.E.), Mecca was polytheistic and idolatrous, a period Muslims call the *jahiliyyah*, a time of ignorance. After receiving the message from God and relating what had been communicated to him, Muhammad began to gain followers, first his wife, Khadija and then others among his family and intimate circle. Eventually, the Prophet began spreading the revelations he received, which included "the oneness of God, the reality of the Last Judgement, and the need for pious God-fearing behavior." The oneness of God is central to Islam, which is confirmed in its statement of belief or *shahada*, "there is no God but God, and Muhammad is His messenger." By ascribing paganism or polytheism to Islam, early modern writers deliberately misrepresented the religion, its history, and its prophet in an attempt to undermine Islam's message, which claimed the same genealogy as Christianity and, therefore, was a source of discomfort.

The Bishop of Carlisle's religio-ethnic markers for Muslims are simultaneously racial markers. Premodern racial formation, like its contemporary manifestations, made human difference meaningful by freighting the physical body of the Other with symbolic, moral, and ethical values, which then operated in a system of material relations that advantaged some while disadvantaging others. Race was also fluid then, as it is now, meaning that racial classifications could change and shift according to the contingencies of power. Although racial systems were beginning to emphasize color-based or phenotypic conceptions of race in the premodern period, with "black" being an especially loaded term, race continued to operate through multiple and intersecting differences, including religion and culture. Early modern European discourses harnessed all of these strategies in their racialization of Islam and Muslims. Not only did their religious "misbelief" situate them outside the bounds of Christian fraternity and salvation, but also their languages, non-European geographic origins, cultures, and customs supported and confirmed their racial alterity. Carlisle's use of "black," to modify "pagans," then, is multivalent—rhetorical and literal—signifying the moral and spiritual bankruptcy and lack of salvation that accompanies Islamic misbelief and the embodied, physical, material mark of human difference. As Anthony Barthelemy demonstrates, "the association of evil with blackness is so much a part of the Western tradition that to catalog it would belabor the point."[55] He explains how this tradition continues uninterrupted from antiquity into the early modern period and how it neatly maps on to the bodies of Black people, making skin a marker of moral and religious value. Barthelemy contends that Black people "came to be seen as creatures beyond the realm of grace and civil society. Viewed in this manner, every aspect of their being was touched by their strangeness, their otherness."[56] Definitionally, this figuring of blackness outside the bonds of society serves to locate civility, goodness, and godliness within whiteness. Islam and Muslims were similarly represented, as Vitkus observes: "whether imagined as a black-skinned African Moor, or as a robed and turbaned Turk, the physical, external difference of the Islamic Other was often read as a sign of demonic darkness and barbaric ignorance."[57] Islamic difference or Otherness cast Muslims as inhuman, evil, and in league with Satanic forces. Such constructions of Muslims bespeak an emerging racial discourse, that renders physical, cultural, and even sumptuary differences (e.g., veils and turbans) strange, in order to exert both discursive and material power over the Other. Similarly, Jeffery Jerome Cohen argues that the Saracen as both a religious and racialized Other facilitates the construction of a raceless (but also white) Christian identity, noting that

> Anatomical appearance, the medical composition of the body, and skin color were in fact essential to the construction of difference throughout much of this period, especially in Christian representation of the Jews who lived in their midst (*gens Judaica*) and of Iberian and eastern Muslims (*Saraceni*).[58]

The Muslim Other, thus, represents both a religious and racial threat, which is also a threat to European imperial and territorial expansion, as the presence of the "Turk" in Europe exposes and the "Moor" in medieval Iberia confirmed. Underlying the fabrication of these Others, then, and the racializing used to depict them, is the competition for material resources and for geographic control of contested lands.

The end of *Richard II* offers an oblique reference to this imperial competition. After Richard has been murdered by Exton and Henry presented with his corpse, Henry disavows the foul act of regicide and vows to purify both the realm and himself by "mak[ing] a voyage to the Holy Land / To wash this blood off from my guilty hand."[59] Like Mowbray's military endeavors against Muslims (also presumably in Jerusalem), Henry intends to seek restitution for Richard's murder (and maybe even his own theft of the crown) by fighting and killing Muslims. During the time represented in the play—1399—and in the early modern period, the Holy Land was under Muslim control. In 1187 Muslim forces under the command of Salah al-Din Yusuf ibn Ayyub—called Saladin in European sources—captured Jerusalem from Latin control, and in 1516 the city passed into Ottoman hands, where it remained until the twentieth century. Shakespeare leaves unmentioned whether this is a pilgrimage of repentance or whether, like Mowbray, Henry will wash Richard's blood from his hands by shedding Muslim blood.[60] The latter seems more plausible, especially given Carlisle's triumphant eulogy for Mowbray in Act 4. Moreover, killing Muslims to restore the honor of Christianity and by extension his own seems a canny way for Henry to absolve himself of responsibility for Richard's downfall and demise. The textual repression of Muslims in the Holy Land is another strategic erasure on Shakespeare's part. It preserves the geography as a wholly Christian space, obscures the Muslim presence and Ottoman dominion of the locale, and stakes territorial Christian rights to a place that the audience knows is no longer under Christian control. The play asserts discursive ownership when reality belies any and all such claims. These final words offer a challenge to Muslim hegemony in that geography and assert English military power and agency. Through the potential domination of the Muslim Other, Henry can resolve the civil tension and treason that has helped his political rise to the throne.

While civil unrest continues to dog Henry IV's reign and Shakespeare's two plays that bear his name, the conclusion of *Henry IV, Part II*, promises political stability because "fair sequence and succession" have been restored with a son succeeding a father to the crown. The moment, which should be a triumph for the regime, is troubled, however, by a remarkable reference to the "Turk." After the young prince Henry has ascended the throne to become king of England, he announces to his court,

> This new and gorgeous garment, majesty,
> Sits not so easy on me as you think.
> Brothers, you mix your sadness with some fear.
> This is the English, not the Turkish court;
> Not Amurath an Amurath succeeds,
> But Harry Harry.[61]

In typical Hal style, he disarms his audience by suggesting his own discomfort in this new role, that it will take some time for him to get accustomed to the accoutrement of monarchy. Immediately following that disclaimer, however, Henry strikes a jarring note, wherein he rouses the specter of the Ottoman sultan as a point of comparison for his own succession.[62] Henry still seeks to assure his brothers that his reign will be a comfort to them. To convey this benevolence, he offers a comparison between the English and Ottoman courts, meant to—through opposition—defuse fears of the possibility of

Henry's own violent and tyrannical rule. Nevertheless, as Richard Hillman aptly notes,

> One of the "odorous" properties of comparisons is that they are impossible to control, proliferating associations beyond their context, and doing so even if they are made in negative terms—in fact, denying a comparison is an especially efficient way of introducing one.[63]

By establishing the contrast, Henry, and Shakespeare, demand that their audiences consider what, exactly, is being juxtaposed.

Henry claims that "this is the English, not the Turkish court; / Not an Amurath a Amurath succeeds, / But Harry Harry," yet lying within his assurance, made more comforting through his use of the diminutive of his name, is the danger contained within the moment of succession, one for which he must mobilize Ottoman imperial practice in order to make it visible and simultaneously to banish it. Henry's allusion to the "fear" his brothers may be feeling, combined with his immediate reference to the Ottoman court accomplishes two things: it recalls the Ottoman practice of imperial fratricide, where the sons of the sultan battle for the imperial crown—the ruling sultan during the composition of this play, Mehmet III, murdered 19 of his brothers to claim his throne—and it deflects and projects political violence onto the Muslim Other and away from the English. This custom also racializes the Ottomans through their perceived barbarism and their devaluing of blood ties. Imperial fratricide renders the Ottomans outside the bounds of civilized society, and this savagery is mapped onto their geographic origin as well as their religion, turning the "Turk" into a symbol of depravity. As witnessed from the vantage point of the primogeniture-practicing English this Ottoman tradition, the routine slaughter of all of the previous sultan's male progeny, suggested not simply their cruelty and barbarism, but also their inhumanity as witnessed through these ritual murders which confirm their lack of familial bonds. Both historical and contemporary English history would disprove Henry's attempt at securing such moral superiority for the English monarchy. As Richmond Barbour points out,

> to assign this violation of nature's law to the Turks was a queasy matter. Executions within the royal family confirmed the Tudor successions, as the beheadings of Lady Jane Grey and Mary Stuart famously recalled. Shakespeare's histories brood over the kin-killing among Plantagenets, his Henry IV for instance haunted by the murder of a cousin, Richard II.[64]

Rather than reassuring his audience, then, Henry's pronouncement of the supposed differences between his rule and that of the "Turk" aligns him with that identity. Even though, "no Murad ever did succeed another," the murderous father is reproduced through the construction "But Harry Harry."[65] Thus, Henry uses the image of the "Turk" to demonize behavior that he disclaims, yet the warning remains for any and all who may oppose him, family or not. The tyrant he seeks to denounce is already present in himself.

The Ottoman reference in this scene is of further utility to the logic of this play and to that of the second tetralogy, which is quite deliberately focused on questioning the moral, political, and religious mandate to rule. When Henry Bolingbroke usurps the crown from his cousin, Richard, he sets a precedent for political instability and rebellion that plagues his reign and seems to be resolved with the ascension of his son to the throne, following the proper protocol of patri-lineal succession. It is not out of bounds to wonder why Shakespeare makes a comparison to the Ottoman court rather than a contemporary European one such as France or Spain. We might posit that the analogy to the "Turk" signals extreme alterity, difference, and Otherness. To be sure, it does, yet the fact that the Ottoman Empire is a point of comparison and an easily accessible trope gestures at its familiarity. The "Turk" is supposed to be recognizable through his barbarism, but there is another form of recognition occurring simultan-eously: that of desire. A Harry succeeding a Harry is novel in Tudor England, where Henry VIII famously married six women in the violent hope of securing a male heir. While his son, Edward did succeed, his short reign resulted in the rule of women, that of Mary and Elizabeth, and a bloody period of religious strife and political upheaval. Shakespeare's play injects stability into a politically harrowing world and the comparison to the "Turk" helps him do that. By referencing the Ottoman Empire in this context, Henry positions England as its political equal, projecting for England the unbroken dynastic lineage that the Ottomans were able to achieve, from their first *ghazi* or warrior leader, Osman, to their current *padishah*, Sultan Mehmet III. When Shakespeare was writing these plays, the Ottomans had successfully passed the imperial crown from father to son for over 300 years. As a point of comparison, then, the English were far from achieving the kind of dynastic history and stability that the Ottomans could claim. Thus, Henry's astute conjuring of the "Turk" allows him to mobilize that history in England's favor: not only does he successfully demonize the "Turks" for their custom of frat-ricide, but he also puts England on equal footing with the colossal power of the Ottoman Empire.

The alignment of England with the "Turk," as elicited through Henry's comparison, is dutifully and judiciously banished at the end of *Henry V*, where lines of culture, custom, and religion are redrawn and reaffirmed to serve the interests of a unified imperial English identity. In his titular play, Henry wages a dubious war of aggression against France, wins that war despite overwhelming odds, and claims both the French crown and princess as his war prizes. At the end of the play, Henry presents himself to Princess Katherine as a conventional lover: "O fair Katherine, if you will love me soundly with your French heart, I will be glad to hear you confess it brokenly with your English tongue."[66] The scene demonstrates that the personal is political, especially the erotic lives of the elite. While Henry puts on a good show for the princess, both parties know that it is just a show. Katherine's consent to the union is irrelevant, and Henry is making it and himself more palatable through his lovesick persona. The numerous repetitions of "France" and "England" and their attendant associations with hearts, tongues, and other body parts firmly map identity onto bodies, erecting boundaries that will be dissolved through the union of France and England, which their future marriage will accomplish. While the national boundaries of Europe are destroyed through this marriage, another is established in order to confirm the dissolution of intra-European difference and locate difference in another more foreign identity and culture, that of the Ottomans. Part of Henry's wooing of Katherine is to sway her toward him by envisioning a glorious martial future for their child, who will engage in war against Muslims: "Shall not thou and I, between Saint Denis and Saint George, compound a boy, half French, half English, that shall go to Constantinople and take the Turk by the beard?"[67] In Henry's imaginings their future child will be a warrior-prince, ready to challenge the power of the "Turk" and reclaim Istanbul for Europe. Shakespeare's reference is anachronistic. Henry V died in 1422 and Mehmet II did not conquer Constantinople until 1453. In Shakespeare's own time, Istanbul had been the seat of Ottoman imperial power for over a century, and so the play is speaking to his own moment and to the threat and might of the Ottoman Empire in the late sixteenth century rather than to the events of the fifteenth. What, then, is the "Turk" doing here?

The reference picks up an important theme that emerges in *Henry V* and in the second tetralogy broadly: that of consolidating political power through warfare, especially through the invasion of foreign lands. In *Henry V*, Henry quashes internal political turmoil in England by pursuing this conflict with France, during the course of which he is able to accomplish a tentative truce between the different identities that fall under the aegis of his crown. In exchange for fighting for him, he promises his troops composed of soldiers representing the body politic from all ranks and ethnicities, including English, Scottish, Welsh, and Irish, kinship, that they will be a "band of brothers." English unity is achieved by projecting internal strife externally, because a foreign war produces cohesion at home. Similarly, unity between England and France will be realized through the imagined future conflict with the "Turk." In Henry's fantasy, then, military aggression against the Ottomans can create a unified European Christian polity, and who better to lead that effort than his half-French half-English son? Through his own lineage, Henry imagines a future English nation that can challenge the Ottoman Empire in its own geography.

Henry's desire to see his future son take on the "Turk" replicates crusade rhetoric which represented Islam as an existential threat and advocated military aggression against Muslims. Crusade rhetoric renders Islam an illegitimate religion and Muslims as radically Other to European Christians. It constructs Islam and Christianity as dueling faiths, locked in an existential struggle for the control of the one true religion and the means to salvation. In this vision of religious conflict there is no possibility of a cross-confessional encounter that is not antagonistic. It is deeply ironic, then, that Henry focuses on his future son's mixed heritage, French and English, as vital for him to beard the "Turk," since both the French and English had successfully negotiated commercial relations with the Ottoman Empire, the French even forming a military alliance with them. These historical, diplomatic arrangements undermined the popular representation of the "Turk" and also violated Papal authority that forbade such agreements with non-Christians. The ideological conflict that Henry desires, in order to establish the might of his own dynastic lineage, is countered by the political alliances that brought the Ottomans into European political affairs. Even as Shakespeare's history plays desperately attempt to limit Islam, Muslims, and the Ottoman Empire to the fringes of Europe and within the realm of perpetual conflict, the shadow of the "Turk" that looms over these plays escapes tidy attempts at containment because the of the centrality of the Ottoman Empire as a political, religious, and cultural force in Europe. The utility of the "Turk," as both a metaphor and a material presence, informs the plot and action of these plays. Indeed, the diplomatic engagements with which I began this chapter demonstrate the convenient fiction of perpetual conflict between Europe and the Ottoman Empire, concealing a more nuanced reality. Even though Shakespeare does not depict a "Turk" onstage, the Ottoman presence proliferates across his works and those of his fellow early modern playwrights. Islam, Muslims, and the Ottoman Empire were part of the cultural milieu and London audiences were eager to consume their stories. In Shakespeare's plays, the Ottoman Empire is an object of curiosity and a culture through and against which he investigates his own society's relation to power, misrule, and political agency. References to the "Turk" are not simply local color or topical flavor; they illustrate contemporary discourses about the Ottoman Empire, and they reflect the kinds of engagement that England was pursuing with the Ottomans in the early modern period. Consequently, the shadow presence of the Ottomans simultaneously demonstrates Shakespeare's interest in Islam and its cultures, and his desire to construct a pan-European polity free of them: a desire to represent England as white and Christian, untouched by the international, inter-religious, and inter-racial intimacies that Queen Elizabeth was cultivating with the Ottomans.

NOTES

1 Samuel Chew, *The Crescent and the Rose* (Oxford: Oxford University Press, 1937), 164. For more on Dallam's organ see Scott Trudell, "An Organ for the Seraglio: Thomas Dallam's Artificial Life," *Renaissance Studies*, 34.5 (2020): 766–83.

2 J. Theodore Bent, "Introduction," *Early Voyages and Travels in the Levant. I.–The Diary of Master Thomas Dallam, 1599–1600. II.–Extracts from the Diaries of Dr John Covel, 1670–1679. With Some Account of the Levant Company of Turkey Merchants*, ed. J. Theodore Bent, Hakluyt Society, First Series, 87. (New York: Burt Franklin, 1893), i. The Turkey Company was established in 1580 and was turned into the Levant Company in 1590.

3 Bent, "Introduction," i.

4 "The Diary of Master Thomas Dallam," in Bent (ed.), *Early Voyages and Travels in the Levant*, ed. Bent, 73. See also Jerry Brotton, *The Sultan and the Queen: The Untold Story of Elizabeth and Islam* (New York: Penguin, 2017), 119.

5 Aygül Ağır, "From Constantinople to Istanbul: The Residences of the Venetian Bailo (Thirteenth to Sixteenth Centuries)," *European Journal of Archaeology* 18.1 (2015): 128–46.

6 "Diary of Thomas Dallam," 18, 59.

7 "Diary of Thomas Dallam," 59.

8 "Diary of Thomas Dallam," 59.

9 Eric L. De Barros, "The Gatekeeping Politics of "Good" Historicism: Early Modern Orientalism and "The Diary of Master Thomas Dallam," *College Literature* (2016), 632.

10 De Barros, "Gatekeeping," 632.

11 *Oxford English Dictionary*, s.v. "infidel (n.)," accessed November 1, 2022.

12 "Diary of Thomas Dallam," 62.

13 "Diary of Thomas Dallam," 62–63.

14 "Diary of Thomas Dallam," 69.

15 "Diary of Thomas Dallam," 71.

16 "Diary of Thomas Dallam," 79, 85.

17 "Diary of Thomas Dallam," 79–80.

18 "Diary of Thomas Dallam," 80.

19 "Diary of Thomas Dallam," 84.

20 Susan A. Skilliter, *William Harborne: The Trade with Turkey, 1578–1582: A Documentary Study of the First Anglo-Ottoman Relations* (London: Oxford University Press, 1977).

21 Lisa Jardine, "Gloriana Rules the Waves: or, The Advantage of Being Excommunicated (and a Woman)," *Transactions of the Royal Historical Society* 14 (2004), 211.

22 De Lamar Jensen, "The Ottoman Turks in Sixteenth Century French Diplomacy," *The Sixteenth Century Journal*, 16.4 (1985): 451–70; Pascale Barthe, *French Encounters with the Ottomans, 1510–1560*, 1st ed. (London: Routledge, 2016).

23 Bernadette Andrea, *Women and Islam in Early Modern English Literature* (Cambridge: Cambridge University Press, 2008), 23.

24 Barthe, *French Encounters*, 19.

25 Matthew Dimmock, "Guns and Gawds: Elizabethan England's 'Infidel' Trade," *A Companion to the Global Renaissance: Literature and Culture in the Era of Expansion, 1500–1700*, ed. Jyotsna G. Singh (Oxford: Wiley Blackwell, 2021), 210.

26 Dimmock, "Guns and Gawds," 210.

27 Quoted in Jardine, "Gloriana Rules the Waves," 215.

28 Jardine, "Gloriana Rules the Waves," 216.

29 Richard Hakluyt, *Principal Navigations: Voyages, Traffiques and Discoveries of the English Nation* [...], 3 (London: J.M. Dent, 1910), 54.

30 Brotton, *The Sultan and the Queen*, 143.

31 Vitkus, Daniel J. "Turning Turk in *Othello*: The Conversion and Damnation of the Moor," *Shakespeare Quarterly*, 48.2 (1997), 152–53.

32 Quoted in Vitkus, "Turning Turk," 124. John Foxe, *Acts and Monuments of Matters Most Special and Memorable, Happening in the Church, with an Universal History of the Same* (London, 1596), 1:675.

33 Brotton, *The Sultan and the Queen*, 144.

34 Andrea, *Women and Islam*, 23–29.

35 Andrea, *Women and Islam*, 28–29.

36 Gerald MacLean and Nabil Matar, *Britain and the Islamic World, 1558–1713* (Oxford: Oxford University Press, 2011).

37 For more on such ambivalent relations, see Daniel Vitkus, *Turning Turk: English Theater and the Multicultural Mediterranean, 1570–1630* (New York: Palgrave-Macmillan, 2003); Jonathan Burton, *Traffic and Turning: Islam and English Drama, 1579–1624* (Newark: University of Delaware Press, 2005); Benedict S. Robinson, *Islam and Early Modern English Literature: The Politics of Romance from Spenser to Milton* (New York: Palgrave-Macmillan, 2007); and Jane Hwang Degenhardt, *Islamic Conversion and Christian Resistance on the Early Modern Stage* (Edinburgh: Edinburgh University Press, 2010).

38 Harborne's memoir, quoted in Brotton, *The Sultan and the Queen*, 145.

39 Brotton, *The Sultan and the Queen*, 145.

40 Wann, Louis, "The Oriental in Elizabethan Drama," *Modern Philology*, 12.7 (1915), 423–47.

41 Wann, "Oriental," 429.

42 Wann, "Oriental," 426.

43 Wann, "Oriental," 439.

44 Wann, "Oriental," 439.

45 F. Aslı Ergul, "The Ottoman Identity: Turkish, Muslim or Rum?", *Middle Eastern Studies*, 48.4 (2012), 629–45.

46 Jerry Brotton, "Shakespeare's Turks and the Spectre of Ambivalence in the History Plays." *Textual Practice*, 28.3 (2013), 522.

47 Gerald MacLean, *Looking East: English Writing and the Ottoman Empire Before 1800* (New York: Springer, 2007), xi.

48 *Open Source Shakespeare: Concordance*, s.v. "Turk (n.)," accessed November 1, 2022, www.opensourceshakespeare.org/concordance/o/?i=767 227&pleasewait=1&msg=sr

49 Brotton, "Shakespeare's Turks," 524.

50 Mark Hutchings, *Turks, Repertories, and the Early Modern English Stage* (New York: Palgrave Macmillan, 2017), 154.

51 William Shakespeare, *Richard II*, ed. Frances Dolan and Stephen Orgel (New York: The Pelican Shakespeare, 2017), 4.1.96–110.

52 Geraldine Heng, *The Invention of Race in the European Middle Ages* (Cambridge: Cambridge University Press, 2018), 110. Additionally, Shokoofeh Rajabzadeh has aptly pointed out that Saracen is an inherently Islamophobic term and should be excised from the contemporary critical lexicon in "The Depoliticized Saracen and Muslim Erasure." *Literature Compass*, 16.9–10 (2019): e12548.

53 Heng, *Invention of Race*, 111.

54 Daniel J. Vitkus, "Early Modern Orientalism: Representations of Islam in Sixteenth and Seventeenth-century Europe," *Western Views of Islam in Medieval and Early Modern Europe*, ed. David R. Banks and Michael Frassetto (New York: Palgrave Macmillan, 1999), 208.

55 Anthony Gerard Barthelemy, *Black Face, Maligned Race: The Representation of Blacks in English Drama from Shakespeare to Southerne* (Baton Rouge: LSU Press, 1987), 2.

56 Barthelemy, *Black Face, Maligned Race*, 6.

57 Vitkus, "Early Modern Orientalism," 225.

58 Jeffrey Jerome Cohen, "On Saracen Enjoyment: Some Fantasies of Race in Late Medieval France and England." *Journal of Medieval and Early Modern Studies*, 31.1 (2001), 116.

59 Shakespeare, *Richard II*, 5.6.49–50.

60 Shakespeare's plays omit the fact that Henry Bolingbroke had traveled to Jerusalem in 1392–1393, not on Crusade but on a pilgrimage. See W.G. Boswell-Stone, ed. *Shakespeare's Holinshed* (London: Lawrence and Bullen, Ltd., 1896).

61 60 5.2. 44–49.

62 Several scholars, starting with Richard Hillman and including Richmond Barbour, Benedict Robinson, Jonathan Gil Harris, Jerry

Brotton, and Mark Hutchings have written about this provocative moment in the play, which signals not only an awareness of Ottoman imperial practice but also informs English monarchial self-fashioning in and through the figure of the "Turk." See Richard Hillman, "'Not Amurath an Amurath Succeeds': Playing Doubles in Shakespeare's Henriad." *English Literary Renaissance*, 21.2 (1991): 161–89; Richmond Barbour, *Before Orientalism: London's Theatre of the East, 1576–1626* (Cambridge: Cambridge University Press, 2003), 23–27; Benedict S. Robinson, "Harry and Amurath," *Shakespeare Quarterly*, 60.4 (2009): 399–424; Jonathan Gil Harris, *Untimely Matter in the Time of Shakespeare* (Philadelphia: University of Pennsylvania Press, 2010), 66–87; Brotton, "Shakespeare's Turks"; Hutchings, *Turks*, 151–93.

63 Hillman, "Not Amurath," 162.

64 Barbour, *Before Orientalism* 23.

65 Hillman, "Not Amurath," 162.

66 William Shakespeare, *Henry V*, ed. Barbara A. Mowat and Paul Werstine. Folger Shakespeare Library: 2020, 5.2.107–10.

67 Shakespeare, *Henry V*, 5.2. 214–17.

REFERENCES

Ağır, Aygül. "From Constantinople to Istanbul: The Residences of the Venetian Bailo (Thirteenth to Sixteenth Centuries)." *European Journal of Archaeology* 18.1 (2015): 128–46. doi:10.1179/1461957114Y.0000000082.

Andrea, Bernadette. *Women and Islam in Early Modern English Literature.* Cambridge: Cambridge University Press, 2008.

Barbour, Richmond. *Before Orientalism: London's Theatre of the East, 1576–1626.* Cambridge: Cambridge University Press, 2003.

Barthe, Pascale. *French Encounters with the Ottomans, 1510–1560*, 1st ed. London: Routledge, 2016.

Barthelemy, Anthony Gerard. *Black Face, Maligned Race: The Representation of Blacks in English Drama from Shakespeare to Southerne.* Baton Rouge: LSU Press, 1987.

Bent, J. Theodore (ed). *Early Voyages and Travels in the Levant. I.–The Diary of Master Thomas Dallam, 1599–1600. II.–Extracts From the Diaries of Dr John Covel, 1670–1679. With Some Account of the Levant Company of Turkey Merchants.* Hakluyt Society, First Series, 87. New York: Burt Franklin, 1893.

Brotton, Jerry. "Shakespeare's Turks and the Spectre of Ambivalence in the History Plays." *Textual Practice* 28.3 (2013): 521–38.

―――. *The Sultan and the Queen: The Untold Story of Elizabeth and Islam*. New York: Penguin, 2017.

Chew, Samuel C. *The Crescent and the Rose: Islam and England during the Renaissance*. Oxford: Oxford University Press, 1937.

Cohen, Jeffrey Jerome. "On Saracen Enjoyment: Some Fantasies of Race in Late Medieval France and England." *Journal of Medieval and Early Modern Studies* 31.1 (2001): 113–46.

De Barros, Eric L. "The Gatekeeping Politics of 'Good' Historicism: Early Modern Orientalism and "The Diary of Master Thomas Dallam." *College Literature* (2016): 619–44.

Dimmock, Matthew. "Guns and Gawds: Elizabethan England's 'Infidel' Trade." In *A Companion to the Global Renaissance: Literature and Culture in the Era of Expansion, 1500–1700*, edited by Jyotsna G. Singh, 276–89. Oxford: Wiley Blackwell, 2021.

Ergul, F. Aslı. "The Ottoman Identity: Turkish, Muslim or Rum?" *Middle Eastern Studies* 48.4 (2012): 629–45. doi: 10.1080/00263206.2012.683337.

Foxe, John. *Acts and Monuments of Matters Most Special and Memorable, Happening in the Church, with an Universal History of the Same...* STC (2nd ed.) / 11226, London, Printed by Peter Short, dwelling on Breadstreete hill at the signe of the Starre, by the assigne of R. Day. 1596.

Hakluyt, Richard. *Principal Navigations: Voyages, Traffiques & Discoveries of the English Nation Made by Sea or Overland to the Remote and Farthest Distant Quarters of the Earth at Any Time within the Compass of These 1600 Years*. 8. London: J.M. Dent, 1927.

Harris, Jonathan Gil. *Untimely Matter in the Time of Shakespeare*. Philadelphia: University of Pennsylvania Press, 2010.

Heng, Geraldine. *The Invention of Race in the European Middle Ages*. Cambridge: Cambridge University Press, 2018.

Hillman, Richard. "'Not Amurath an Amurath Succeeds': Playing Doubles in Shakespeare's Henriad." *English Literary Renaissance* 21.2 (1991): 161–89.

Hutchings, Mark. *Turks, Repertories, and the Early Modern English Stage*. New York: Palgrave Macmillan, 2017.

Jardine, Lisa. "Gloriana Rules the Waves: or, The Advantage of Being Excommunicated (and a Woman)." *Transactions of the Royal Historical Society* 14 (2004): 209–22.

Jensen, De Lamar. "The Ottoman Turks in Sixteenth Century French Diplomacy." *The Sixteenth Century Journal* 16.4 (1985): 451–70. https://doi.org/10.2307/2541220

MacLean, Gerald. *Looking East: English Writing and the Ottoman Empire Before 1800.* New York: Springer, 2007.

MacLean, Gerald and Nami Matar, *Britain and the Islamic World, 1558–1713.* Oxford: Oxford University Press, 2011.

Robinson, Benedict S. "Harry and Amurath." *Shakespeare Quarterly* 60.4 (2009): 399–424.

Shakespeare, William. *Richard II.* Edited by Frances Dolan and Stephen Orgel. New York, The Pelican Shakespeare, 2017.

———. *Henry V.* Edited by Barbara A. Mowat and Paul Werstine. Washington, D.C.: Folger Shakespeare Library, 2020.

Skilliter, Susan A. *William Harborne. the Trade with Turkey, 1578–1582: A Documentary Study of the First Anglo-Ottoman Relations.* London: Oxford University Press, 1977.

Trudell, Scott. "An Organ for the Seraglio: Thomas Dallam's Artificial Life." *Renaissance Studies* 34.5 (2020): 766–83.

Vitkus, Daniel J. "Turning Turk in *Othello*: The Conversion and Damnation of the Moor." *Shakespeare Quarterly* 48.2 (1997): 145–76.

———. "Early Modern Orientalism: Representations of Islam in Sixteenth and Seventeenth-Century Europe." In *Western Views of Islam in Medieval and Early Modern Europe,* edited by David R. Banks and Michael Frassetto, 207–30. New York: Palgrave Macmillan, 1999.

Wann, Louis. "The Oriental in Elizabethan Drama." *Modern Philology* 12.7 (1915): 289–456.

The "Moor" You Know

Shakespeare's Nation of Islam

Three

On July 21, 2008 *The New Yorker* magazine ran a controversial cover featuring then-Democratic presidential candidate Barack Obama and his wife Michelle in the Oval Office—a cartoon image that leaned heavily into anti-Black, anti-Muslim narratives that right-wing outlets had been spreading during the primary campaign. First among these was that Obama himself was Muslim. Obama had just secured the nomination, becoming the first Black man to represent a major political party in the United States.[1] Being Muslim would not have barred him from running for office, but in 2008, at the height of the War on Terror, even the imputation of Islamic identity was a serious political liability. Obama has repeatedly affirmed that he is not a Muslim, but upwards of 30% of the American electorate continued to claim uncertainty about his religion.[2] Enter *The New Yorker* cover, which depicted the Obamas fist bumping in the sacred sanctum of the Oval Office. The celebratory hand gesture replicated a moment from June 10, 2008, after Obama effectively clinched the presidential nomination, which had then raised a firestorm of media coverage, from a "fist-bump that Rocks the Nation," to "terrorist fist jab."[3] Not content to merely reproduce that moment, *The New Yorker* cover incorporated all of the stereotypes about the Obamas circulating in the mainstream US culture (dominant white culture). Standing on a carpet featuring the Seal

DOI: 10.4324/9781003213581-4

of the President, the fist-bumping pair are dressed in ways that communicate their antagonistic position to the United States. Michelle Obama is dressed as a Black militant or separatist, in fatigues and combat boots, with an AK-47 strapped to her back, and wearing a natural or afro hairstyle. Beside her, presented in profile, Barack Obama is wearing a long tunic or thobe, pants that hit above his ankles, and his feet in slippers. On his head is a large white turban. The cover also illustrates how the couple has redecorated the Oval Office: a state portrait of a turbaned and bearded brown man—in the style of a sheikh or imam and an allusion to Osama bin Laden—hangs above the fireplace, where an American flag is being burned. The cover deliberately employs stereotypes in an attempt to critique right-wing hysteria and propaganda. However, in a political and cultural moment rife with anti-Blackness and anti-Muslim racism the cover badly misses its mark. Instead of questioning the validity of the stereotypes attached to the Obamas and the racism underwriting them, it naturalizes them.

The representation of the Obamas on The New Yorker cover—Michelle as Black nationalist and Barack as Islamic terrorist—emphasizes the dominant white culture's suspicion of identities that are allegedly alien, foreign, or Other to mainstream American—read white—identity. Michelle Obama came under considerable scrutiny during and after Obama's campaign, for reasons that were, as many scholars have pointed out, rooted in her race.[4] As a Black woman, Obama's personhood was already politicized: meaning that her speech and actions acquired significance not because of her abilities and qualifications but because of her raced and gendered identity. Anything she said was suspicious because it seemed to carry with it the agenda of her Black womanhood. Michelle

Obama's caricature conjures the "angry Black woman" stereotype as it traffics in imagery of Black radical movements that were deemed dangerous and inimical to the United States. For example, the image recalls the cultural memory of activists like Angela Davis, a civil rights icon, who was once one of the FBI's most wanted and put on trial for conspiracy to murder, among other capital felony charges.[5] By representing Michelle Obama as a gun-toting commando, the cover transforms her valid critique of the country's racist past—"for the first time in my adult lifetime, I am really proud of my country"— into anti-American militancy, something right-wing critics pounced on in the wake of her remarks.[6]

Barack Obama's clothing similarly signified his Otherness. Obama's generic Muslim costume alluded to a photograph that circulated during the campaign of him in traditional Somali clothing. It was taken during a trip to Kenya in 2006, which was described at the time as a personal and humanitarian mission: "Mr. Obama, a freshman Democratic senator from Illinois, was in Kenya's capital on Friday as part of a tightly scripted four-country tour in Africa to raise awareness for AIDS and to reconnect with his roots."[7] Two years, later, however, the pictures from that trip became fodder for the right-wing grist mill. The photograph that caused the most stir was one in which Obama is wearing a white wrap with two pieces of fabric crossing over his chest and a white turban on his head. In the picture, Obama has his head slightly bowed as he listens to an elder, whose hand grasps his. While it is a common custom for (white) diplomats to wear the traditional clothing of the countries they visit, on Obama the clothing reinforced his alterity through race, geography, and religion.[8] Obama's Kenyan father and Indonesian stepfather were both Muslim, and his name,

Barack Hussein Obama, further identified him with Islam. In 2008, this close connection was exploited by Obama's political opponents to suggest his un-Americanness and to link him with "radical Islamic fundamentalists."[9] *The New Yorker* cover offers a palimpsest of Black and brown threats to the country, from the domestic insurgency of the 1960s Black nationalist movement—which was spearheaded by groups like the Nation of Islam and figures like Malcolm X—to the more contemporary national security threat posed by the foreign Muslim Other represented by groups like al-Qaeda. Writing about this intersection of Muslim identity, race, and national security, Su'ad Abdul Khabeer exposes the shifting construction of "the Muslim" in the US imaginary:

> The racialization of the Muslim as Brown and foreign is a departure from the mid-twentieth century, when the "Black Muslim" was the dominant face of Islam in America. The Black Muslim designation was shorthand for the Nation of Islam and for a practice of Islam that was considered heterodox and seen as a dangerous form of Black protest. Like the "Muslim" of today, the Black Muslim was known by specific bodies and behaviors: black skin, bow ties, and preaching "hate." Likewise, the Black Muslim was also under intense state surveillance under the COINTELPRO program (an FBI Counter Intelligence Program), which included the use of agent provocateurs to destabilize Black Muslim communities. Therefore, although the racial time associated with Muslimness has changed from Black to Brown, there is also continuity: the Muslim continues to be seen as a threat to the state that is managed not only through state surveillance but also through notions of multiculturalism.[10]

Khabeer's analysis of the differently racialized Muslim—from Black to brown—demonstrates the palimpsest of "Muslim" identities that *The New Yorker* image conveys. Similarly, Suhail Daulatzai points out, "to be Black is one thing in America that marks you as un-American, but to be Black and Muslim is quite another, as it marks you as anti-American."[11] *The New Yorker* cover brands both groups as terrorists who threaten disruption to and dissolution of (white) American values. It fastens Otherness to both Blackness and Islam suturing them to related forms of anti-Americanness.

The strategy mobilized by Obama's political opponents was to question his Americanness and his patriotism. Whether that was lodged in his "funny name," his supposed foreign birth, or his lack of a US flag lapel pin, it was always set against the whiteness of the dominant US culture to which his Blackness had to be appropriately calibrated and made legible.[12] Poking fun at white fears of the Black and foreign Other seizing the highest elected office of the land seems to be the subject of this cartoon, but the editorial choice ultimately ended up corroborating, rather than dispelling, those fears.

While the cover failed to critique the anxiety generated by Obama's candidacy for white Americans, it understood how the dominant culture perceived Black political success: as a threat to the status quo. By changing the décor of the Oval Office, hanging a portrait of a "fundamentalist" Muslim cleric, and burning the American flag, Black occupancy of the White House would—as the narrative goes—destroy the pristine halls of democracy, violate its norms, and replace the symbols of whiteness with Blackness and foreignness. Manufacturing the different diasporic forms of Black identity that Barack and Michelle Obama claim, the image chose to align them with the specific forms of dangerous Otherness that each posed in the white imaginary. Nonetheless, their alterity was rooted in their Blackness. Race, then, was the crucial problem the American electorate had with the Obamas, yet, given the logics of "colorblind racism" and emergent post-raciality, race was precisely the thing that could not be mentioned by name.[13] Thus, over the course of Obama's two campaigns his opponents introduced other attacks through his multicultural or cosmopolitan background and identity. The political strategy was to make Obama's difference, rather than his policies, undesirable for the vast majority of the predominantly white American electorate without commenting explicitly on his Blackness.

Thus, Obama's name and heritage were seized upon to highlight his non-western roots, as was his early upbringing in Indonesia. Conservative media and politicians emphasized *Hussein* when they used Obama's name before confidently spouting erroneous claims that he attended a *madrassa*—the Arabic word for school—as a young boy.[14] In the post-9/11 climate in which he was running for the presidency, these facts were manipulated to render Obama sympathetic to Islam and Muslims at best and a Muslim himself at worst. As conservative journalist Juan Williams deemed it in January of 2007,

> in terms of Obama and race, I still think that there's—and don't forget the idea that, you know, he comes from a father who was a Muslim and all that. I mean, I think that, given that we're at war with Muslim extremists, that presents a problem.[15]

Williams's pivot to religion to discuss Obama's race reveals how both discourses are being mobilized in order to demonize him for Williams' audience. Obama is presumed

Muslim because of his ancestry and father's ethnicity. Neither of these identity categories is a disqualifier for the presidency, yet Williams' insistence that Obama's candidacy is a "problem" because "we" are at "war with Muslim extremists" easily obscures that fact. Instead, it points not only to Obama being a secret Muslim but also an extremist. For Williams and many others, the race question was inextricably tied to the religious question, neither one of which was found to be commensurate with their America.

These and other political attacks—such as his supposed foreign birth—lobbed against Obama during his two successful presidential campaigns exposed the fiction at the heart of "colorblind" discourses that claimed that racism was no longer a problem in the nation because of the advances of Civil Rights liberalism and de jure equality. Obama's election brought white identity politics to the fore, especially as they cohered around an increasingly narrow definition of "American," which was rooted in white Christianity. The anti-Muslim racism and xenophobic tensions that animated opposition to Obama were not new. Indeed, they seemed to harness hostilities and antagonisms upon which the west was built: those of cultural purity established through conflict with racial and religious Otherness. In 2012, during Obama's second campaign for the presidency, Republican congressman Louie Gohmert proclaimed that Obama was ushering in a new Ottoman Empire:

> Thank you President Barack *Hussein* Obama, this will be quite a legacy for you. And I'm not one of those who says he's not a Christian. All I know is that's between him and God, but what I do know is he has helped jump start a new Ottoman Empire. [...] You look across Tunisia, Libya, and

Egypt, and Iraq, and Iran, and in Syria, Lebanon, you look at these countries and come on over to Afghanistan, that this president is losing as we speak. And Pakistan, which has been harming us all they could while still taking our money. [...] You look and you say oh my gosh this is the making, this is the beginning, a massive beginning of a new Ottoman Empire that President Obama can take great credit for.[16]

Before getting to the topic of his screed on Obama's Ottoman Empire, Gohmert adds an unnecessary disclaimer about Obama's religion being "between him and God." By calling into question Obama's own statements about his faith, Gohmert can more easily link Obama first to Islam, and then to one of the most powerful Muslim empires in the world, whose territories stretched across Africa, Asia, Europe, and the Mediterranean. Gohmert's focus is not on the many cultures and geographies that comprised the Ottoman Empire. He narrows his geographical ambit to North Africa, West Asia, and South Asia, and collapses these diverse populations into a single monolithic Muslim world—a seething mass of unrest and antagonism toward the United States, with Obama as its figurehead. To be sure, Gohmert is spewing polemic, yet his words conjure the idea of an Islamic menace that seems to pose an existential threat to the west and Christianity. Moreover, the link Gohmert establishes relies on a long tradition of Islamic Otherness, which is constructed along both racial and religious lines. Obama, then, is the perfect avatar for this Otherness, never mind his own religious and national affiliations. Obama can be aligned with the Ottoman Empire precisely because his difference, in the view of his detractors, yokes him more closely with the foreign, encroaching Other, than it does with the domestic (white) American subject.

"MOORS" IN THE EARLY MODERN PERIOD

I take this route through contemporary US politics in order
to arrive at Shakespeare's "Moors" because Obama's complex,
multicultural, and multiracial identity suggests the difficulties of incorporating racial and religious difference into the
body of the white nation.[17] The fact that Obama's birthplace
became controversial reveals as much, given that his opponent
in 2008, John McCain was born on a naval base in the Panama
Canal Zone (therefore outside of the contiguous region of
the United States, like Obama, who was born in Hawaii).[18]
McCain's birthplace was never an issue, yet Obama's was, to
the extent that even during the 2012 campaign his Republican
rival, Mitt Romney stated "no one's ever asked to see my
birth certificate," referencing birther conspiracy theories that
Obama was ineligible to be president because he was not
born in the United States.[19] Obama's foreignness was somatically located and then made meaningful through his name and
heritage. He presented an epistemological problem for both
his critics and the logics of whiteness at large because he was
like and unlike, acceptable and objectionable, based on the
cosmopolitanism that made him a viable candidate but also
rendered him suspicious.[20] Obama embodied the hybridity
of multicultural society, yet that multiculturalism uneasily
existed in relation to whiteness which requires that difference
be identifiable and stable.

Obama, as I have argued elsewhere, was in effect a "Moor"
of America: his identity tested and disturbed the liberalism of a
multicultural democracy because it seemed to rub up against its
limits and borders.[21] Twenty-first-century US politics and early
modern English drama are temporally, geographically, socially,
politically, discursively, and culturally vastly different; however,
the ways in which our current moment reflects tensions and

anxieties that are similar to the ways that early modern culture manufactured and managed racial and religious Otherness opens up important and vital opportunities to think through race and the process of racial formation.[22] Moreover, the ubiquity of Shakespeare in the US political arena, the many references to his plays by journalists, intellectuals, and cultural historians indicate how Shakespeare has shaped cultural and racial understanding and responses.[23] Obama's candidacy and presidency resulted in obvious and basic comparisons to Othello, which relied upon Obama's exceptional rise to the apogee of an almost all white US political milieu (usually disregarding the damaging narrative of racist abuse and domestic violence that the play rehearses) and his beautiful oratory that seemed resonant with Othello's speech before the Venetian senate.[24] Obama presented social, cultural, and political problems for a white supremacist society intent on obscuring the structural and institutional mechanism that kept whiteness at the top of the racial and political hierarchy through its embrace of race neutrality. Othello, too, suggests Venetian cosmopolitanism and tolerance of racial difference through Venice's acceptance of "the Moor" within its domains and as its most valued and "valiant" general. Nonetheless, the play simultaneously emphasizes the limits of cultural acceptance and assimilation; its plot turns on the anxieties generated by the inclusion of the foreign, non-white, non-European "Moor" into the pristine white body of the nation, emblematized by Desdemona. Thinking about the representation of these characters in early modern English culture and drama in tandem with the tensions elicited by Obama's identity exposes points of affinity and contact, where temporal folds meet across the centuries to disclose the long process of racialization and the manufacturing of Otherness by the white imaginary.

Shakespeare's depiction of the "Moor," like that of the "Turk," harnesses the polysemy of that identity in early modern English culture, wherein the term "Moor" contained the marks of physical and religious Otherness, which indicated that "Moor" was an identity that was racialized as non-white, non-European, and non-Christian. "Moor" enters the English lexicon through Spanish, Moro, and Portuguese, Mouro, which in turn derived from "the Latin Maurus, an inhabitant of Mauretania, the Roman designation for the region of the Maghreb," which we would identify as North Africa.[25] Thus, it is a western, European, Latin, or Roman term for people Othered by their geographic origin. In the early modern period, "Moor" had extremely strong associations with Islam, particularly because of the long history of Islamic Iberia or al-Andalus, which had come to an end almost a century before Shakespeare began writing his plays with the last Nasrid kingdom of Grenada conquered in 1492. However, Moriscos (converted Muslims) remained in Spain (until their eventual expulsion in 1609) along with the memory of al-Andalus, which was kept alive through Spanish festivals, drama, games, and dance.[26] Thus, Iberian Muslims and their culture had contemporary resonance for Shakespeare and his audiences, shaped by medieval encounters with Muslims during the Crusades and the recent situation in Spain, which positioned "Moors" as hostile and antagonistic toward Christian European identity. Furthermore, "Moors" offered a ready example of internal foreigners, whose history was part of the formation of European culture—through the history of Muslim Iberia and through the burgeoning trade in enslaved Africans in which several European nations, including England, Spain, and Portugal were engaged. Iberian discourses about "Moors," like their English counterparts, demonstrated forms of racial thinking by utilizing the term as a catch-all for the many internal cultural differences between the Muslim communities of *al-Andalus*, conflating Arabs, Africans, North Africans, and Slavic Muslims under the banner of "Moor."[27] In his critically vital study "The Moors?," Ross Brann investigates the meaning of the term within medieval Iberia finding that "Moor is problematic because of its shifting significance," moving from a geographic and ethnic term to also signaling color or blackness.[28] The yoking of geography to religion to color is perhaps most explicit, as Brann demonstrates, in *Primera Crónica General*, a thirteenth-century chronicle, part of which rehearses the events of 711, the Muslim landing in Iberia. The construction of "Moors" in this text exhibits the negative associations of this identity that continue to cohere around it as it moves from Iberia to England:

> The Moors of the host wore silks and colorful cloths which they had taken as booty, their horses' reigns were like fire, their faces were black as pitch, the handsomest among them was black as a cooking-pot, and their eyes blazed like fire; their horses swift as leopards, their horsemen more cruel and hurtful than the wolf that comes at night to the flock of sheep. The vile African people who were not wont to boast of their strength nor their goodness, and who achieved everything by stealth and deceit, and who were...at that moment raised on high.[29]

Brann's analysis uncovers the term's utility in locating diffe-rence in "Moors" and weaponizing that difference in order to demonize Muslim Otherness by Iberian Christian writers and polemicists. Moreover, Brann notes that "Moor" was explicitly a term used by non-Muslims to define and fix Iberian, Muslim identity. He concludes that the term

> underscored for Christian readers not only Muslims' religious and cultural otherness but also and more particularly their "foreign," racialized African origins: their misplaced and thus temporary presence as outsiders supposedly without roots in Castile. Having come from another, darker place, the Moors surely belonged somewhere else.[30]
>
> By this calculus, Afro-Muslims are rendered foreign and Other to Iberia and Europe.

Archival evidence has documented the long history of African people in early modern England and the political responses engendered by their presence, which included an official edict from Queen Elizabeth I.[31] The proclamation, which offered a rationale for the deportation of this African population, announced:

> After our hearty commendations; whereas the Queen's majesty, tending the good and welfare of her own natural subjects, greatly distressed in these hard times of dearth, is highly discontented to understand the great number of Negros and blackamoors which (as she is informed) are carried into this realm since the troubles between her highness and the King of Spain; who are fostered and powered here, to the great annoyance of her own liege that which co[vet] the relief which these people consume, as also for that most of them are infidels having no understanding of Christ or his Gospel.[32]

The ostensible reason for the proposed deportation of this "blackamoor" population is that they are consuming resources that rightly belong to the queen's "natural subjects." They are framed as a drain on the country, and their claims to succor are illegitimate because they are foreign. Blackness or non-whiteness becomes incompatible with native or "natural" English identity. In addition to their physical difference from English subjects, the proclamation also emphasizes religious difference, noting that "most of them are infidels." As I have already detailed in Chapter Two, the word "infidel" was frequently used by English and European writers to undermine Islam as a religion by questioning its religious and theological claims. Moreover, by emphasizing that these African people have come into the realm due to hostilities between the English and Spanish crowns, the proclamation suggests that they are Spain's rather than England's problem. The connection being established here operates on two levels: firstly, it gestures toward Spanish involvement in the African slave trade; and secondly, it implies the racialization of Spain because of its own recent Islamic past. Both somatic difference and religious difference are mobilized by the writers of the proclamation to Otherize this African population and render them unfit for residency within the realm. The strategy of racialization on display shores up English cultural purity through the identification and banishment of these "blackamoor" Others. In many ways, "Moor" was a recognizable and familiar Other for English and European culture, at once an insider and outsider, that could have no place in the culture being formed in the period, which located Blackness and Islam outside of its borders.

SHAKESPEARE'S "MOORS"

Shakespeare turns to the figure of the "Moor" in three plays, *Titus Andronicus* (1594), *The Merchant of Venice* (1598), and *Othello*

(1603), which demonstrate his most sustained engagement with a non-white racialized Other identity. These representations are not static; however, they change across the different plays, with the figure performing different ideological and culture work in each. I argue the racial composition of "Moor" relies on both physical or bodily markers *and* religious markers of identity. The racialization of the "Moor"—in Shakespeare's work and the period more broadly—relies upon the intersection of these markers and upon the meanings that get attached to them by the culture that is manufacturing racialized relations of power. Shakespeare's construction of "Moors" layers these differing discourses atop one another to emphasize the alterity of Muslims and black Africans within European culture. His depictions make religious difference visible through the body, constructing race. His depictions make the body the site/sight of cultural contest and Otherness, constructing race. Racial formation operates through multiple discourses, adjusting and adapting to changing historical and political circumstances and the exigencies of power. Shakespeare's "Moors" reflect the fluidity of racial discourses and expose the different ways they can be mobilized and the manifold uses to which they can be put. They signal the multiple axes along which racialization occurs, through the registers of color, culture, custom, region, and religion. In this way, "the Moor" is the perfect avatar for locating race in the period and also dislocating race, if (as has been the common view of early modern studies) race is taken as biology and skin color and the period's collusion with damaging systems of colonial and imperial oppression are to be obscured or denied.[33] Examining Shakespeare's "Moors" in the context of racialized Islam exhibits the strategies of white supremacy that undergirded England's emerging imperial ambitions, but also

Shakespeare's own global awareness, wherein the "Moor" was among the many "things of darkness," that had no place in his worldmaking project.[34]

The term "Moor" and the identities associated with it present an opportunity to consider Shakespeare's most explicit engagement with Muslim identity as well as the ways in which the processes of racialization in the period intersected with religious difference and cultural foreignness in order to signal the alterity of that identity. Shakespeare was not the first early modern English dramatist to depict the figure of "Moor" onstage.[35] His plays followed a long tradition that included medieval mystery plays and more contemporary work by playwrights such as Thomas Kyd, Christopher Marlowe, and George Peele.[36] The "Moor" on the English stage was complex, simultaneously signaling somatic or racial difference (through black skin) as well as religious Otherness (through affiliation with Islam). Michael Neill, in his examination of how these characters are constructed, observes that they "could not so easily disguise their difference," because it announced itself through the visual register.[37] He further points out, however, that "Moorish" identity was not only a matter of skin, but rather "notoriously indeterminate" in polysemous ways:

> Insofar as it was a term of racial description, it could refer quite specifically to the Berber-Arab people of the part of North Africa then rather vaguely denominated as "Morocco," "Mauritania," or "Barbar;" or it could be used to embrace the inhabitants of the whole North African littoral; or it might be extended to refer to Africans generally (whether "white," "black," or "tawny" Moors); or, by an even more promiscuous extension, it might be applied (like "Indian") to almost any dark-skinned peoples—even, on

occasion those of the New World. [...] But *Moor* could often be deployed (in a fashion perhaps inflected, even for the English, by memories of the Spanish *Reconquista*) as a religious category. Thus Muslims on the Indian subcontinent were habitually called "Moors," and the same term is used in East India Company literature to describe the Muslim inhabitants of Southeast Asia, whether they be Arab or Indian traders, or indigenous Malays.[38]

I quote Neill at length because his important catalogue demonstrates the mobility and fluidity of racial discourses, particularly in understanding the category of "Moor," wherein race is constructed through religion and physical or phenotypic markers, such as skin color. Neill's account emphasizes how early modern discourses were attempting to define, categorize, and taxonomize human difference and the connections or linkages they were making across various non-European geographies through the term "Moor." The flexibility of "Moor"—its ability to be a meaningful descriptor in several different contexts—betrays how the process of race-making operates not in a coherent or uniform fashion, but relationally through groupings of people based on shared or presumably shared characteristics, customs, features, manners, and beliefs. Neill's historical overview also makes explicit the geographic and religious foreignness carried within the term, yet he concludes that "in such contexts it is simply impossible to be sure whether *Moor* is a description of color or religion or some vague amalgam of the two."[39] Neill's overarching claim through his examination of "Moor" is that race as we know it now did not exist in the period, and that "Moor" encapsulates these problems because of its shifting application by Englishmen across the globe. Neill's argument veers close

The "Moor" You Know

to a claim advancing the construction of race in the period when he notes the discourse's nimble fluidity, the construction of categories of humans, and the emphasis on somatic markers of difference, but he ultimately seeks to disentangle race from colonial domination, arguing for English insecurity in the face of mercantile contact with the foreign Other.[40] To arrive at such a conclusion, however, Neill must traverse the inchoate and incoherent ways in which race was being formed in the period: located in bodies of non-white, non-European, and non-Christian Others, which also performed the inverse by constructing whiteness in European Christians. Indeed, as his citation of Purchas exposes, whiteness also had to be made legible through color-coded means in the period: "the tawney Moor, the black Negro, duskie, Libyan, ash-colored Indian, olive-colored American....with the whiter European."[41] Skin, then, was one technology of racialization, which often operated through a visual episteme but it worked in and through other articulations of race, such as religion. For Neill, this becomes an either/or, rather than an intersectional schema, wherein race is biologically rooted, rather than a social construct that functions through multiple, various, and interlocking discourses of power and subordination.

In *Shakespeare through Islamic Worlds* I insist on an understanding of race as a social construction that locates differences between humankind to construct asymmetrical systems of power underpinned and enabled by racism. To focus on one without the other elides the symbolic and material results produced by race. As theorists Karen and Barbara Fields contend, "*race* is the principal unit and core concept of *racism*" and "*racism* is first and foremost a social practice, which means that it is an action and a rationale for action or both at once."[42] What Fields and Fields succinctly demonstrate is that race cannot function outside of a racist framework, which requires hierarchized human difference in order to advantage some and disadvantage others. Race comes into being in specific temporalities and geographies to accomplish local and particular ends. Nor are all racisms the same across time and space; the malleability of race corroborates what Stuart Hall calls its discursive quality. Noting how human difference is transformed into race, Hall argues that,

> It's only when these differences have been organized within language, within discourse, within systems of meaning, that the differences can be said to acquire meaning and become a factor in human culture and regulate conduct. That is the nature of what I'm calling the discursive concept of race. It's not that nothing exists of differences, but that what matters are the systems we use to make sense, to make human societies intelligible. The system we bring to those differences, how we organize those differences into systems of meaning, with which, as it were, we could find the world intelligible [...] I think these are discursive systems because the interplay between the representation of racial difference, the writing of power and the production of knowledge is crucial to the way in which they are generated, and the way in which they function.[43]

Human difference becomes race when it has been assigned meaning within a system that hierarchically organizes society and culture. Hall's emphasis on "the interplay," of representation, power, and knowledge untethers race from biology and elucidates its constructed nature that allows race to nimbly adapt to the mandates of power. Kim F. Hall has similarly argued for the salience of race as a technology of power: "the insistent association of 'black' as a negative signifier of different cultural and religious practices with physiognomy and skin color is precisely what pushes this language into the realm of racial discourse."[44] Underscoring the persistent use of a "language of race in the early modern period," Hall notes that

> language itself creates differences within social organization and that race was then (as it is now) a social construct that is fundamentally more about power and culture than about biological difference. Most theorists of race do agree that racist thought involves a degree of classification and exclusion used to exercise or to justify control over (or exploitation of) people of other cultures.[45]

Race is discursively fabricated but its effects are material; therefore, to think through race in all of its shifting manifestations requires thinking about the benefits and harms of racialization. More recently, Geraldine Heng has synthesized the precepts of race theory to show how race in the European Middle Ages "has no singular or stable referent: that *race is a structural relationship for the articulation and management of human differences, rather than a substantive content*."[46] Race, then, operates within social systems and structures wherein difference is produced in order to be controlled and that difference can be somatic and physical or religious and cultural.

While Shakespeare's "Moors" are not explicitly identified as Muslim, his plays demonstrate how Islamic identity shadows these characters. The application of the label of Muslim is redundant for "Moorish" identity; for example, the geographic origin of a character like the Prince of Morocco in *The Merchant of Venice* allows for no other religious affiliation except that of Islam. Thus, the claim that there are no

Muslims in Shakespeare's plays because he has not labeled them as such is misleading at best and disingenuous at worst because it reinforces the erasure of Islam from the cultures of the Mediterranean about which Shakespeare was writing.[47] Shakespeare's engagement with an identity that had strong associations with Islam—"Moor"—and his attempted evacuation of Islam from that same identity reveals the tension underpinning his attempts at depicting the cultural plurality of the Mediterranean while also attempting to promote and establish the power and cultural supremacy of white European Christianity. The figure of the "Moor," much like the "Turk" discussed in the prior chapter, allows Shakespeare to flirt with various forms of difference—physical, cultural, and religious—and to emphasize the absolute alterity of this figure. As Barbara Fuchs points out, "Moorish" and *Morisco* identities were racialized in the service of Spanish cultural hegemony, but their residue, the history of *al-Andalus* facilitated the racialization of the Spanish for other European powers, such as the English, exposing the fault lines through which race was produced and showing how the Islamic presence troubled the project of nation building and cultural purity.[48] The Muslim subtext of Shakespeare's "Moors" is found in sumptuary and stage properties, geography, and elliptical or mysterious histories and origins, exhibiting one of Shakespeare's strategies to simultaneously conjure and marginalize Islam from his works. By bounding Islam in this way, Shakespeare successfully disappears it from the cultural geographies in which it operated in the early modern period, marking it as peripheral to the early modern world.

Aaron in *Titus Andronicus* would appear to have the least to do with Islam and Muslims. The play is, after all, set in the classical past, before the advent of Islam in the seventh century.

One of Shakespeare's earliest plays, *Titus Andronicus* recounts a violent internecine struggle for power within imperial Rome, which begins before the arrival of the titular Titus and his captives, the enemy Goths against whom he has been on a decade-long military campaign. The presence of these "barbarous" foreigners, which include their queen Tamora, her sons, Chiron and Demetrius, and Aaron, "the Moor," threatens the disintegration, not only of Titus's family but of Rome itself.[49] Order is eventually restored through the violent deaths of these outsiders, ensuring the security of the state by projecting disorder upon the bodies of racialized Others who are then purged from the body politic.[50] Within the military and cultural conflict between the Romans and the Goths, Aaron occupies a third position. His non-white and non-European racialization renders him hypervisible and makes his color a significant part of his character. Aaron's blackness provides an external sign of his inner villainy, which is made explicit in his first speech and then exhibited throughout the play, from his scheme to plot Lavinia's rape, to his mind games with Titus, and finally to his illicit sexual dalliance with Tamora, which results in a mixed-race child. Through his villainy, Aaron, bears a close resemblance to other stage "Moors," such as Muly Hamet in George Peele's *The Battle of Alcazar* (1594) and Ithamore in Christopher Marlowe's *The Jew of Malta* (1590). Thus, Shakespeare's character conforms to a popular stage tradition that depicted blackness as a type, one where external markers corroborate internal morality. Aaron is black and a villain, but he is not labeled a Muslim as these other characters are. Aaron's "Moorish" identity contains a layer of otherness beyond that of his skin color. As Noémie Ndiaye asserts, "in *Titus Andronicus*, Jewishness, Moorishness, and blackness are also woven together in the Hebraic name of the Blackamoor, Aaron."[51] Ndiaye uncovers multiple layers of signification attached to Aaron's racialized Otherness and its specific connection to Spain, observing that "the Goths also evoked the Christian kingdom of the Visigoths who ruled Hispania until the Moorish invasion in the early eighth century;" and pointing to Spain as a counter-example for the English on how to manage difference, particularly blackness, within their political domains.[52] Aaron's complex identity, his physical blackness coupled with a Hebrew name, signal various interlocking forms of Othering at work in his construction. In *Figuring Racism in Medieval Christianity*, Lindsay Kaplan details how medieval constructions of "Jewish inferiority" racialize Jews in ways that are also subsequently used to racialize Muslims and Africans. She argues that medieval ecclesiastical laws establish an "ontological" Jewish difference or "inferiority," and

create a racial status of inherent Jewish subordination. [...] The development of this racial construction within the multivalent system of typology enables the reapplication of these figures to similarly justify and subordinate other infidels: Muslims and the pagan inhabitants of Africa.[53]

Identifying Aaron's Jewish construction along with his blackness also raises the shadow of Muslim identity, not simply because the strategies of racialization were similar, but also because the Spanish context demonstrates how both religious identities troubled the construction of a unified and racially pure Spanish Christendom. Indeed, anti-Muslim and anti-Semitic propaganda linked both groups in the early modern period, so much so that Christian writers frequently advanced the narrative that the Prophet Muhammad's parents were Jewish and framed both religions as false, linked by their apparent hostility to Christianity.[54]

These internal elements of Aaron's character are supplemented by external markers or props, as seen in Act 4, when Tamora orders him to kill their child because its skin color betrays their illicit love affair. The baby poses a significant danger to the Goths, yet for Aaron, the baby is his family, representing his blood, lineage, and futurity. While Tamora's other sons, Chiron and Demetrius curse the child as "the offspring of so foul a fiend," Aaron celebrates his child's beauty "is black so base a hue? / Sweet blowse, you are a beauteous blossom, sure."[55] Protecting his child from its brothers' murderous intentions, Aaron warns, "He dies upon my scimitar's sharp point / That touches this my first-born son and heir!".[56] A scimitar is a single-edged, curved sword commonly used in medieval and early modern Islamicate cultures.[57] Its appearance as a stage prop, therefore, in a scene overloaded with color-coded, racialized imagery that challenges popular associations of blackness, hints at a familiar Otherness lurking within the identity of "Moor," that of Muslim. Aaron's scimitar materially signals Islamic identity, particularly its resonances with bloodthirsty violence. The sword also ties him to his stage brethren, who almost without exception claimed a Muslim identity and were racialized as black and African, pointing to the racialization of Islam in the period and the ways that blackness was deliberately situated outside the boundaries of white Christian Europe.

Like Aaron, the Prince of Morocco in *The Merchant of Venice*, is a threatening racialized Other whose alterity resides in both his color—a "complexion of the devil," according to the play's heroine Portia—and his exotic Islamic origin. Portia's Belmont is besieged by international suitors from England to France to Germany, yet Morocco is the first to hazard the casket trial designed by her late father to choose her husband. Morocco's long journey—from the western Mediterranean to its eastern borders—and arrival in Belmont attest to Portia's value as a prized object. Her father's will requires her to entertain all suitors, even those outside of the boundaries of white European Christendom, and Morocco's arrival on the scene shows that geography's significance within European and Mediterranean socio-political relations. Indeed, at the time of *The Merchant of Venice*'s composition in 1598, England already had a lucrative trading relationship with Morocco, made official through the establishment of the Barbary Company in 1580. Moreover, the queen had a diplomatic relationship with the kingdom which culminated in the Moroccan embassy to Elizabeth's court in 1600.[58] These Anglo-Moroccan political ties along with the long tradition of representing "Moors" on the English stage communicate the familiarity of Morocco to English audiences and explain why the Prince of Morocco's religious affiliation does not require explicit mention. Indeed, the play seems to actively repress Morocco's religious identity by emphasizing his physical and phenotypic difference from Portia, who quips, on hearing of his arrival, "If he have the condition of / a saint and the complexion of a devil, I had rather / he should shrive me than wive me."[59] On the surface it is possible to read Portia's construction of the Prince as an exasperated complaint about her lack of agency in choosing her husband; yet her use of racialized language challenges such an easy dismissal. While Portia has been critical of her other suitors for their culture-specific flaws, her criticism of Morocco is rooted in his complexion and skin color, which reveals how racialized Otherness, non-whiteness, makes color and culture one and the same.

Within the play, the focus on Morocco's color obscures his religious difference. As the common usage of "Moor" in the period advances, his Muslim identity is already embedded inside of that appellation, and in the geography through which he is identified. Shakespeare chooses, however, to highlight Morocco's color as the reason he is unfit for Portia. Morocco's introduction announces both the problem of his color within the world of Belmont, and his own awareness of it:

> Mislike me not for my complexion,
> The shadowed livery of the burnished sun,
> To whom I am a neighbor and near bred.
> Bring me the fairest creature northward born,
> Where Phoebus' fire scarce thaws the icicles,
> And let us make incision for your love
> To prove whose blood is reddest, his or mine.
> I tell thee, lady, this aspect of mine
> Hath feared the valiant; by my love I swear
> The best regarded virgins of our clime
> Have loved it too. I would not change this hue
> Except to steal your thoughts, my gentle queen.[60]

Mobilizing early modern climate theory to explain away the fact of his skin color, which he understands may be unappealing to his Belmont audience, Morocco instead points to the mutual bonds of humanity that should exist between them: their shared red blood. Morocco boasts that his blood is as red as that of any "fairest creature northward born," this internal sameness obviating his external difference. A little later in the play, Shylock, the Jewish moneylender who finances Bassanio's suit to Belmont, will proffer a similar argument for his shared humanity with white Christian Venetians, but to vastly different ends when he queries "if you prick us do we not bleed."[61] Shylock's appeal to commonality is a defense of his desire for revenge, yet it is telling that both a Muslim and a Jew apply the logic of blood to argue for mutual humanity in a play that adamantly refuses such gestures from those deemed outside of the humanity accorded by white Christianity. Ian Smith has noted that Morocco approaches his audience with Portia through an internalized conception of his racial inferiority:

> Morocco displays his body for scrutiny and immediately submits an apology for his physical difference. [...] Morocco's plea betrays his visible exception as a difference that is understood within the cultural world of Venice as a physiological defect, an imperfection that situates him on the margins as a profoundly flawed and unassimilable figure.[62]

Within the white supremacist logics of the play, which seek to excise all forms of difference, most importantly religious difference through its depiction of Shylock, Morocco's posturing in this way makes sense; however, within the space of the Mediterranean, particularly the eastern Mediterranean of Venice and the western Mediterranean of Morocco, with its economy of cultural exchange and difference, such positioning has little purchase. Venice's location in the eastern Mediterranean and its political success depends, as the play exhibits, on the strategic incorporation of religious and racial difference, yet when it comes to the matter of marriage, lineage, and bloodlines, miscegenation—among the elite—is firmly out of the question.[63] Consequently, Morocco's appeal to blood as a sign of his sameness and his status contravenes rather than corroborates his suitability.

As many early modern race scholars have argued, race in the early modern period often meant blood and lineage and was tied to rank, nobility, and class.[64] By vouchsafing his red blood, Morocco seeks to obliterate the difference represented by his skin, yet his blood announces another kind of difference, that of his religion. Notions of blood purity, particularly in relation to Muslim and Jewish identities were well developed in early modern culture. In Iberia, where the *Reconquista* ushered in new modes of taxonomizing, hierarchizing, and regulating identity based on prior non-Christian religious identity, blood purity laws transformed blood into

> a vehicle for the transmission of not just physical but also cultural traits: moral, characterological, spiritual. Blood, as a powerful proxy for linage or descent, acquired a kind of religious racial significance, expressed in (among many others) the Castilian word *raza*.[65]

Therefore, rather than demonstrating his fitness for Portia's hand and his commensurability with European Christian culture, Morocco's blood would, in fact, testify to his unfitness by signaling his Muslim religion. Prioritizing complexion in this scene undermines how somatic markers such as skin and blood work in tandem with anti-Muslim discourses to racialize Islam and make its difference legible in the spectral economy of the early modern stage. Junaid Rana has pointed out that Spain's blood purity laws relied on Muslim difference as much as Jewish difference to articulate notions of race and to establish legislation based on the difference of blood to legalize racism.[66] Consequently, anti-Muslim racism was central to the formation of race in the premodern period.

Shakespeare underscores Morocco's religious affiliation alongside his boasts of masculine military prowess. In contrast to Portia's favored suitor Bassanio, Morocco is a man of action, swearing "by this scimitar," fighting in the field against the Persian "Sophy" and winning "three fields of Sultan Solyman."[67] The weapon and the Muslim empires to which Morocco refers, those of the Safavids and the Ottomans, place the Prince firmly within the material and conceptual geographies of Islam. His conflict with these imperial forces illustrates the real political antagonisms between these regimes in the early modern period and the multiple geographies and religious orientations that Muslim cultures occupied, given that Safavid Iran unlike the Ottoman Empire and Saadi Morocco practiced Shi'a rather than Sunni Islam. His hostility toward other Muslim regimes declares his valor and suggests political leanings that veer toward an alliance with European powers, as his suit of Portia expresses. Queen Elizabeth's amity with the Moroccan sultan Ahmad al-Mansūr implies a contemporary corollary for Shakespeare's plot. The two monarchs had exchanged a long diplomatic correspondence and were allied in their antipathy toward Spain and its military aggression in the Atlantic and western Mediterranean. They even schemed to unite in a military venture to overthrow Spanish holdings in the Caribbean and bring those territories under Anglo-Moroccan rule, "for our intent is not only to enter upon the land to sack it and leave it, but to possess it and that it remain under our dominion forever."[68] The plot never materialized, however, because both Elizabeth I and al-Mansūr died in 1603. However, their alliance threatened to disrupt the hegemony of Europe, particularly Spain and

Portugal, in the Atlantic; moreover, their proposed political union divulged how Muslim political regimes exerted power in European affairs of state. Thus, the Prince of Morocco may be a foreign, non-European, non-white, and implicitly Muslim presence within the world of *The Merchant of Venice*, yet the culture, race, and religion that he represents is one that is familiar, not only through the historical experience of Muslim contact and habitation in Europe but also through contemporary geopolitics.

Just as the Prince of Morocco is a familiar stranger, so too is Othello, "the Moor of Venice." Shakespeare's last and most sustained engagement with "Moorish" identity is also the play that makes most explicit the geopolitical threat of Islam. *Othello* begins with news of an impending Ottoman invasion into Venetian territories, but the specter of Islam seems to be restricted to political and geographic markers, such as whether the "Ottomites" make for "Rhodes" or "Cyprus," locations that evoke a long history of Ottoman imperial aggression in the eastern Mediterranean. The Ottomans took control of Rhodes in 1522, during a campaign led by Sultan Süleyman, ejecting the Knights of St. John from their base on that island. They gained Cyprus in 1571, after their defeat at the hands of the Holy League in the Battle of Lepanto earlier that same year. Shakespeare's references to these lost territories set Othello's action either in the early sixteenth century, before these locations came under Ottoman dominion, or in an imagined early modern present, where the Ottoman Empire's military conquest of this geography did not succeed. Indeed, the providential tempest that banishes the Ottoman threat before it has the chance to take material form on his stage suggests a Shakespearean intervention into eastern Mediterranean history, where the threat of Islam can be kept off his stage and outside of the borders of his constructed Europe. Many scholars, including myself, have spilled much ink on the Ottoman and Muslim presence in *Othello* (1603). These studies have ranged from uncovering the Ottoman, Islamic specter in Othello's character, to the manifestation of Ottoman imperial praxis in the play's treatment of Othello's colonized subjectivity, to the romance origins of Othello's character as a convert to Christianity.[69] While Othello's race, his blackness, has troubled some critics in terms of his construction as a "Moor," Islamic cultures in the early modern period encompassed many geographies and ethnicities, including across the northern and western parts of the African continent. Blackness in all of its cultural and somatic variations is not at all incompatible with Islam; in fact, it is central to it particularly when we accept that Hajra or Haggar, Sara's bondwoman with whom Abraham fathered Ismail or Ishmael was a black African woman.[70] Moreover, as I have discussed earlier the capaciousness of the term "Moor" incorporates Muslim and African identities.

Both of Shakespeare's Venetian plays feature characters whose religious and racial identities trouble the normative whiteness and Christianness of that society. Unlike the Prince of Morocco who is an outsider to Belmont, Othello is a cultural insider. He is an esteemed general in Venice's military and accepted into the highest echelons of Venetian society, as evidenced by his frequent visits to Brabantio's home as a much-valued guest. Othello oversteps—or tests the limits of—his position, however, when he elopes with Desdemona, setting off a social and political firestorm that is echoed by the turmoil of the Ottoman attack. By absconding with Desdemona (without her father's approval) Othello trespasses the elite racial and cultural conventions of Venice. He opens up his character to Brabantio's baseless accusations of abuse and witchcraft, which seem to highlight the opacity of his character for his Venetian audience. Defending their marriage before the Senate and pleading to go to Cyprus with Othello, Desdemona confesses,

My heart's subdued
Even to the very quality of my lord.
I saw Othello's visage in his mind,
And to his honors and his valiant parts
Did I my soul and fortunes consecrate.[71]

Desdemona's words reveal a tension between Othello's external visage and the "visage in his mind," pointing out that his internal character, "his honors and his valiant parts" are the reasons behind her desire to marry him. On the one hand, she may seek to defuse and undermine her father's accusations by highlighting Othello's moral virtues; on the other hand, by focusing on the incongruity between Othello's internal character and external features, Desdemona attests to the illegibility of Othello's face. It is not a transparent sign of "his honors and his valiant parts," unlike the one in his mind. Not only does this reflect early modern notions of physiognomy—that physical signs, especially the face, displayed internal character—it also suggests that Othello's face reveals and conceals, that parts of his identity remain opaque for his Venetian and theatrical audience.[72] No matter how much of an insider Othello may be, as the play's subtitle "Moor of Venice," exhorts, Othello's "Moorishness," as blackness and as a religious signifier problematizes his belonging.

Instead of traversing the familiar ground of the crypto-Muslim inside of Othello, in this section I would like to showcase the Islamic backstory for one of the most important objects in the play: Othello's handkerchief. By reinscribing the handkerchief within African and Ottoman cultural geographies, I explore how the prop, a remnant of Othello's pre-conversion life, manufactures Muslim identity in Othello, which explains his tyrannical and lethal misogyny. Ian Smith has masterfully argued for a critical reframing of the handkerchief as a black object and textile that is connected to the racial prosthetics that manufactured the black body on the early modern stage. According to Smith, racial impersonation on the early modern stage was fabricated through black cloth: "The prosthetic black cloth covers and masks the body beneath; its primary function is to materialize the imagined and absent real black subject and to give it meaning."[73] The theatrical black body, for Smith is "a material or textile body," which is reproduced in miniature in the talismanic handkerchief which, "dyed in mummy," would have mimicked Othello's fabricated black body.[74] Smith emphasizes that "this arresting color is a graphic reminder of the handkerchief's function as a visible metonym for Othello, the portable object that Desdemona carries around as a constant reminder of her black African love."[75] Smith's study responds to an established critical tradition that has associated the handkerchief with Desdemona's whiteness and as a violated sign and symbol of her innocence and fidelity.[76] Extending Smith's focus on the handkerchief's African provenance, I take my hermeneutic route through the handkerchief's Islamic geographies, where it functioned as a sign of sexual desire and purity. In this way, Othello's handkerchief, like the "Moor" himself, ambivalently reflects the character's racial and religious heritage. Smith includes a reference to a passage in Leo Africanus's *Geographical History of Africa* where Africanus—whose resemblance to

Othello, including both a thrilling backstory and a Christian conversion, has struck a number of scholars—describes marriage rites in Fez.[77] Africanus provides a detailed sketch of the marriage ritual, that includes a riotous parade through the streets for the bride, "with great noise of trumpets, pipes, and drums, and with a number of torches," followed by the bridal train's arrival at the groom's home where

> the father, brother, and uncle of the bride lead her unto the chamber door, and there deliver her with one consent unto the mother of the bridegroom: who, as soon as she is entered, touches her foot with his, and forthwith they depart into a several room by themselves. In the mean season the banquet is coming forth: and a certain woman stands before the door, expecting till the bridegroom having deflowered his bride reaches her a napkin stained with blood, which napkin she carries incontinent and shows to the guests, proclaiming with a loud voice, that the bride was ever till that time an unspotted and pure virgin. This woman together with other women her companions, first the parents of the bridegroom and then of the bride do honorably entertain. But if the bride be found not to be a virgin, the marriage is made frustrate, and she with great disgrace is turned home to her parents.[78]

Africanus's description demonstrates the public nature not only of a wedding but also the consummation of a marriage: a woman's chastity is a matter of concern, interest, celebration, or condemnation for her family and broader community. The bloodied napkin immediately circulated among the bridal party publishes and secures the bride's virtue and chastity, just as an unspotted napkin would perform the opposite, loudly proclaiming the bride's sexual promiscuity on its pristine fabric. In *Othello*, the issue is not whether the handkerchief is spotted or not (as some critics would have it); but rather its loss signals Desdemona's free and easy circulation in the hands of many. Whether the handkerchief represents Othello's value or Desdemona's chastity, it is an object laden with erotic expectation within the context of a marital union. In both Shakespeare and Africanus, the handkerchief represents patriarchal concerns over women's chastity. Whether or not it is a metonym for Othello's body specifically, as Smith argues, Othello freights the handkerchief with his masculine honor, and seeing it in the hands of his erotic rival, Cassio, confirms his wife's infidelity and his dishonor. Thus, the prop functions as a symbol of African, Moroccan, and Muslim cultural practice rendered even more public than what Africanus rehearses in his narrative, and Desdemona's punishment is much more severe than a return to her father's home.

In early modern European writing about Muslim cultures, handkerchiefs play an important role in the sexual exploits of the Ottoman sultans as well. Ottaviano Bon's *A Description of the Grand Signor's Seraglio; or the Turkish Emperor's Court* (1650), translated into English by John Greaves, provides a first-hand account of the customs inside the Ottoman court, from the administration of the Ottoman bureaucracy to the intimate details of the sultan's private harem. Bon was the bailo, the chief diplomatic official from Venice, in Istanbul from 1604 to 1609, and penned his reflections on his time in Istanbul after his return to Venice. Writing after Shakespeare's composition of *Othello*, Bon's narrative nonetheless reflects common early modern stereotypes of Ottoman culture, particularly the European obsession with sex-segregated spaces like the harem. Moreover, because Ottoman dynastic tradition eschewed marriage in favor of concubinage, and granted political legitimacy to all of the sultan's children born from this system, the harem was an intriguing site because of the presumed salacious acts that occurred there and the political power wielded by its inhabitants. Bon's harem narrative overflows with details that render the scene to which neither he nor any outsider would be able to witness both accurate and taboo. Writing about how the sultan chooses the concubine with whom he will spend the night, Bon elaborates,

> The King doth not at all frequent, or see, these virgins,
> unless it be at that instant when they are first presented
> unto him; or else in case that he desire one of them for
> his bed-fellow, or to make him some pastime with music,
> and other sports. Wherefore when he is prepared for a
> fresh mate, he gives notice to the said Kahiya Cadun of his
> purpose; who immediately bestirs herself like a crafty bawd,
> and chooses out such as she judges to be the most amiable,
> and fairest of all; and having placed them in good order in
> a room, in two ranks, like so many pictures, half of the one
> side, and half on the other; she forthwith brings in the King,
> who walking four or five times in the midst of them, and
> having viewed them well, taketh good notice within himself
> of her that he best likes, but says nothing; only as he goes
> out again, he throws a handkerchief into that virgin's hand;
> by which token she knows that she is to lie with him that
> night.[79]

Bon's description reveals how the sex life of the sultan is governed by elaborate ritual practice. Sex in the harem is a bureaucratic process with no place for intimacy, privacy, or love, only erotic desire, contained in the handkerchief

thrown to the sultan's preferred odalisque. The handkerchief is the symbol of both his power and sexuality, yet within the narrative, bound as the sultan is by ritual practice, his agency is circumscribed and limited, ironically emasculating him. In *Othello*, the handkerchief is an object invested with Othello's love and desire, but also with his heritage, passed down to him from his mother, with an Egyptian backstory of magic woven into its fabrication and design.[80] The handkerchief's origin locates it in the Muslim and Islamicate cultures of North Africa, which at the time of Othello's writing were under Ottoman dominion. Consequently, it carries within it an Otherness that bespeaks its multiple religio-racial and cultural origins.

The handkerchief's circulation within the play, as an object that signals Othello's love for Desdemona, which is then transformed by Iago's schemes into a symbol of Desdemona's faithlessness, mimics Othello's own transformation, from the noble and valiant "Moorish" general into the murderous and bloody "Moor" who kills his wife to restore his honor. In this way, *Othello's* ending echoes the popular early modern narrative of Sultan Mehmet II's obsession with the Greek maiden, Irene. George Peele's lost play, *The Turkish Mahamet and Hyrin the Fair Greek* (1594), may be a possible source for Shakespeare's later tragedy, with Othello taking the place of the Ottoman sultan. William Painter's *Palace of Pleasure* (1566) also offers a version of the story of "Mahomet one of the Turkish Emperors executes cursed cruelty upon a Greek maiden whom he took prisoner, at the winning of Constantinople."[81] The story as it circulated in several sources, including Richard Knolles *General History of the Turks* (1603), describes Sultan Mehmet II (conqueror of Constantinople) as enfettered by his desire for a young Greek captive, Irene. The sultan becomes so obsessed with her that he neglects his imperial duties and is confronted by his janissaries who demand that he kill her. Facing mutiny from his soldiers, Mehmet conquers his debilitating desire, and reclaims his masculine and imperial agency by slaughtering his beloved. Mehmet's murder of Irene restores his honor among his trusty circle of soldiers and advisors and exhibits the tyranny of Ottoman masculinity, which values women only in their capacity to satiate men's desire, as erotic objects that can either support or harm the sultan's image. Othello's murder of Desdemona is also an honor killing. As he justifies the act, he says that he could have tolerated all manners of "sores and shames," even being made into "a fixed figure for the time of scorn, / To point his slow unmoving finger at," but to have given his love to Desdemona and have it "be discarded thence" or kept as a "cistern for foul toads / to knot an gender in," is beyond bearing for him.[82] Through her alleged infidelity, Desdemona is transformed into a grotesque vessel of monstrous sexuality. Her perceived betrayal befouls not only her, but also Othello, and so he must kill her to regain his masculine power and honor,

It is the cause, it is the cause, my soul.
Let me not name it to you, you chaste stars.
It is the cause. Yet I'll not shed her blood,
Nor scar that whiter skin of hers than snow,
And smooth as monumental alabaster.
Yet she must die, else she'll betray more men.[83]

Othello's oblique "it" is his honor and her apparent dishonor. Indeed, as he reiterates his reason for why Desdemona must die, he makes his logic crystal clear: "she must die, else she'll betray more men." Her death will restore male honor because she will no longer have the capacity to betray them with her sexual appetites. Othello's equation of Desdemona's sexuality with his dishonor and his murder of her as a way to reclaim that honor hints at the latent Muslim identity undergirding his representation. The play's renewed emphasis on Othello's racial identity, with Emilia and others almost exclusively referring to him as "Moor," reinforces the link between his Otherness and Muslim patriarchal tyranny. Indeed, even Othello, after he has been confronted with how he has been manipulated by Iago, says, "he that was Othello. Here I am," in brutal recognition that his prior identity, that of the noble Venetian general is lost to him, and now he is simply a "Moor," as others have designated him.[84]

Othello's suicide returns the play's focus to the religio-imperial conflict that inaugurated its action, a move that supplements and underscores the shadowy Islamic presence that haunts Othello's character. In his final speech, Othello offers his own eulogy and reclaims his identity from the dangerous specter of Islam,

> And say besides, that in Aleppo once,
> Where a malignant and a turbaned Turk
> Beat a Venetian and traduced the state,
> I took by th' throat the circumcisèd dog,
> And smote him, thus.[85]

Within this arena of imperial contest, Othello signals his cultural affiliation with the beleaguered Venetian and against "the turbaned" and "circumcised" "Turk," but in killing the "Turk," he also destroys himself, complicating the tidy binary he attempts to establish.[86] Thus, the specter of the Muslim undergirding his character endures.

Despite Shakespeare's deliberate excision of Islam from his plays, particularly *Othello* which turns on imperial antagonism between Venice and the Ottoman Empire, Muslim identity continues to haunt his "Moors" because for early modern culture, "Moor" was almost always synonymous with Islam. Shakespeare's disengagement with Islam and his multiple engagements with Moors demonstrates his investment in constructing a Europe where Muslim identity has no place. Indeed, all of these characters—Aaron, the Prince of Morocco, and Othello—are excised from the cultures in which they participate or encroach, indicating the limits of Shakespeare's worldmaking.

The "Moor," in his multiple manifestations in Shakespeare's plays, reflects English attitudes about alien, strange, foreign, and Muslim Others. Indeed, in early modern Venice, Othello would not have been "an extravagant and wheeling stranger / of here and everywhere" since the city hosted large numbers of non-Venetian and non-Christian people including Muslims and Jews in the sixteenth and seventeenth centuries.[87] Othello is rendered both foreign and exotic through his racial identity and his race also gestures toward an inherent or "natural" religious identity contained in the marker of "Moor" that pushes against his Christian conversion. In many ways, Aaron, the Prince of Morocco, and Othello operate as double agents whose motives and allegiances are put into question because of their religio-racial position. Their identities smuggle Islam into Shakespeare's plays despite the playwright's attempts to restrict Islam to the margins of his corpus and the Mediterranean about which he writes. Shakespeare's Muslim "Moors" offer an early modern corollary to the suspicion engendered by Barack Obama in his presidential campaign in the United States and to the western perception of Muslims which often constructs them as incompatible with liberal western "values" and suggests that they are "fundamentalist" "home grown" sleeper cell agents of terror, who must be surveilled and controlled to ensure the safety of the white Christian nation. This socio-political ideology demands that Islam be kept at bay, on the peripheries of the western worldmaking project. Such repression reveals the limits and borders of liberal humanism and its claims to universal humanity. Furthermore, it exposes how central Islam and Muslims are to the western culture's self-image and self-representation.

NOTES

1   In this chapter I use Black, black, and African to signal the different identities that comprise blackness in America and globally. When I use Black, I am referring to the deliberate political construction of Black identity in resistance to white supremacist regimes as we have them in the United States, for example. I use black when quoting early modern texts that may be utilizing color-coded language to construct African identities. Finally, I use African to locate both geographic origin and somatic difference from white Europeans. I adopt this naming practice not simply for the sake of specificity, but also to acknowledge the ways that early modern people from Africa or of African descent may have thought about their own identities. In this I follow Kim F. Hall who explains the terms she uses and the political reasons for her own preference in *Things of Darkness* for the term "black," which she argues may open her up "to the charge of reifying the very binarism I am trying to deconstruct," yet is necessary because the "term opposes the dominance of white / light and [...] foregrounds the role of color in organizing relations of power." Kim F. Hall, *Things of Darkness* (Ithaca: Cornell University Press, 1995), 7.

2   Tom Rosentiel, "No Decline in Belief that Obama Is a Muslim: Nearly One-in-Five White Evangelicals Think So," *Pew Research Center*, April 1, 2009, www.pewresearch.org/2009/04/01/no-decline-in-belief-that-obama-is-a-muslim/

3 Rachel Skalar, "Obama Fist-Bump Rocks the Nation!" *Huffington Post*, June 14, 2008, www.huffpost.com/entry/obama-fist-bump-rocks-the_n_105490; "Fox Anchor Calls Obama Fist Pound a 'Terrorist Fist Jab'," *Huffington Post*, June 17, 2008, www.huffpost.com/entry/fox-anchor-calls-obama-fi_n_106027

4 Carmen R. Lugo-Lugo and Mary K. Bloodsworth-Lugo, "Bare Biceps and American (in) Security: Post-9/11 Constructions of Safe (ty), Threat, and the First Black First Lady," *Women's Studies Quarterly*, 39.1/2 (2011), 200–17; Koritha Mitchell, *From Slave Cabins to the White House: Homemade Citizenship in African American Culture* (Chicago: University of Illinois Press, 2020), 188–211.

5 Angela Y. Davis, "Afro Images: Politics, Fashion, and Nostalgia." *Critical Inquiry*, 21.1 (1994), 37–45.

6 Audie Cornish, "Michelle Obama Recounts Struggle to Find Her Place in the World in 'Becoming'," *NPR: All Things Considered*, November 12, 2008, www.npr.org/2018/11/12/667118244/michelle-obama-recounts-struggle-to-find-her-place-in-the-world-in-becoming

7 Jeffrey Gettleman, "Obama Gets a Warm Welcome in Kenya," *The New York Times*, August, 26, 2006. www.nytimes.com/2006/08/26/world/africa/26obama.html

8 "Photo of Obama Causes Stir on Internet," *NBC News*, February 25, 2008, www.nbcnews.com/id/wbna23337141

9 Bryan Adamson, "The Muslim Manchurian Candidate: Barack Obama, Rumors, and Quotidian Hermeneutics," *St. John's Journal of Civil Rights and Economic Development*, 25.4 (2010), 581; Michael D. Giardina, "Barack Obama, Islamophobia, and the 2008 US Presidential Election Media Spectacle," *Counterpoints*, 346 (2010), 135–57; Tope, Daniel, Brittany D. Rawlinson, Justin T. Pickett, Amy M. Burdette, and Christopher G. Ellison. "Religion, Race, and Othering Barack Obama," *Social Currents*, 4.1 (2017), 51–70.

10 Su'ad Abdul Khabeer, *Muslim Cool: Race, Religion, and Hip Hop in the United States* (New York: NYU Press, 2016), 25.

11 Suhail Daulatzai, *Black Star Crescent Moon: the Muslim International and Black Freedom Beyond America.* (Minneapolis: University of Minnesota Press, 2012), xv.

12 "Skinny Kid with a Funny Name Rallies Democrats," *NBC News*, July 28, 2004, www.nbcnews.com/id/wbna5537216; Stanley Renson,

"The Political Mind: Obama Denounces Flag-Pin Patriotism," *Politico*, October 27, 2007, www.politico.com/story/2007/10/the-political-mind-obama-denounces-flag-pin-patriotism-006502

13 Eduardo Bonilla-Silva, "The Structure of Racism in Color-blind, 'Post-Racial' America," *American Behavioral Scientist*, 59.11 (2015), 1358–76.

14 Adamson, "Muslim Manchurian Candidate," 586–91; Giardina, "Barack Obama," 136–37.

15 Quoted in Adamson, "Muslim Manchurian Candidate," 588.

16 "Rep. Gohmert: Obama's Ottoman Empire," *CNN*, September 22, 2012, www.youtube.com/watch?v=OJK7QE9YdfQ; For a satirical take on this moment, see Stephen Colbert, "Obama's Ottoman Empire," *The Colbert Report*, September 26, 2012, www.cc.com/video/pnhcq0/the-colbert-report-obama-s-ottoman-empire

17 I put "Moor" in quotation marks to draw attention to the discursive fabrication of religious and racial difference in early modern English constructions of this identity, particularly on the early modern stage. These are not real Moors—if such an identity exists outside of European white supremacist and Christological frameworks—they are deliberately manufactured in order to make Muslim, African, and black Otherness legible and visible.

18 *Encyclopaedia Britannica Online*, s.v. "John McCain," accessed November 9, 2022. www.britannica.com/biography/John-McCain

19 Felicia Sonmez, "Mitt Romney: 'No One's Ever Asked to See My Birth Certificate'." *The Washington Post*. August 24, 2012. www.washingtonpost.com/news/post-politics/wp/2012/08/24/mitt-romney-no-ones-asked-for-my-birth-certificate/

20 Homi K. Bhabha, *The Location of Culture* (London: Routledge, 2012).

21 Ambereen Dadabhoy. "The Moor of America: Approaching the Crisis of Race and Religion in the Renaissance and the Twenty-First Century." In *Teaching Medieval and Early Modern Cross-Cultural Encounters*, ed. Karina F. Attar and Lynn Shutters (New York: Palgrave, 2014), 123–40.

22 Michael Omi and Howard Winant, *Racial Formation in the United States* (London: Routledge, 2014).

23 See, for example, Kim C. Sturgess, *Shakespeare and the American Nation* (Cambridge: Cambridge University Press, 2004); Linda Charnes, *Hamlet's Heirs: Shakespeare and the Politics of a New Millennium* (London: Routledge, 2006); Alden T. Vaughan, and Virginia Mason

Vaughan, *Shakespeare in America* (Oxford: Oxford University Press, 2012); Michael D. Bristol, *Shakespeare's America, America's Shakespeare (Routledge Revivals)* (London: Routledge, 2014); James Shapiro, *Shakespeare in a Divided America: What His Plays Tell Us About Our Past and Future* (New York: Penguin, 2021).

24 Venetia Thompson, "Obama Is an Othello for Our Times," *The Spectator*, February 23, 2008, www.spectator.co.uk/article/obama-is-an-othe llo-for-our-times/; Maureen Dowd, "McCain's Green Eyed Monster," *The New York Times*, April 6, 2008, Lexis, November 20, 2022; Christina Kearney, "Examining Shifting Black Culture," *The Leader Post*, August 27, 2008, Lexis, November 20, 2022; Neal Conan, "Rethinking 'Othello' in the Age of Obama," *Talk of the Nation*, September 29, 2009, www. npr.org/templates/story/story.php?storyId=113169694;   Andrew Haydon, "Memo to RSC Obama Is Not Othello," *The Guardian*, January 21, 2009, www.theguardian.com/stage/theatreblog/2009/jan/21/ rsc-obama-othello

25 Nandini Das, João Vicente Melo, Haig Smith, and Lauren Working, *Keywords of Identity, Race, and Human Mobility in Early Modern England* (Amsterdam: Amsterdam University Press, 2021), 40. https:// library.oapen.org/viewer/web/viewer.html?file=/bitstream/han dle/20.500.12657/50188/9789048552283.pdf?sequence= 1&isAllowed=y

26 Mayte Green-Mercado, "The Forced Conversions and the Moriscos," *The Routledge Handbook of Muslim Iberia*, ed. Maribel Fierro (London: Routledge, 2021), 552–71; Olivia Remie Constable, *To Live Like a Moor: Christian Perceptions of Muslim Identity in Medieval and Early Modern Spain* (Philadelphia: University of Pennsylvania Press, 2017).

27 Brann, Ross, "The Moors?," *Medieval Encounters*, 15 (2009), 307–18.

28 Brann, "The Moors?," 311.

29 Brann, "The Moors?," 311.

30 Brann, "The Moors?," 312.

31 For a detailed study of Black people in early modern England see Imtiaz Habib, *Black Lives in the English Archives, 1500–1677: Imprints of the Invisible* (London: Routledge, 2017).

32 *Tudor Royal Proclamations*, ed. Paul L. Hughes and James F. Larkin, vol. 3 (New Haven, CT: Yale University Press, 1969), 221. For more on the connection between the proclamations and early modern English

race making, see Emily Weissbourd, "'Those in Their Possession' Race, Slavery, and Queen Elizabeth's 'Edicts of Expulsion'," *Huntington Library Quarterly*, 78.1 (2015), 1–19; and Ambereen Dadabhoy, "Barbarian Moors: Documenting Racial Formation in Early Modern England," *The Cambridge Companion to Shakespeare and Race*, ed. Ayanna Thompson (Cambridge: Cambridge University Press, 2021), 30–46.

33 Emily C. Bartels, "Making More of the Moor: Aaron, Othello, and Renaissance Refashionings of Race," *Shakespeare Quarterly*, 41.4 (1990), 433–554; Bartels, "Othello and Africa: Postcolonialism Reconsidered," *The William and Mary Quarterly*, 54.1 (1997), 45–64; Michael Neill, "'Mulattos,' 'Blacks,' and 'Indian Moors': Othello and Early Modern Constructions of Human Difference," *Shakespeare Quarterly*, 49.4 (1998), 361–74.

34 For more on globalization and race in Shakespeare, see Noémie Ndiaye, "Shakespeare, Race, and Globalization: Titus Andronicus," *The Cambridge Companion to Shakespeare and Race*, ed. Ayanna Thompson (Cambridge: Cambridge University Press, 2021), 158–74.

35 I make this distinction because medieval mystery plays used color-coded visual imagery to distinguish between good (white) and evil (black). "Moor," as I will argue in this chapter, signals racialization that encompasses religious difference, specifically Islamic Otherness. For more on the history of Blackness in early modern English drama, see Virginia Mason Vaughan, *Performing Blackness on English Stages, 1500–1800* (Cambridge: Cambridge University Press, 2005).

36 See Vaughan, *Performing Blackness*; Louis Wann, "The Oriental in Elizabethan drama," *Modern Philology*, 12.7 (1915), 423–47; Emily C. Bartels, *Speaking of the Moor: From "Alcazar" to "Othello"* (Philadelphia: University of Pennsylvania Press, 2010).

37 Neill, "'Mulattos,' 'Blacks,' and 'Indian Moors'," 364.

38 Neill, "'Mulattos,' 'Blacks,' and 'Indian Moors'," 364–65.

39 Neill, "'Mulattos,' 'Blacks,' and 'Indian Moors'," 365.

40 Neill, "'Mulattos,' 'Blacks,' and 'Indian Moors'," 369–74.

41 Neill, "'Mulattos,' 'Blacks,' and 'Indian Moors'," 369.

42 Barbara J. Fields and Karen E. Fields, *Racecraft: The Soul of Inequality in American Life* (London: Verso, 2014), 17.

43 Stuart Hall, "Race, the Floating Signifier: What More Is There to Say about 'Race'?" *Selected Writings on Race and Difference*, ed. Paul Gilroy

and Ruth Wilson Gilmore (Durham, NC: Duke University Press, 2021), 364.

44 Kim F. Hall, *Things of Darkness: Economies of Race and Gender in Early Modern England* (Ithaca, NY: Cornell University Press, 1995), 6.

45 Hall, *Things of Darkness*, 6.

46 Geraldine Heng, *The Invention of Race in the European Middle Ages* (Cambridge: Cambridge University Press, 2018), 19. Italics in source.

47 Matthew Dimmock, "Shakespeare's Non-Christian Religions," *Shakespeare and Early Modern Religion*, ed. David Loewenstein and Michael Witmore (Cambridge: Cambridge University Press, 2015), 280–99.

48 See Barbara Fuchs, "The Spanish Race," *Rereading the Black Legend: The Discourses of Religious and Racial Difference in the Renaissance Empires*, ed. Margaret R. Greer, Walter D. Mignolo, and Maureen Quilligan (Chicago: The University of Chicago Press, 2007), 88–98.

49 The word "barbarous" appears seven times in *Titus Andronicus*, the most in any of Shakespeare's plays. It is applied twice to the Romans as a collective, and once to the Goths. For specific characters, it is applied to Tamora once and to Aaron three times. These differing applications show that everyone has the capacity for barbarism in the play; however, it is more frequently a trait associated with the outsider Goths, and particularly Aaron. See *Open Source Shakespeare: Concordance*, s.v. "barbarous," accessed November 20, 2022.

50 For more on the racializing of the Goths see: Francesca T. Royster, "White-Limed Walls: Whiteness and Gothic Extremism in Shakespeare's Titus Andronicus," *Shakespeare Quarterly*, 51.4 (2000), 432–55.

51 Noémie Ndiaye, "Aaron's Roots: Spaniards, Englishmen, and Blackamoors in *Titus Andronicus*," *Early Theatre*, 19.2 (2016), 63.

52 Ndiaye, "Aaron's Roots," 61.

53 Lindsay Kaplan, *Figuring Racism in Medieval Christianity* (Oxford: Oxford University Press, 2018), 2–3.

54 Nabil Matar, "Britons and Muslims in the Early Modern Period: From Prejudice to (a Theory of) Toleration," *Patterns of Prejudice*, 43.3–4 (2009), 217.

55 William Shakespeare, *Titus Andronicus*, ed. Barbara Mowat and Paul Werstine (Washington, D.C.: Folger Shakespeare Library, 2013), 4.2.83; 4.2.74–75.

56 Shakespeare, *Titus Andronicus*, 4.2.95.

57 Ladan Niayesh, "Of Pearls and Scimitars: The Shakespearean Bazaar of Oriental Props," *Actes des congrès de la Société française Shakespeare* 27 (2009), 84.

58 For more on Anglo-Moroccan relations see: Nabil Matar, *Turks, Moors, and Englishmen in the Age of Discovery* (New York: Columbia University Press, 2000); Gustav Ungerer, "Portia and the Prince of Morocco," *Shakespeare Studies*, 31 (2003), 89–126; Nabil Matar, "Queen Elizabeth I Through Moroccan Eyes," *Journal of Early Modern History*, 12.1 (2008), 55–76; Jerry Brotton, *This Orient Isle: Elizabethan England and the Islamic World* (London: Penguin, 2016); Jerry Brotton, "Global Interests in the Shakespearean World," *The Art of Cultural Exchange: Translation and Transformation between the UK and Brazil (2012–2016)*, ed. Paul Heritage and Ilana Strozenberg (Wilmington, DE: Vernon Press, 2019), 28–41.

59 William Shakespeare, *The Merchant of Venice*, ed. Barbara Mowat and Paul Werstine (New York: Simon and Schuster, 2010), 1.2.129–31.

60 Shakespeare, *Merchant*, 2.1.1–12.

61 William Shakespeare, *The Merchant of Venice*, ed. Barbara Mowat and Paul Werstine (New York: Simon and Shuster, 2015), 3.1.63.

62 Ian Smith, "The Textile Black Body: Race and 'Shadowed Livery' in *The Merchant of Venice*," *The Oxford Handbook of Shakespeare and Embodiment: Gender, Sexuality, and Race*, ed. Valerie Traub (Oxford: Oxford University Press, 2016), 170–85.

63 Kim F. Hall, "Guess Who's Coming to Dinner? Colonization and Miscegenation in 'The Merchant of Venice,'" *Renaissance Drama* 23 (1992), 87–111.

64 See *Race in Early Modern England: A Documentary Companion*, ed. Ania Loomba and Jonathan Burton (New York: Palgrave Macmillan, 2007); Ayanna Thompson, *Performing Race and Torture on the Early Modern Stage* (London: Routledge, 2013); Jean Feerick, *Strangers in Blood: Relocating Race in the Renaissance* (Toronto: University of Toronto Press, 2010).

65 María Elena Martínez, David Nirenberg, and Max-Sebastián Hering Torres, eds., *Race and Blood in the Iberian World* (Münster: LIT Verlag, 2012), 1.

66 Junaid Rana, "The Story of Islamophobia," *Souls*, 9.2 (2007), 148–61. For more on anti-Muslim racism in see Hassana Moosa. "Marking Muslims: The Prince of Morocco and the Racialization of Islam in

The Merchant of Venice." In *Global Shakespeare and Social Justice*. Eds. Chris Thurman and Sandra Young. 120–41. (London: Bloomsbury, 2023).

67 Shakespeare, *Merchant*, 2.1.25–27.

68 Quoted in Samia Errazzouki, "Partners in Empire: Sultan Ahmad al-Mansur and Queen Elizabeth I," *The Journal of North African Studies*, (2021), 10. See also, Matar, *Turks, Moors, and Englishmen* (New York: Columbia University Press, 2000).

69 See Daniel J. Vitkus, "Turning Turk in *Othello*: The Conversion and Damnation of the Moor," *Shakespeare Quarterly*, 48.2 (1997), 145–76; Ambereen Dadabhoy, "Two Faced: The Problem of Othello's Visage," *Othello: The State of Play*, ed. Lena Cowen Orlin (London: Bloomsbury, 2014), 121–48; Dennis Austin Britton, *Becoming Christian: Race, Reformation, and Early Modern English Romance* (New York: Fordham University Press, 2014), 112–41. This list is by no means exhaustive, simply representative of some of the ways Islam and Muslim cultures have been examined in relation to *Othello*.

70 Sheymaa Ali Nurein and Humera Iqbal, "Identifying a Space for Young Black Muslim Women in Contemporary Britain," *Ethnicities*, 21.3 (2021): 433–53.

71 William Shakespeare, *Othello*, ed. Barbara Mowat and Paul Werstine (New York: Simon and Schuster, 2017), 1.3.285–89.

72 See the following essays in *Shakespeare and the Power of the Face*, ed. James A. Knapp (London: Routledge, 2016): Sean Lawrence, "The Two Faces of Othello," 61–74; Vanessa Corredera, "Complex Complexions: The Facial Signification of the Black Other in Lust's Dominion," 93–114; and Farah Karim-Cooper, "Fashioning the Face: Embodiment and Desire in Early Modern Poetry," 29–42.

73 Ian Smith, "Othello's Black Handkerchief," *Shakespeare Quarterly*, 64.1 (2013), 1–25.

74 Smith, "Othello's Black Handkerchief," 20.

75 Smith, "Othello's Black Handkerchief," 20.

76 Lynda E. Boose, "Othello's Handkerchief: 'The Recognizance and Pledge of Love'," *English Literary Renaissance*, 5.3 (1975), 362.

77 Lois Whitney, "Did Shakespeare Know Leo Africanus?" *PMLA*, 37.3 (1922): 470–83; Bartels, "Making More of the Moor"; Phyllis Natalie Braxton, "Othello: the Moor and the metaphor," *South Atlantic Review*, 55.4 (1990), 1–17; Andrew Hadfield, "Race in 'Othello': The 'History

and Description of Africa' and the Black Legend," *Notes and Queries*, 45.3 (1998), 336–39; Jonathan Burton, "'A Most Wily Bird': Leo Africanus, Othello and the Trafficking in Difference," *Post-Colonial Shakespeares*, ed. Ania Loomba and Martin Orkin (London: Routledge, 2003), 55–75.

78 Leo Africanus, *A Geographical Historie of Africa, Written in Arabicke and Italian by Iohn Leo a More, Borne in Granada, and Brought Vp in Barbarie. [...] Translated and Collected by Iohn Pory, Lately of Goneuill and Caius College in Cambridge.* London: 1600, 143–45.

79 Ottaviano Bon, *A Description of the Grand Signour's Seraglio, or Turkish Emperours Court.: By John Greaves, Late Professor of Astronomie in the University of Oxford,* translated by Robert Withers (London: Jo. Ridley, 1653), 49–51.

80 Shakespeare, *Othello*, 3.4.81.

81 William Painter, *The Palace of Pleasure* (London, 1566), quoted in "Turkish Mahomet and Hiren the Fair Greek," *The Lost Plays Database*, accessed December 2, 2022, https://lostplays.folger.edu/Turkish_Mahomet_and_Hiren_the_Fair_Greek,_The. See also Fahd Mohammed Taleb Saeed Al-Olaqi, "The Uxoricide Legend of the Sultan and His European Wife in Elizabethan Drama," *Arts and Social Sciences Journal*, 8.1 (2017), doi: 10.4172/2151-6200.1000240.

82 Shakespeare, *Othello*, 4.3.63–72.

83 Shakespeare, *Othello*, 5.2.1–6.

84 Shakespeare, *Othello*, 5.2.334. See all of Acts 4 and 5 of the play for the renewed focus on "Moor" in the play.

85 Shakespeare, *Othello*, 5.2.413–17.

86 I have written more about this scene and Othello's position as Moor within the Venetian–Ottoman contest in Dadabhoy, "Two Faced."

87 Shakespeare, *Othello*, 1.1.151–52. For more on foreigners in Venice, see Benjamin Ravid, "Venice and Its Minorities," *A Companion to Venetian History, 1400–1797* (Leiden: Brill, 2013), 449–86.

REFERENCES

Adamson, Bryan. "The Muslim Manchurian Candidate: Barack Obama, Rumors, and Quotidian Hermeneutics." *St. John's Journal of Civil Rights and Economic Development* 25.4 (2010): 581–624.

Africanus, Leo, *A Geographical Historie of Africa, Written in Arabicke and Italian by Iohn Leo a More, Borne in Granada, and Brought Vp in Barbarie. Wherein He*

Hath at Large Described, Not Onely the Qualities, Situations, and True Distances of the Regions, Cities, Townes, Mountaines, Riuers, and Other Places Throughout all the North and Principall Partes of Africa; but also the Descents and Families of their Kings ... Gathered Partly Out of His Owne Diligent Obseruations, and Partly Out of the Ancient Records and Chronicles of the Arabians and Mores. before which, Out of the Best Ancient and Moderne Writers, is Prefixed a Generall Description of Africa, and also a Particular Treatise of all the Maine Lands and Isles Vndescribed by Iohn Leo. ... Translated and Collected by Iohn Pory, Lately of Goneuill and Caius College in Cambridge. London: 1600. Accessed via Early English Books Online.

Al-Olaqi, Fahd Mohammed Taleb Saeed. "The Uxoricide Legend of the Sultan and his European Wife in Elizabethan Drama." *Arts and Social Sciences Journal.* 8.1 (2017). doi: 10.4172/2151-6200.1000240.

Bartels, Emily C. "Making More of the Moor: Aaron, Othello, and Renaissance Refashionings of Race." *Shakespeare Quarterly* 41.4 (1990): 433–54.

———. "Othello and Africa: Postcolonialism Reconsidered." *The William and Mary Quarterly* 54.1 (1997): 45–64.

———. *Speaking of the Moor: From "Alcazar" to "Othello."* Philadelphia: University of Pennsylvania Press, 2010.

Bhabha, Homi K. *The Location of Culture.* London: Routledge, 2012.

Bon, Ottaviano. *A Description of the Grand Signour's Seraglio, or Turkish Emperours Court.: By John Greaves, Late Professor of Astronomie in the University of Oxford.* Translated by Robert Withers. London: Jo. Ridley, 1653. Accessed via Early English Books Online.

Bonilla-Silva, Eduardo. "The Structure of Racism in Color-blind, 'Post-Racial' America." *American Behavioral Scientist* 59.11 (2015): 1358–76.

Boose, Lynda E. "Othello's Handkerchief: 'The Recognizance and Pledge of Love'." *English Literary Renaissance* 5.3 (1975): 360–74.

Brann, Ross, "The Moors?," *Medieval Encounters*, 15 (2009), 307–18.

Braxton, Phyllis Natalie. "Othello: The Moor and the Metaphor." *South Atlantic Review* 55.4 (1990): 1–17.

Bristol, Michael D. *Shakespeare's America, America's Shakespeare (Routledge Revivals).* London: Routledge, 2014.

Britton, Dennis Austin. *Becoming Christian: Race, Reformation, and Early Modern English Romance.* New York: Fordham University Press, 2014.

Brotton, Jerry. *This Orient Isle: Elizabethan England and the Islamic world.* London: Penguin UK, 2016.

————. "Global Interests in the Shakespearean World." In *The Art of Cultural Exchange: Translation and Transformation between the UK and Brazil* (2012–2016), edited by Paul Heritage and Ilana Strozenberg, 28–41. Wilmington, DE: Vernon Press, 2019.

Burton, Jonathan. "'A Most Wily Bird': Leo Africanus, Othello and the Trafficking in Difference." In *Post-Colonial Shakespeares*, edited by Ania Loomba and Martin Orkin, 55–75. London: Routledge, 2003.

Charnes, Linda. *Hamlet's Heirs: Shakespeare and the Politics of a New Millennium*. London: Routledge, 2006.

CNN. "Rep. Gohmert: Obama's Ottoman Empire." September 22, 2012. Video clip. www.youtube.com/watch?v=OJK7QE9YdfQ

Colbert, Stephen. "Obama's Ottoman Empire." *The Colbert Report*. September 26, 2012. www.cc.com/video/pnhcq0/the-colbert-report-obama-s-ottoman-empire

Conan, Neal. "Rethinking 'Othello' in the Age of Obama." *Talk of the Nation*. September 29, 2009. www.npr.org/templates/story/story.php?storyId=113169694

Constable, Olivia Remie. *To Live Like a Moor: Christian Perceptions of Muslim Identity in Medieval and Early Modern Spain*. Philadelphia: University of Pennsylvania Press, 2017.

Cornish, Audie. "Michelle Obama Recounts Struggle to Find Her Place in the World in 'Becoming'." *NPR: All Things Considered*. November 12, 2008. www.npr.org/2018/11/12/667118244/michelle-obama-recounts-struggle-to-find-her-place-in-the-world-in-becoming

Corredera, Vanessa. "Complex Complexions: The Facial Signification of the Black Other in Lust's Dominion." In *Shakespeare and the Power of the Face*, ed. James A. Knapp, 93–114. London: Routledge, 2016.

Dadabhoy, Ambereen. "The Moor of America: Approaching the Crisis of Race and Religion in the Renaissance and the Twenty-First Century." *Teaching Medieval and Early Modern Cross-Cultural Encounters*, edited by Karina F. Attar and Lynn Shutters, 123–40. Palgrave Macmillan, New York, 2014.

————. "Two Faced: The Problem of Othello's Visage." *Othello: The State of Play*, edited by Lena Cowen Orlin, 121–48. London: Bloomsbury, 2014.

————. "Barbarian Moors: Documenting Racial Formation in Early Modern England." In *The Cambridge Companion to Shakespeare and Race*, edited by Ayanna Thompson, 30–46. Cambridge, Cambridge University Press, 2021.

Das, Nandini, João Vicente Melo, Haig Smith, and Lauren Working, *Keywords of Identity, Race, and Human Mobility in Early Modern England* (Amsterdam: Amsterdam University Press, 2021), 40. https://library.oapen.org/viewer/web/viewer.html?file=/bitstream/handle/20.500.12657/50188/9789048552283.pdf?sequence=1&isAllowed=y

Daulatzai, Suhail. *Black Star Crescent Moon: The Muslim International and Black Freedom Beyond America*. Minneapolis: University of Minnesota Press, 2012, xv.

Davis, Angela Y. "Afro Images: Politics, Fashion, and Nostalgia." *Critical Inquiry* 21.1 (1994): 37–45.

Dimmock, Matthew. "Shakespeare's non-Christian Religions." In *Shakespeare and Early Modern Religion*, edited by David Loewenstein and Michael Witmore, 280–99. Cambridge: Cambridge University Press, 2015.

Dowd, Maureen. "McCain's Green Eyed Monster." *The New York Times*. April 6, 2008. Lexis. November 20, 2022.

Errazzouki, Samia. "Partners in Empire: Sultan Ahmad al-Mansur and Queen Elizabeth I." *The Journal of North African Studies* 3 (2021): 1–18.

Feerick, Jean. *Strangers in Blood: Relocating Race in the Renaissance.* Toronto: University of Toronto Press, 2010.

Fields, Barbara J., and Karen E. Fields. *Racecraft: The Soul of Inequality in American Life*. London: Verso, 2014.

Fuchs, Barbara. "The Spanish Race." In *Rereading the Black Legend: The Discourses of Religious and Racial Difference in the Renaissance Empires*, edited by Margaret R. Greer, Walter D. Mignolo, and Maureen Quilligan, 88–98. Chicago: The University of Chicago Press, 2007.

Gettleman, Jeffrey. "Obama Gets a Warm Welcome In Kenya." *The New York Times*. August, 26, 2006. www.nytimes.com/2006/08/26/world/africa/26obama.html

Giardina, Michael D. "Barack Obama, Islamophobia, and the 2008 US Presidential Election Media Spectacle." *Counterpoints* 346 (2010): 135–57.

Green-Mercado, Mayte. "The Forced Conversions and the Moriscos." In *The Routledge Handbook of Muslim Iberia*, edited by Maribel Fierro, 552–71. London: Routledge, 2021.

Habib, Imtiaz. *Black Lives in the English Archives, 1500–1677: Imprints of the Invisible*. London: Routledge, 2017.

Hadfield, Andrew. "Race in 'Othello': the 'History and Description of Africa' and the Black Legend." *Notes and Queries* 45.3 (1998): 336–39.

Hall, Kim F. "Guess Who's Coming to Dinner? Colonization and Miscegenation in 'The Merchant of Venice.'" *Renaissance Drama* 23 (1992): 87–111. www.jstor.org/stable/41917285

———. *Things of Darkness: Economies of Race and Gender in Early Modern England.* Ithaca, NY: Cornell University Press, 1995.

Hall, Stuart. "Race, the Floating Signifier: What More Is There to Say about 'Race'?" In *Selected Writings on Race and Difference*, edited by Paul Gilroy and Ruth Wilson Gilmore, 359–73. Durham, NC: Duke University Press, 2021.

Haydon, Andrew, "Memo to RSC Obama Is Not Othello," *The Guardian.* January 21, 2009. www.theguardian.com/stage/theatreblog/2009/jan/21/rsc-obama-othello

Heng, Geraldine. *The Invention of Race in the European Middle Ages.* Cambridge: Cambridge University Press, 2018.

Huffington Post. "Fox Anchor Calls Obama Fist Pound a 'Terrorist Fist Jab'." June 17, 2008. www.huffpost.com/entry/fox-anchor-calls-obama-fi_n_106027

Hughes, Paul L., and James F. Larkin (eds.). *Tudor Royal Proclamations.* 3 vols. New Haven, CT: Yale University Press, 1969.

Kaplan, Lindsay. *Figuring Racism in Medieval Christianity.* Oxford: Oxford University Press, 2018.

Karim-Cooper, Farah. "Fashioning the Face: Embodiment and Desire in Early Modern Poetry." In *Shakespeare and the Power of the Face*, ed. James A. Knapp, 29–42. London: Routledge, 2016.

Kearney, Christina. "Examining Shifting Black Culture." *The Leader Post.* August 27, 2008. Lexis. November 20, 2022.

Khabeer, Su'ad Abdul. *Muslim Cool: Race, Religion, and Hip Hop in the United States.* New York: NYU Press, 2016, 25.

Lawrence, Sean. "The Two Faces of Othello." In *Shakespeare and the Power of the Face*, ed. James A. Knapp, 61–74. London: Routledge, 2016.

Loomba, Ania, and Jonathan Burton, eds. *Race in Early Modern England: A Documentary Companion.* New York: Palgrave Macmillan, 2007.

Lugo-Lugo, Carmen R., and Mary K. Bloodsworth-Lugo. "Bare Biceps and American (in) Security: Post-9/11 Constructions of Safe (ty), Threat, and the First Black First Lady." *Women's Studies Quarterly* 39.1/2 (2011): 200–17.

Martínez, María Elena, David Nirenberg, and Max-Sebastián Hering Torres, eds. *Race and Blood in the Iberian World*. Münster: LIT Verlag, 2012.

Matar, Nabil. *Turks, Moors, and Englishmen in the Age of Discovery*. New York: Columbia University Press, 2000.

———. "Queen Elizabeth I Through Moroccan Eyes." *Journal of Early Modern History* 12.1 (2008): 55–76.

———. "Britons and Muslims in the Early Modern Period: From Prejudice to (a Theory of) Toleration." *Patterns of Prejudice* 43.3–4 (2009): 213–31.

Mitchell, Koritha. *From Slave Cabins to the White House: Homemade Citizenship in African American Culture*. Champaign, IL: University of Illinois Press, 2020.

Moosa, Hassana. "Marking Muslims: The Prince of Morocco and the Racialization of Islam in *The Merchant of Venice*." In *Global Shakespeare and Social Justice*. Eds. Chris Thurman and Sandra Young. 120–41. London: Bloomsbury, 2023.

NBC News. "Skinny Kid with a Funny Name Rallies Democrats." July 28, 2004. www.nbcnews.com/id/wbna5537216

———. "Photo of Obama Causes Stir on Internet." February 25, 2008. www.nbcnews.com/id/wbna23337141

Ndiaye, Noémie. "Aaron's Roots: Spaniards, Englishmen, and Blackamoors in *Titus Andronicus*." *Early Theatre* 19.2 (2016): 59–80.

———. "Shakespeare, Race, and Globalization: Titus Andronicus." In *The Cambridge Companion to Shakespeare and Race*, edited by Ayanna Thompson, 158–74. Cambridge: Cambridge University Press, 2021.

Neill, Michael. "'Mulattos,' 'Blacks,' and 'Indian Moors': Othello and Early Modern Constructions of Human Difference.' *Shakespeare Quarterly* 49.4 (1998): 361–74.

Niayesh, Ladan. "Of Pearls and Scimitars: The Shakespearean Bazaar of Oriental Props." *Actes des congrès de la Société française Shakespeare* 27 (2009): 83–98.

Omi, Michael, and Howard Winant. *Racial Formation in the United States*. London: Routledge, 2014.

Rana, Junaid. "The Story of Islamophobia," *Souls* 9.2 (2007), 148–61.

Ravid, Benjamin. "Venice and Its Minorities." In *A Companion to Venetian History, 1400–1797*, edited by Eric R. Dursteler, 449–86. Leiden: Brill, 2013.

Renshon, Stanley. "The Political Mind: Obama Denounces Flag-Pin Patriotism." *Politico.* October 27, 2007. www.politico.com/story/2007/10/the-political-mind-obama-denounces-flag-pin-patriotism-006502

Rosentiel, Tom. "No Decline in Belief that Obama Is a Muslim: Nearly One-in-Five White Evangelicals Think So." *Pew Research Center.* April 1, 2009. www.pewresearch.org/2009/04/01/no-decline-in-belief-that-obama-is-a-muslim/

Royster, Francesca T. "White-Limed Walls: Whiteness and Gothic Extremism in Shakespeare's Titus Andronicus." *Shakespeare Quarterly* 51.4 (2000): 432–55.

Shakespeare, William. *The Merchant of Venice.* Edited by Barbara Mowat and Paul Werstine. New York: Simon and Schuster, 2010.

———. *Titus Andronicus.* Edited by Barbara Mowat and Paul Werstine. Washington, D.C.: Folger Shakespeare Library, 2013. https://shakespeare.folger.edu/downloads/pdf/titus-andronicus_PDF_FolgerShakespeare.pdf

———. *Othello.* Edited by Barbara Mowat and Paul Werstine. New York: Simon and Schuster, 2017. https://shakespeare.folger.edu/downloads/pdf/othello_PDF_FolgerShakespeare.pdf

Shapiro, James. *Shakespeare in a Divided America: What His Plays Tell Us About Our Past and Future.* New York: Penguin, 2021.

Skalar, Rachel. "Obama Fist-Bump Rocks the Nation!" *Huffington Post.* June 14, 2008. www.huffpost.com/entry/obama-fist-bump-rocks-the_n_105490

Smith, Ian. "Othello's Black Handkerchief." *Shakespeare Quarterly* 64.1 (2013): 1–25.

———. "The Textile Black Body: Race and 'Shadowed Livery' in *The Merchant of Venice*." In *The Oxford Handbook of Shakespeare and Embodiment: Gender, Sexuality, and Race,* edited by Valerie Traub, 170–85. Oxford: Oxford University Press, 2016. https://doi.org/10.1093/oxfordhb/9780199663408.013.9

Sonmez, Felicia. "Mitt Romney: 'No One's Ever Asked to See My Birth Certificate'." *The Washington Post.* August 24, 2012. www.washingtonpost.com/news/post-politics/wp/2012/08/24/mitt-romney-no-ones-asked-for-my-birth-certificate/

Sturgess, Kim C. *Shakespeare and the American Nation*. Cambridge: Cambridge University Press, 2004.

Thompson, Ayanna. *Performing Race and Torture on the Early Modern Stage*. London: Routledge, 2013.

Thompson, Venetia. "Obama Is an Othello for Our Times." *The Spectator*. February 23, 2008. www.spectator.co.uk/article/obama-is-an-othello-for-our-times/

Tope, Daniel, Brittany D. Rawlinson, Justin T. Pickett, Amy M. Burdette, and Christopher G. Ellison. "Religion, Race, and Othering Barack Obama." *Social Currents* 4.1 (2017): 51–70.

Ungerer, Gustav. "Portia and the Prince of Morocco." *Shakespeare Studies* 31 (2003): 89–126.

Vaughan, Alden T., and Virginia Mason Vaughan. *Shakespeare in America*. Oxford: Oxford University Press, 2012.

Vaughan, Virginia Mason. *Performing Blackness on English Stages, 1500–1800*. Cambridge: Cambridge University Press, 2005.

Vitkus, Daniel J. "Turning Turk in *Othello*: The Conversion and Damnation of the Moor." *Shakespeare Quarterly* 48.2 (1997): 145–76.

Wann, Louis. "The Oriental in Elizabethan Drama." *Modern Philology* 12.7 (1915): 289–456.

Weissbourd, Emily. "'Those in Their Possession' Race, Slavery, and Queen Elizabeth's 'Edicts of Expulsion'." *Huntington Library Quarterly* 78.1 (2015): 1–19.

Whitney, Lois. "Did Shakespeare Know Leo Africanus?" *PMLA* 37.3 (1922): 470–83.

Turkish Delight

Twelfth Night's *Harem Life*

Four

Shipwrecked upon an unfamiliar shore in the opening of *Twelfth Night* (1602), Viola asks "what country, friends, is this," in a desperate attempt to orient herself.[1] For many scholars, the answer she receives, "Illyria," has suggested a "magical" no-place, a fantastic "fairyland" or "a scarcely familiar territory, more significant, perhaps, for its evocation of like-sounding exotica—Elysium, delirium—than for concrete geopolitical associations."[2,3] The latter critical evaluation presumably responds to Viola's double lament, "what should I do in Illyria? / My brother he is in Elysium," bemoaning her fate and the likely demise of her brother.[4] More recently, critics have challenged the supposed blank slate of Illyria by tracing the geography's classical and early modern provenance to argue that Shakespeare's audiences may well have been familiar with it. Illyria registers in early modern England in several ways, from a specific geopolitical location on the Adriatic Coast, to its historical importance at a crossroad of trade and pilgrimage routes, to its contemporary resonances as a contact zone of between the Ottoman Empire and Europe.[5] In Shakespeare's play, Illyria is a palimpsest, simultaneously elusive and sedimented with layers of history and culture specific to the eastern Mediterranean, and consequently to the Muslim societies that had long inhabited its environs. Building upon the important work of scholars who have limned the contours

DOI: 10.4324/9781003213581-5

of Illyria as a cultural and symbolic geography, I argue that Ottoman imperial praxis, particularly the same-sex organization of Ottoman societies, influences the spatial arrangements of *Twelfth Night*. Just as the literal ground of the play, Illyria, was a geography occupied by the Ottomans, so, too, does Shakespeare conjure the Ottoman Empire through the two households—Orsino's and Olivia's respective courts—that dominate the play. Illyria's geography allows Shakespeare to evoke the sex-segregated spaces of the Ottoman Empire, specifically the locale of the harem, as a setting for the comic play in and of sex and gender in *Twelfth Night*. In other words, Shakespeare harnesses popular representations of Ottoman domestic spaces and the goings on within those forbidden places to effect his characters' own transformations of identity. Investigating the play's geography exposes how Shakespeare mobilizes Ottoman and Islamic Otherness at the same time that he evacuates this culture from this geography, reconstituting these spaces as void of Islamic influence.

CONTESTED GEOGRAPHIES

Scholars have traced the sources of *Twelfth Night* to several key texts, including Plautus's *Menaechmi* and one of the stories from Barnabe Riche's collection *His Farewell to the Military Profession* (1594). The latter is of particular importance because its eastern Mediterranean setting and evocation of the "Turk" firmly embed the Ottoman Empire within the conceptual framework of the play.[6] The second story in Riche's collection, "Apolonius and Silla," chronicles the romantic adventures of the titular couple, which include Silla dressing as a man in an attempt to get closer to Apolonius, and Apolonius then sending her to woo the woman he desires, Julina, who promptly falls in love with Silla (disguised as Silvio). Riche's short story contains the rudimentary plot architecture of Shakespeare's play, but is set in Constantinople and Cyprus, two locales that at the time of Riche's writing were associated with—indeed occupied by—the Ottoman Empire. As Riche notes at the start of the tale, Apolonius has been fighting the "Turks" in an unnamed frontier, and it is on his return journey to Constantinople that his ship is blown off course to Cyprus:

> During the time that the famous City of Constantinople, remained in the hands of the Christians, amongst many other noble men, that kept their abiding in that flourishing City, there was one whose name was Apolonius, a worthy Duke, who being but a very young man, and even then new come to his possessions which were very great, levied a mighty band of men, at his own proper charges, with whom he served against the Turk, during the space of one whole year, in which time although it were very short, this young Duke so behaved himself, as well by prowess and valiance shewed with his own hands, as otherwise, by his wisdom and liberality used towards his Soldiers, that all the world was filled with the fame of this noble Duke. When he had thus spent one year's service, he caused his Trumpet to sound a retreat, and gathering his company together, and embarking themselves he set sail, holding his course towards Constantinople: but being upon the Sea, by the extremity of a Tempest which suddenly fell, his fleet was deserved some one way, and some another, but he himself recovered the Isle of Cyprus.[7]

In addition to detailing the eastern Mediterranean geography of his story—a hinterland military frontier and the critical locales of Constantinople and Cyprus—Riche's opening specifically harkens back to an earlier time when Constantinople was still under Byzantine rule. Riche's representation of Constantinople as a "famous" city which "remained in the hands of Christians" declares the city's glory and mourns its transfer from Christian hands into Muslim ones.

Setting the narrative in the recent past reminds readers of the Christian history, genealogy, and claims to this geography that predate the current Ottoman and Muslim domination of this space. Indeed, the unidentified war that Apolonius engages in with the "Turk" recalls the encroaching danger at the borders of the region, obliquely referencing the threat of Islam, even as it is sidelined, so as not to intrude on the main narrative. The Duke's martial bravery against the "Turk" shows him to be a worthy and virile man, whose thoughts appropriately turn toward the erotic after he has already proven himself on the field of battle. Thus, the "Turk" further operates as a foil through which European masculinity proves its bellicose and amorous prowess. While actual "Turks" do not appear in Riche's comic-erotic narrative, their menace contextualizes the geography in which his romantic intrigues occur. Moreover, the long-standing conflict in which Apolonius takes part—though only for a year—displays the constant, ubiquitous, and dangerous presence of the Ottoman Empire in the region.

I stress the importance of this seemingly inconsequential background material because geography is more than location in both Riche's narrative and Shakespeare's play. For Riche, the evocation of Constantinople as a "Christian" city activates nostalgia for its Christian past and for the Christian dominance of the eastern Mediterranean. Furthermore, his romance plot reclaims this geography for a western European Christian audience—one that was quite different from the Greek eastern Orthodox Christian culture of the city. Riche's rhetorical maneuver invokes the fantasy of a unified Christendom, located in and through Constantinople and the Mediterranean via Cyprus, allied against the common enemy embodied by the "Turk." Geography provides Riche with a tidy shorthand through which to lay out the ideological stakes of his story, wherein men can turn to affairs of the heart after they have secured affairs of the state, particularly against an encroaching Other like the "Turk."

By 1594, Constantinople had been renamed Istanbul and been the capital of the Ottoman Empire for well over a century. Fatih Sultan Mehmet (the Conqueror) besieged the city in April of 1453 and successfully routed Byzantine forces by May of that same year. The fall of Constantinople reverberated throughout Europe with some contemporary rulers unwilling to believe the Ottoman victory and others hastening to make peace with its new overlords.[8] For the contemporary Greek chronicler Kritovoulos, the loss of the city equaled and surpassed the sack of Troy, Babylon, Carthage, Rome, and Jerusalem because it was "a disaster the like of which had occurred in no one of the great renowned cities of history," with "overwhelming and unheard-of horror" accompanying its defeat.[9] He concludes his elegy for the city by lamenting,

> And the City which had formerly ruled with honor and glory and wealth and great splendor over many nations was now ruled by others, amid want and disgrace and dishonor and abject and shameful slavery. While it had been an example of all good things, the picture of brilliant prosperity, it now had become the picture of misfortune, a reminder of sufferings, a monument of disaster, and a by-word for life.[10]

Kritovoulos's requiem for Constantinople demonstrates the symbolic contours of the geography. Constantinople was the seat of the Eastern Roman Empire, representing the history and culture of that classical inheritance, which was now "ruled by others," lost to non-European and non-Christian invaders. The fall of Constantinople signaled to other European powers their own vulnerability in the face of a possible Ottoman onslaught. The conquest of Constantinople indicated to the Ottomans their right to European and world empire. Constantinople as a place and an idea contained real and figurative power. It offered a gateway into Europe for the Ottomans as well as imperial legitimacy, while furthering their own worldmaking project.[11]

Constantinople was simultaneously a specific geographical location, with coordinates that could be fixed on a map, and it was also a cultural geography, a space produced by the cultures that inhabited and conquered it and—as Riche's example illustrates—the cultures that wrote about it. Cultural geography considers how space is produced and "perpetuated" through social norms; therefore, culture informs spatial arrangements, just as spatial arrangements reinforce or contest cultural norms.[12] Thinking through space requires attending to "how particular sites acquire meanings and how places and sites are used by cultures."[13] The geographies through which Riche's characters traverse, then, are more than mere exotic settings: they specifically gesture toward the imminent threat of the "Turk" and the transformation of European Christian spaces into "foreign" Muslim ones.

In *Twelfth Night* Shakespeare shifts the location for his comedy from the Mediterranean itinerary of Riche's story to Europe's Adriatic. Illyria, as it was known in the early modern period, cannot be neatly mapped onto current nation states;

however, it nebulously covered much of what is now called the Balkans, a landmass that includes Croatia, Albania, Bosnia & Herzegovina, Serbia, Bulgaria, and Romania among other countries.[14] In the early modern period, Illyria was variously identified with all or some parts of this geography, so that Richard Knolles in his monumental study of the Ottoman Empire, *The General History of the Turks* (1603), declares "BOSNA (in time past called ILLYRIA)," and at other times aligns Illyria with other principalities such as Serbia or Hungary, and still at others mentions it by itself.[15] Despite these geographic inconsistencies, Knolles's *General History* demonstrates how much of this region was under the control of the Ottoman Empire and how much of it was contested territory. Ottoman incursions into southeastern Europe began in the mid-fourteenth century, with Sultan Murad I's advances into Albania, Bosnia, and Dubrovnik in 1386 and his successors' battles in Hungary and the Danube, which continued well into the seventeenth century.[16] Under Sultan Süleyman, the western frontier of the empire continued to be of critical importance:

> In 1526 he defeated the Hungarians in the Battle of Mohács and briefly took Buda. Three years later, he lad another army into Hungary, occupied the entire country, and even besieged Vienna for three weeks. The Ottomans, however, found it difficult to hold what was conquered. The distance between Istanbul and these provinces, the custom of retreat after each campaign season, and the abilities of the Habsburgs to organize and mobilize opposing forces may have contributed to the Ottomans' shaky position. It was in fact not until the 1540s that the Ottomans felt secure enough to organize the regions around the towns of Buda and Temesvár [Timișoara, Romania] into provinces. Furthermore, a relatively stable

"march" area emerged between the Habsburg and Ottoman domains, which demarcated an unacknowledged but very real border between the two empires.[17]

Süleyman's and his successors' military advances into the region created Ottoman suzerainties and outposts in the Balkans, but those strongholds were embattled, contested, and disputed. Ottoman imperial dominion was not secure, yet its presence was a near-constant reality.

At the time that *Twelfth Night* was first performed, then, Illyria would have invoked a variety of literal and symbolic geographies. The landmass associated with it comprised all or part of the areas that were either under Ottoman dominion or imperiled by the looming specter of Ottoman invasion. Shakespeare's sleight of hand in substituting Illyria for Constantinople is an attempt to repress and obscure the Ottoman presence and Islam from his play, yet their long history in the region demonstrates the difficulty, if not the outright impossibility, of such a move. In one of the first essays to investigate the presence of the "Turk" in *Twelfth Night*, Constance Relihan contrasts the Constantinople / Illyria dyad to expose how Shakespeare "erases the East from the text so that we may explore more fully the nature of Elizabethan masculinity."[18] For Relihan, Shakespeare's experimentation with same-sex desire and the underlying homoeroticism of the play relies on the "liminal realm" of his Illyria, a place where "[e]ast and [w]est mingle with some degree of safety."[19]

While Relihan gestures toward Shakespeare's displacement of Constantinople for Illyria as an exchange in the familiar for the unfamiliar, Patricia Parker has persuasively argued that Illyria was well known to early modern English audiences due to mercantile relationships between Ragusa and London, and the notoriety of Illyria within discourses about the "Turk" found in a variety of texts, from travel to religious writing.[20] Parker's broad archival focus uncovers a vast array of European discourses on Illyria and the centrality of Ottoman culture to these depictions, particularly Ottoman tyranny. Following Parker, Su Fang Ng has argued that the "frontier" location of Illyria "draws together religion and geography to explore the politics of border zones and the consequent dizzying shifts of perspectives."[21] As Ng explores, the mutability of the frontier facilitates the experimentation with identity that is so central to the play's action. By changing the geography of his play from Constantinople to Illyria, Shakespeare swaps one Ottoman setting for another, a move designed—perhaps—to defamiliarize, yet one that depends upon and exploits the Ottoman presence and its domestic spatial arrangements to ascribe meaning to the play's many transformations.

While Shakespeare may have transferred the setting of his play from the Mediterranean to the Adriatic, *Twelfth Night* still displays the characteristics of a staged Mediterranean play. As I explored in Chapter One, the staged Mediterranean is a sub-genre in early modern English drama, which is concerned with the traffic and exchanges encouraged and facilitated by the fluid geography of the region. These plays center European encounters with racial and religious Otherness. They further test the limits of identity by teasing out the possibility of transformation through conversion, religious or otherwise. Staged Mediterranean plays construct a simulacrum of the geography through which this contact zone can reinforce the power and legitimacy of European cultural, political, and religious norms. In this way, the staged Mediterranean is a safe arena for play and experimentation, wherein boundaries can be pushed, dangers of contact with the Other can be performed, the thrill of the Other can be witnessed close at hand, and the familiar social norms and mores can be asserted and restored in the final act. *Twelfth Night* exhibits the qualities of a staged Mediterranean play because of its own experimentation with identity in response to contact and exchange with foreign difference. Even though all of the characters in the play are ostensibly European, white, and Christian—some even English—the play's flirtation with "the east," the Other, the Muslim, and the Ottoman arises in and through its displacement of geography, of the Mediterranean for Illyria, which then facilitates further displacements of gender, rank, culture, and custom. Shakespeare's initial substitution of the Mediterranean for the Adriatic signals other changes and shifts that point to the impossibility of evacuating the Ottoman presence from this geography.

OTTOMAN GEOGRAPHIES

Twelfth Night is often designated as a particularly English play. From its titular reference to the eve of Epiphany to the buffoonish knights, Sir Toby Belch and Sir Andrew Aguecheek, and their rivalry with the "Puritan" Malvolio, the play accesses English Christian observance and stock character types. However, its topical Englishness sits cheek-by-jowl with the Ottoman presence haunting the setting and is crystalized in the spatial arrangements that structure its action. Expelled from the Adriatic Sea onto Illyria's coast, Viola receives an abbreviated history of the two ruling households that hold sway in this unfamiliar place. Learning that Olivia, "a virtuous maid" and "the daughter of a count," is also recently bereaved of a brother, Viola hopes to serve her but is thwarted because Olivia "will admit no kind of suit."[22] Viola then opts to disguise herself as "an eunuch" and serve the duke, Orsino, a plan to which the ship's captain responds, "Be you his eunuch, and your mute I'll be."[23] Shakespeare's early references to the figures of eunuchs and mutes, exotic figures often associated with the Ottoman Empire in early modern European discourses, aligns Orsino's court with Ottoman elite culture. The initial reference, which is not repeated in the play, contextualizes and lends local color to Orsino's court. The play's bifurcation of Duke Orsino's and Countess Olivia's households further delineates the separation of masculine and feminine realms, another distinguishing feature of Islamicate societies.

The gendered division of space alluded to in this early scene establishes how space will be mobilized in the play to imbue the action with cultural difference that draws upon Ottoman customs and mores. Moreover, this scene follows upon the opening of the play, wherein Shakespeare presents Orsino as an effete, luxuriant, and emotionally overwrought lover. Twelfth Night's famous opening lines "If music be the food of love, play on / Give me excess of it, that surfeiting, / The appetite may sicken and so die," hint at Orsino's immoderate consumption of sensual pleasure and, more darkly, his desire to kill or destroy the love which he is unable to possess.[24] To be sure, the play is establishing Orsino's narcissistic love of himself in love, but as Susanne Wofford has pointed out, Orsino's passion throughout the play alludes to a kind of eastern, Islamic, and Ottoman emotional instability and tyranny.[25] For Wofford, Orsino's emotional state emblematizes his "foreign" or "translated character," yet in the context of the liminal, layered, and palimpsestic geography of Illyria, Orsino's character is Othered only insofar as the repressed Ottoman presence arises in his affect and in the highly ritualized and same-sex space of his court. In other words, both Orsino and his court are structured around and through Ottoman customs and practices that enable and further the play's interest in identity and transformation, which are only overtly referenced in this brief moment when Shakespeare mentions "eunuchs" and "mutes."

By entering into Orsino's employ having metamorphosed into the eunuch Cesario, Viola becomes part of his noble household whose structures of servitude mimic those of Ottoman imperial culture. Viola becomes Orsino's close and constant companion, learning the secrets of his heart—an intimacy that fosters her own affection and desire for him. "Cesario" is re-introduced to the audience through another courtier, Valentine's, observation, "If the Duke continue these favors towards you, Cesario, you are like to be much advanced. He hath known you but three days, and already you are no stranger."[26] Viola's swift rise in rank, status, and access to the duke circumvents traditional court hierarchies and serves the play's investigation into same-sex (or presumed same-sex) desire by alluding to the confined spaces of the Ottoman imperial household. Furthermore, her usurpation of customary rank mimics the structure of Ottoman bureaucracy and court culture where birth was not a necessary factor for access to privileged rank. The elite of Ottoman society, unlike the European aristocracy, was not determined by birth. Ottomanist historian Halil Inalcık explains:

> According to Ottoman theory all subjects and lands within the realm belonged to the Sultan. This principle abolished all local and inherited rights and privileges in the Empire, and it was formulated essentially to confirm the Sultan's absolute authority and to show that all rights stem from his will.[27]

In the Ottoman Empire, then, not all ranks and hierarchies were eliminated, but hereditary power belonged almost exclusively to the sultan and his family.

All other rankings within the empire were subject to the sultan's "will." His total and complete authority over his subjects was a sign of his absolute power and a mechanism through which to foster loyalty and devotion only to his person and to the Ottoman dynasty. As Leslie P. Peirce notes, the *kul* (enslaved people) who served in the sultan's household were among "the top military forces of the empire: generals and their lieutenants as well as the soldier-statesmen who served the empire as provincial governors and, at the pinnacle, the sultan's viziers."[28] Many of these *kul* entered the Ottoman body politic through the *devşirme* system, which collected children as tax or tribute (usually) from the empire's Christian populations, converted them to Islam, and turned them into Ottoman subjects who served the imperial bureaucracy, military, or administration. The practice has been variously described as

> the forcible removal, in the form of a tribute, of children of the Christian subjects from their ethnic, religious, and cultural environment and their transplantation into the Turkish-Islamic environment with the aim of employing them in the service of the Palace, the army, and the state, whereby they were on the one hand to serve the Sultan as slaves and freedmen and on the other to form the ruling class of the State.[29]

The brutality of *devşirme* in severing children from their homelands, families, and cultures is juxtaposed with the political power that these enslaved youths were ultimately able to achieve from their service within the imperial household. Out of the thousands of boys between the ages of 10 and 15 who were collected by Ottoman officials and converted to Islam en route, "several scores" were conscripted into the sultan's service at Topkapı Sarayı, where they entered rigorous training as pages for their future roles within the Ottoman elite bureaucracy.[30] The ability of enslaved youth to eventually rise in rank as high as the sultan's second-in-command demonstrates how the Ottoman state absorbed its Others into itself in order to construct an Ottoman polity. At the same time, it exhibits the existential danger that the Ottoman Empire posed to those it sought to incorporate because it required that all prior identities be shed in order to perpetuate its own.

Early modern European observers of this practice lamented the loss of Christian youth to Ottoman enslavement, but they transformed that loss into a point of pride by noting that the privileged ranks of Ottoman society were comprised of former Christians. Their social and political elevation became a sign of Christian superiority over that of the "natural Turks." Writing about the expansion of the *devşirme* under Sultan Murad II (1404–1451), Knolles relates how the sultan managed to steer the loyalty of his subjects to him by curbing the power of the "natural Turks," and vesting power in converted Christians:

> he as a man of great wisdom and judgement, to keep them
> under, in the beginning of his reign, by manifold favors
> began to bind unto himself men of strange and foreign
> countries, [as] his servants; and by ordering of his most
> weighty affairs by their authority, so by little and little to
> cast off the service of his natural Turks […] he, seeing by
> experience how serviceable those new kind of soldiers were,
> began forthwith to plot in his head, how to make himself an

army all together of such able persons, his own creatures [...]. And to that end, by his officers appointed for that purpose, took from the Christians throughout his dominions, every fifth child: *the fairest and aptest of whom, he placed in his own Seraglio* [...] where they were by sufficient teachers, first instructed in the principles of the Mahometan religion, and then in all manner of activity and feats of arms. Of these, when they were grown to man's state, he made horsemen, gave them great pensions, and sorting them into divers orders appointed them also to guard his person; honoring the better sort of them with the name of Spahi-Oglani, that is to say, His sons the knights. And of these he began to make his Bashas, his Generals of his armies, and the Governors of his provinces and cities, with all the great offices of the state. The rest and far the greatest part of these tribute children taken from their Christian parents, and not brought up in these Seraglios, he caused to be dispersed into every city and country of his dominion in ASIA, there for certain years to be brought up in all hardness and painful labor, never tasting of ease or pleasure: out of which hard brood so inured to pains, he made choice of so many of the most lusty and able bodies fittest for service, as he thought good; who kept in continual exercise, and by skillful men taught to handle all manner of weapons, but especially the bow, the piece, and the scimitar, were by him as occasion served added to the other Janissaries, and appointed for the guarding of his person: calling them commonly by the names of his sons.

The remainder of these tribute children, as unfit for the wars, he put unto other base occupations and ministries. But unto those martial men of all sorts so by him ordained, he appointed a continual pay, according to their degrees and places: and by great benefits and liberties bestowed upon them, bound them so fast unto him, as that he might now account himself to have of them so many sons, as he had soldiers: *For they together with the Christian religion, having forgot their parents and country, and knowing no other lord and master but him, and acknowledging all that they had to come and proceed of his free grace only, remained ever bound and faithful unto him.*[31]

I quote Knolles at length here because of the exactness of his description, the political calculus he attributes to the expansion of the *devşirme* under Murad II, and his lament for Christian youth lost to their religion, culture, and heritage but privileged under the new polity to which they now belonged. Knolles is accurate in noting the extensive learning program that *devşirme* youth underwent: training in military, religious, and courtly subjects which prepared them for the kinds of service that they were to perform for the empire. He further records the payment that these youth receive, which, along with their rise in social rank, may—for him and his readers—explain their devotion to their ruler and their willingness to abjure their former religion and families. In addition to improvements in their daily, material conditions of life, these youths were able to rise socially and politically almost to the very pinnacle of the Ottoman Empire, often to the position of the grand vizier, the chief administrative officer of the realm, whose commands were second only to those of the sultan. Indeed, Karen Barkey points out that, "at the height of the *devşirme* between the mid-fifteenth and sixteenth centuries, only five grand viziers out of forty-seven were of Turkish origin; the others were of Albanian, Greek, or Slavic origin and had risen from the *devşirme*."[32] Systems of enslavement like the *devşirme* were vital to the empire's survival and longevity, and the *kul* who were conscripted into this service often originated from the geography over which *Twelfth Night* traverses. Viola's rapid rise in Orsino's court and her great intimacy with him displays how Ottoman political arrangements are echoed in Shakespeare's play.

Viola's plan to disguise herself as an eunuch points to a more specialized form of service than what was performed by the general *kul* population. The Ottomans were not the only empire to employ eunuchs in their administrative, bureaucratic, and military apparatus. Indeed, in many ways, they inherited eunuch service and enslavement from their Roman and Byzantine counterparts as well as from other Islamic regimes, such as the Mamluks and Abassids.[33] Eunuchs were chiefly employed in the sultan's service in the imperial household. Palmira Brummett theorizes that the Ottoman imperial household should be conceived of "in terms of the intersections between the military-administrative and domestic household, with all their attached economic and cultural ramifications."[34] In addition to being a domestic space and location of dynastic reproduction, the imperial household was also a political, social, and economic place, where internal and external struggles for power were conducted, particularly in and through access to the sultan's personage.[35] For centuries, eunuchs played an integral part in the running of the sultan's household, as Jane Hathaway highlights; "at the time of the Ottoman emirate's emergence and early expansion Byzantine slaves, including eunuchs were pervasive in Anatolia."[36] She relates the medieval Muslim traveler, Ibn Battuta's (1304–1377) reaction at seeing these enslaved youth in the emir of Aydin's residence:

When we reached the vestibule, we found about twenty of his
servants of strikingly beautiful appearance and dressed in
silk garments. Their hair was parted and hanging down, and
their color was radiant white tinged with red. "Who," I asked
the jurist, "are these beautiful forms?" "These," he replied,
"are Greek eunuchs."[37]

Ibn Battuta is struck by the fair beauty of the eunuchs he
encounters and the delight their vision offers him, suggesting
the homoerotic dimension of eunuch servitude which
became more transparent as the empire and harem developed
into a more institutionalized structure relegated by gendered
and racial segregation.

Eunuchs patrolled both the men's and women's quarters
of the harem, policing and ensuring the sexual purity of
those spaces. Writing about the structure and organization
of the imperial household, Ottaviano Bon, the Venetian Bailo
to Istanbul from 1604 to 1607, obliquely remarks on the
mechanisms for maintaining the chastity of kul youth through
eunuch surveillance:

Neither are they [kul] permitted, so long as they are in these
three Odas [rooms], to be familiar with any but themselves,
and that with great modesty too; so that it is a matter of
great difficulty for any stranger to speak with them, or see
them, which if it be obtained, it must be by express leave
from the Capee Agha [Gate Agha], who causes an Eunuch
to be there present, so long as any stranger shall be in the
company of the said youths. Nay, when they have occasion
to go to the Bano [bath], or the like businesses, the eunuchs
are always at hand, that so by all means they may be kept
from lewdness. And in their bedchambers, which are long

rooms, and hold about thirty or forty in each of them, (for they sleep near one another upon the Sofas,) there are every night lamps burning, and eunuchs lying by them to keep them in awe, and from lewd and wanton behavior.[38]

Gesturing toward the homoerotic dimension of the same-sex spaces within the Ottoman imperial household, Bon's narrative demonstrates and emphasizes the liminal position of eunuchs, who are presented here as guardians of the morality, chastity, and virtue of kul youths. The primary role of eunuchs in the imperial household was simultaneously to oversee kul progress in "education, training, and practical service" and to guard the sanctity of the women's quarters and the sultan's apartments in the harem, the management of which was the duty of black African eunuchs.[39] Regarding the number of imperial eunuchs and the method of castration, Bon observes that

all the eunuchs in the Seraglio may be in number about two hundred, what with old ones, middle aged, and young ones: they are all of them not only gelt, but have their yards also clean cut off, and are chosen of those Renegado youths, which are presented from time to time to the Grand Signor, as aforesaid: few, or none of them are, gelt and cut against their will. For then, as the master workmen in that business do affirm, they would be in great danger of death: wherefore, to get their consent thereto, they promise them fair, and shew unto them the assurance they may have, in time, to become great men; all which must be done when they are very young, at their first coming into the Seraglio. For it is a work not to be wrought upon men of years.[40]

Bon's description notes the diverse ages of the eunuch population, which accords with other historical evidence about the hierarchies of service and the priority of place given to age and experience. Moreover, his detailed explanation of the process and dangers of castration satisfies the prurient interest of his European audience, particularly about people they primarily associated with eastern Otherness and sexual deviance. Bon also emphasizes the apparent agency of men and boys who undergo this process, especially for the European men who make this choice. Bon's informant about this practice may have been his compatriot, the Venetian-born eunuch and Kapı Aghası, Gazanfer Agha (d. 1602), who was kidnapped along with his mother, sisters, and brother by pirates. While his mother and sisters were ransomed, Gazanfer and his brother Cafer entered into Sultan Süleyman's service. Upon the accession of Selim II (1524–1574), the brothers "voluntarily underwent castration so that they could remain close to him, for no uncastrated male outside the imperial family would be allowed such close contact with the sultan."[41] Gazanfer's access to the sultan, and the power he amassed through that access, depended upon him becoming an eunuch, and his social elevation meant that one of his sisters and her sons "joined him at Topkapı. The sister served as a key intermediary between the Venetian ambassador and the Ottoman court."[42] Gazanfer's history demonstrates the important political power that eunuchs were able to amass in the Ottoman Empire, especially those close enough to the sultan to control access to his person.

The intimacy that the Ottoman household promoted between eunuchs and the sultan was also found between the sultan and his "mutes," enslaved deaf people who commonly populated the Ottoman imperial court. Shakespeare exposes his knowledge of these figures when he has the captain bind himself to Viola's service by promising to be her "mute:" "When my tongue blabs, then let mine eyes not see."[43,44] The captain's promise is another provocative reminder of the Ottoman subtext the play's action will exploit. Enslaved deaf people were familiar companions of Ottoman sultans, who in the sixteenth century began to cultivate a public and private image of seclusion, communicating via emissaries and through a specialized and secret sign language that was understood only by their intimate circle of mutes. Like eunuchs, "mutes" in the Ottoman Empire were enslaved deaf people who served the sultan and were classed as exotic or luxury slaves of the empire by foreign European visitors.[45] As the Ottoman sultans began to mystify the nature of their rule and increasingly surround themselves with the enslaved peoples of their households, like their eunuchs, dwarves, and mutes, they also developed a language system that allowed for further secrecy. Gülru Necipoğlu notes that "sign language was first introduced to the palace by two mute [sic] brothers during the reign of Süleyman. Finding this form of communication very respectful, the sultan ordered it to be used by pages in his Privy Chamber," but it transformed into a mode of communicating imperial power that asserted the sultan's might, vanity, and arrogance.[46] Necipoğlu further suggests the sultan exhibited his power through

> signs instead of words, in his refusal to appear at all in
> public, as if mere mortals were not worthy to look upon him,
> in his refusal to address ambassadors, and in his sitting like
> a statue during audiences.[47]

Deaf people, then, became indispensable to the running of the empire, particularly in translating the will of the sultan.

In European writings about the Ottoman Empire, deaf people—exclusively referred to as "mutes"—had a more sinister function: they were the sultan's silent assassins. The most infamous political incident, one that was broadcast far and wide in Europe was the murder of the young Şehzade (prince) Mustafa, Sultan Süleyman's firstborn son, in 1553. For most European observers, the murder of Mustafa was another sign of Ottoman barbarism. These writers blamed the sultan's second wife, Hürrem Sultan, or Roxelana as she was known in Europe, for instigating a feud between Süleyman and his eldest son—accusing Mustafa of plotting with the Janissaries to overthrow his father—because she wanted one of her own sons to inherit the empire.[48] Mustafa, ignorant of the plots laid against him, thought he was simply meeting his father and was instead strangled by Süleyman's assassins.[49] Knolles' lengthy rehearsal of the murder emphasizes the prince's extreme nobility and innocence, and the heartless cruelty of his father and executioners:

> He came unto his father's camp, and [...] suited himself
> all in white, in token of his innocence, [...] came with great
> reverence towards the tent of his father, fully resolving to
> have kissed his hand, as their usual manner is. But when he
> was come to the entrance of the tent, remembering that he
> had yet his dagger girt to him, he entered not until he had
> put it off; because he would not come into his father's sight
> with any weapon, if happily so he might clear himself of his
> father's needless suspicion. So when he was come into the
> more inward rooms of the tent, he was with such honor
> as belonged to his state cheerfully received by his father's
> eunuchs. But seeing nothing else provided but one seat
> whereon to sit himself alone, he perplexed in mind stood
> still a while musing, at length asked where the emperor

his father was? Whereunto they answered, That he should
by and by see him: and with that casting his eye aside, he
saw seven Mutes (these are strong men, bereft of their
speech, whom the Turkish tyrants have always in readiness,
the more secretly to execute their bloody butchery) coming
from the other side of the tent towards him: at whose sight
stricken with a sudden terror, said no more, but Lo my
death; and with that, arising, was about to have fled: but
in vain, for he was caught hold on by the eunuch and
Mutes, and by force drawn to the place appointed for his
death: where without further stay the Mutes cast a bow
string about his neck, he poor wretch still striving, and
requesting that he might speak but two words to his father
before he died. All which the murderer (for no addition is
sufficient significantly to express his unnatural villainy)
both heard and saw by a travers from the other side of the
tent: but was so far from being moved with compassion,
that thinking it long till he were dispatched, with a most
terrible and cruel voice he rated the villains inured to blood,
saying, Will you never dispatch that I bid you? will you never
make an end of this traitor, for whom I have not rested one
night these ten years in quiet? Which horrible commanding
speeches yet thundering in their ears, those butcherly
Mutes threw the poor innocent prince upon the ground, and
with the help of the eunuchs forcibly drawing the knotted
bow string both ways, by the commandment of a most
wicked father strangled him.[50]

For Knolles, Süleyman's "unnatural" murder of his first-
born is made even more so by the agents who carry out his
lethal mandate. Despite the "magnificence" through which
Süleyman was represented in European discourses, his filicide

diminishes the glory of his reign. Ottoman sultans, as such narratives would have it, are made impotent through their intimacies with and reliance upon eunuchs and "mutes." The difference of these enslaved people highlights the "unnaturalness" of the Ottoman Empire and normalizes—according to Knolles—the degeneracy of the regime. The figure of the "mute" and the violence associated with it licenses the Othering of deaf and disabled identity and the empire with which it was ubiquitously aligned.

Twelfth Night mobilizes these figures to advance its comic purpose. Indeed, after its initial conjuring, the play seems to forget this plot point, focusing instead on the different trajectories of sexual desire that will instead animate its subsequent action. Nonetheless, it remains haunted by the specter of the Ottoman presence through those desires and the spaces—the sex-segregated precincts of its twin households—wherein those desires will be given free reign. Cesario's disguise, establishes the Ottoman character of Orsino's court. In addition to being populated with stock figures firmly associated with the empire in the European imaginary and in popular discourses, Orsino's household is a site of indolent luxury, vanity, and narcissism. In other words, his court is an ersatz or displaced harem, in which he, as the sultan, is surrounded by his corps of eunuchs, jesters, and entertainers, a loyal retinue who obey only his will.

The norms of Ottoman spatial arrangements, like the same-sex locations established in spaces such as the imperial palace, as well the inhabitants therein, provide context for Twelfth Night's plot structure. The dual courts of Orsino and Olivia are at the center of the play's action, yet the only points of intersection between them are the movements of Cesario, the eunuch, and Feste, the clown, liminal border-crossing figures within the social hierarchy of Illyria. The masculine and feminine spheres of the play, and these characters' ability to move between the two realms, hint at how the play's geography—literal, symbolic, and cultural—organizes and influences the plot. In other words, while obscured by the "European" geography of Illyria, the Ottoman context returns through the social spaces that the play constructs to achieve its comic confusions and inversions, which encompass rank, sexuality, and desire. The Ottoman Empire serves as the repressed subtext for Shakespeare's investigations because its structure likewise contained unorthodox—in the European imaginary—norms and hierarchies. As Orsino's erotic emissary, Cesario easily moves from the Duke's masculine domain into the feminine sphere of Olivia's court. His fluid movements are sanctioned by his eunuch disguise, which both explains his androgynous physique and eliminates him as a possible rival for Olivia's affections. Ironically, it is his unbearded face and the sentiments he expresses on behalf of his master that sway Olivia toward him rather than Orsino. Described by Malvolio as "not yet old enough for a man, nor young enough for a boy," Cesario's ambivalent gender facilitates his access to Olivia, who otherwise shuns all male company other than that of those already occupying her household, such as her scoundrel uncle, Sir Toby, his gullible friend, Sir Andrew, and her stern steward, Malvolio.[51] Olivia acquiesces to an audience with Cesario, and once in his company, she is moved by his words, which scorn her hard refusal to bend to Orsino's desires.[52] Olivia relents to Cesario's surrogate suit, requesting that Orsino, "send no more / Unless, perchance, you come to me again / To tell me how he takes it."[53] Both Cesario's ambiguous social location and Olivia's same-sex desire for Cesario-cum-Viola insinuate a sexuality associated with the Ottomans, especially in the precincts of the harem which was frequently the subject of the lurid gaze and curiosity of European discourses about the empire.

As a figure able to move between the masculine and feminine domains of the play, Cesario rehearses the in-between social and gender position of harem eunuchs. The structure of the Ottoman palace at Topkapı imitates, as Necipoğlu has argued, the structure of power within the regime: moving inwards from the outer courts of the palace—each of which had particular functions—required crossing various thresholds that would ultimately lead to the sultan, access to whom was highly guarded.[54] The third court of the Ottoman imperial palace was "where the sultan lived with his family and inner households," including his mother, wives, concubines, enslaved men and women, and the eunuchs, teachers, servants, and guardians who oversaw the administration of this court.[55] For European audiences, the harem represented a site of sexual degeneracy, characterized by the depraved lechery of the sultan, whose lust could only be accommodated by the hundreds of concubines who were believed to be at his beck and call. For these writers, the lewd sexuality contained within the harem emblematized the immorality of the empire.[56] However, in Ottoman culture, while the harem was the space of dynastic reproduction, the word itself "did not connote a space defined exclusively by sexuality."[57] Peirce clarifies this double meaning:

> A harem is by definition a sanctuary or a sacred precinct. By implication, it is a space to which general access is forbidden or controlled and in which the presence of certain individuals or certain modes of behavior are forbidden.[58]

Thus defined, the harem possess a sacral and religious element as well as its "gender-specific" character as it relates to the apartments and quarters belonging to women within a household.[59] Peirce points out that the term *haremi hümayûn*, "the imperial harem", initially referred to the sultan's own rooms, specifically "the inner precinct of the royal palace, inhabited only by males." Near the end of the sixteenth century, when

> the sultan established a second set of private quarters in the palace precinct to house women and children of the royal household, the latter area also began to be referred to as "the imperial hareem" because of the presence there not of the women but of the sultan.[60]

Contrary to Ottoman constructions of this space as sacred because of the presence of the sultan, European discourses represented it almost exclusively as a site of sexual degeneracy, transforming its character to suit their needs.[61] Indeed, the sex-segregated nature of the space probably contributed to the fascination that this site aroused. The all-male and all-female spaces within the harem were guarded by eunuchs (who could move between the two), while the sultan was the only man allowed into the women's space.

The European discursive transformation of the harem from the private quarters of the sultan, where administrative business also took place, into a location associated with sexual degeneracy served to discredit the Ottoman Empire through its sexual mores and practices, which did not align with European Christian dynastic or monarchial norms. In the mid-fifteenth century, the Ottoman sultans stopped taking legal wives for a number of reasons, including a desire to consolidate and protect the family line through centralized patrilineage with no competing alliance.[62] Thus, concubinage was the primary means through which to secure the futurity of the dynasty. As the site of this dynastic reproduction, the harem housed the sultan's mother, his *hasekis*, "favorite consorts," as well as other concubines, and when viewed by outsiders, the space prompted immense prurient interest as well as condemnation.[63]

Through Cesario, *Twelfth Night* offers a glimpse inside the forbidden geography of Olivia's harem. Unlike Orsino's ostensibly same-sex household, Olivia's court contains male figures, yet their real and pseudo-emasculation and her social power link the geography of her home with the feminine geography of the Ottoman harem. The women's spaces in the Ottoman Empire were generally same-sex, except for the person of the sultan and the eunuchs who guarded access to these quarters. Indeed, as Abdulhamit Arvas has incisively pointed out, "the eunuchs' movement between the different gendered spaces of the court clearly indicated that they existed outside the boundaries of adult masculinity, and even beyond the gender binary altogether."[64] In *Twelfth Night* Cesario, as an eunuch, offers a further challenge to the play's gender regimes—that are already called into question by its multiple iterations of same-sex and homoerotic desires— and his movements throughout the different social and cultural geographies in the play mimic the mobility allowed to eunuchs within Ottoman culture. Eunuchs posed little threat to the sexual purity of the harem; however, the use of black and white eunuchs within the imperial harem reveals, as George Junne has suggested, that a further mechanism for the surveillance of chastity within this space was necessary. By employing black eunuchs as the guardians of the women's harem, and white eunuchs as the custodians of the all-male spaces, the Ottoman regime ensured that any sexual impropriety between the occupants, which might result in a child, would apparently be visible.[65] This racialized division of labor in the Ottoman Empire points to the emergence and maintenance of race-based and racist ideologies in early modern Islamicate cultures.[66]

Shakespeare manipulates the repressed sexuality contained within the figure of the eunuch and transforms it into the seemingly transgressive and comic same-sex desire between Olivia and Viola.[67] In this relationship, Olivia becomes a sexually aggressive woman. No longer abiding by her vows of mourning, she actively manipulates circumstances to bring Cesario into her presence and woo him. Olivia's sexuality echoes that of Muslim women, particularly the women of the harem as represented in European discourses. Ottoman women's sexuality was constructed as rapacious, particularly because of their confinement within the same-sex spaces of their households and their limited access to men. Thus, European writers dwelled with prurient delight on the sexual exploits they believed were inherent to such geographies. In the *Anatomy of Melancholy*, Robert Burton notes that "wives" of the "Grand Signor" [sultan] are

> so penned up they may not confer with any living man, or converse with younger women, have a cucumber or carrot sent into them for their diet, but sliced, for fear & c. and so live and are left along to their unchaste thoughts all the days of their lives.[68]

Harem women's sexual appetites are represented as excessive and degenerate to the extent that their food must be specially prepared so as not to be used as ersatz dildoes. In fact, even conversation with "younger women" is presented as dangerous since the ear also could become an erotic organ and elicit forbidden desires.[69]

European writers were preoccupied—to the point of obsession—with Muslim women's geographies to which they did not have access. Like the harem, the hamam (bathhouse) was another site wherein they located Muslim women's supposed degenerate and aggressive sexuality. Writing in the mid-sixteenth century, Nicolas de Nicolay claims that Ottoman women's seclusion facilitated the sexual deviance they enjoyed within the hamam:

> They so familiarly wash one another, whereby it cometh to pass…sometimes become so fervently in love the one of the other as if it were with men, in such sort that perceiving some maiden, or woman of excellent beauty, they will not cease until they have found means to bathe with them, and to handle and grope them everywhere at their pleasures, so full are they of luxuriousness and feminine wantonness.[70]

The same-sex spaces of Muslim societies, such as the harem and hamam, became recurring and fetishized sites of perceived Islamic sexual permissiveness and Muslim women's "unnatural" and immoral sexuality. George Sandys in *Relation of a Journey* (1615) writes "much unnatural and filthy lust is said to be committed daily in the remote closets of the darksome bannias [baths]: yea, women with women: a thing incredible, if former times had not given thereunto both detection and punishment."[71] Ottoman women's geographies engendered much curiosity, even as they became eroticized and demonized projections of European sexual fantasy. Olivia's socially disruptive same-sex desire for

Cesario is transferred to Viola's twin, Sebastian, a displacement that achieves the play's sanctioned heteronormativity by re-routing Olivia's sexual appetites outside of the Ottoman frame and toward a more appropriately European and male object of desire.

In *Twelfth Night*, Olivia's household is much more chaste than what was attributed to women's spaces in Islamicate societies; however, because the space lacks a patriarch, it is a site of both gender confusion and transgression in terms of rank and authority. In this way, Olivia's court also mirrors the power wielded by elite and ostensibly free Ottoman women, particularly the power harnessed by harem women during the so-called sultanate of women.[72] While Hürrem Sultan, the wife of Süleyman, amassed a tremendous amount of political power from her legal marriage to the sultan, the sultanate of women is generally a term used for a later period in Ottoman history, from the reign of Murad III onwards, during which the Valide Sultan (the mother of the sultan) garnered imperial power and—according to some contemporary historians—began to rule through her son.[73] Despite being "confined" in the imperial harem, "high-ranking women of the harem lived at the very heart of political life" because they were in charge of the princes' political education and then became trusted advisors when their sons ascended to the throne.[74] Harem women harnessed and wielded material power in the empire to the extent that the English ambassador Thomas Roe noted that Sultan Ahmet was "governed by his mother [Kösem sultan], who governed his father, a man of spirit and wit."[75] Women's political power in this case was simultaneously a breach in propriety and an object of extreme curiosity, particularly given the masculinist popular construction of the Ottoman Empire.

In her own court, Olivia too has social and political power; however, the unruly members of her household undermine that power. Consequently, Shakespeare seems to suggest that political stability can only be achieved if and when Olivia is properly married. Furthermore, *Twelfth Night* marks several threats to Olivia's female-ruled harem, not only through the carousing of Sir Toby and his commitment to riotous behavior, but also in the social-climbing of Olivia's dour steward Malvolio. While Malvolio is called "a kind of puritan" by Maria, a reference to his disdain for the loud, disorderly, and boisterous antics initiated by Sir Toby, he is also identified with Mediterranean Islamic Otherness.[76] After Malvolio has been gulled by the forged letter, and believes Olivia to be in love with him, Maria tells Sir Toby that their plan has worked and that "yon gull Malvolio is turned heathen, a very renegado, for there is no Christian means to be saved by believing rightly can ever believe such impossible passages of grossness."[77] Maria's use of "turn" in the context of Malvolio's transformation is provocative because of the common early modern idiom "turning Turk," which connoted betrayal of faith and nation, and crucially referred to the literal act of conversion to Islam. Similarly, a "renegado," in the popular parlance of the day, was also a figure who had reneged on religion and converted to Islam. In fact, renegados frequently populated the early modern English stage in staged Mediterranean plays. Consequently, as both Patricia Parker and Su Fang Ng have detailed about this moment, Malvolio's desire for Olivia aligns him with Christians who have converted to Islam for social mobility and the material wealth Muslim cultures seemed to have offered them.[78] Indeed, as Parker points out, when Malvolio seems to recognize the handwriting as Olivia's and declares, "By my life, this is my lady's hand. These be

207 **Turkish Delight**

her very c's, her u's, and her t's," the letters read as "cut," referring obscenely to Olivia's genitalia, but also to the "cut" of circumcision or castration, which was commonly given to kul who were conscripted into the Ottoman Empire and to Christian converts in the Mediterranean.[79] Malvolio's in-between position in Olivia's household, as the male authority figure who was also under the authority of a woman, suggests affinities between him and Cesario, which position him as the play's other eunuch. His attempt at ascending in rank through marriage to Olivia follows the pattern of political and social advancement allowed by Ottoman imperial praxis, which facilitated the sometimes spectacular rise of the sultan's enslaved subjects to positions of power within the imperial administration and marriage within the sultan's family. The play mocks and punishes his attempted overreach, however, because of its repression of its Ottoman sphere of influence. The Ottoman specter haunting the play is firmly banished by a return to normative heteropatriarchy through mixed rather than sex-segregated spatial arrangements.

Shakespeare's many displacements in *Twelfth Night* emphasize the importance of place within this ambiguously located play. Beginning with the consequential question, "what country friends is this"—ambivalently answered with "Illyria"—the play's location is not only a palimpsest or contested geography, but it is also a substitute geography for Shakespeare's source, Constantinople. Such exchanges abound in *Twelfth Night*, particularly in their engagement with and elision of Ottoman cultural geographies and praxis. While Ottoman and Islamic material in the play is limited to referents such as "eunuch," "mute," "Sophy," and "renegado," these keywords are codewords, placeholders tethering the play to the geography over which it traverses. *Twelfth Night*'s displacements, transformations, and subversions operate through the repression of Ottoman culture that had a long history in Illyria and among the people of that region. Shakespeare's neat excision of an overt or explicit Ottoman presence accords with the kind of Mediterranean which his corpus of plays represents, a geography in which the Ottoman Empire and other Islamicate regimes and cultures are either peripheral or absent. Thus, building on the long history of cultural contact, exchange, and conflict in the region, which Shakespeare mobilizes in his use of this geography, the shadow of the Ottoman Empire is both in and out of place in *Twelfth Night*.

NOTES

1 Roger Warren and Stanley Wells, "Introduction," *Twelfth Night*, ed. Roger Warren and Stanley Wells (Oxford: Oxford University Press, 2008), 1.2.2.

2 Warren and Wells, "Introduction," 9.

3 Leah S. Marcus, *Puzzling Shakespeare: Local Reading and Its Discontents*, The New Historicism, 6 (Berkeley, CA: University of California Press, 1988), 161.

4 *Twelfth Night*, 1.2. 3–4.

5 See Constance Relihan, "Erasing the East from *Twelfth Night*," *Race, Ethnicity, and Power in the Renaissance*, ed. Joyce Green MacDonald (Vancouver: Fairleigh Dickinson University Press, 1997), 80–94; Goran Stanivukovic, "Illyria Revisited: Shakespeare and the Eastern Adriatic," *Shakespeare and the Mediterranean: The Selected Proceedings of the International Shakespeare Association World Congress Valencia, 2001*, ed. Tom Clayton, Susan Brock, and Vicente Forés (Newark, DE: University of Delaware Press, 2001), 400–15; Patricia Parker, "Was Illyria as Mysterious and Foreign as We Think?" *The Mysterious and the Foreign in Early Modern England*, ed. Helen Osstovich, Mary V. Silcox, and Graham Roebuck (Newark, DE: University of Delaware Press, 2008), 209–34; Su Fang Ng, "The Frontiers of *Twelfth Night*," *Early Modern England and Islamic Worlds*, ed. Bernadette Andrea and Linda McJannet (New York: Palgrave Macmillan, 2011), 173–96; and Lea Puljcan Juric, *Illyria in Shakespeare's England* (New York: Rowman & Littlefield, 2019).

6   Warren and Wells, "Introduction," 14–22.

7   Barnabe Riche, "Apolonius and Silla," *His Farewell to Militarie Profession.* (London: Robart Walley, 1583).

8   For European reactions to the loss see, Nancy Bisaha, "European Reactions to the Fall of Constantinople," *Routledge Handbook on Christian–Muslim Relations* (London: Routledge, 2017), 219–26.

9   Michael Kritovoulous, *History of Mehmed the Conqueror*, trans. Charles T. Riggs (Princeton, NJ: Princeton University Press, 1954), 77.

10 Kritovoulous, *History of Mehmed*, 80.

11 Robert Ousterhout, "The East, the West, and the Appropriation of the Past in Early Ottoman Architecture," *Gesta* 43.2 (2004): 165–76; Nancy Bisaha, *Creating East and West: Renaissance Humanists and the Ottoman Turks* (Philadelphia, PA: University of Pennsylvania Press, 2006); Kaya Şahin, "Constantinople and the End Time: The Ottoman Conquest as a Portent of the Last Hour," *Journal of Early Modern History* 14.4 (2010): 317–54; Gavin D. Brockett, "When Ottomans Become Turks: Commemorating the Conquest of Constantinople and Its Contribution to World History, "*The American Historical Review* 119.2 (April 2014), 399–433; Jerry Brotton, *Trading Territories: Mapping the Early Modern World* (Ithaca, NY: Cornell University Press, 1998).

12 Mike Crang, *Cultural Geography* (London: Routledge, 2013), 3.

13 Crang, *Cultural Geography*, 5.

14 Juric, *Illyria in Shakespeare's England*, 14.

15 Richard Knolles, *The generall historie of the Turkes from the first beginning of that nation to the rising of the Othoman familie: [...] digested into one continuat historie vntill this present yeare 1603* (London: Adam Islip, 1603), 197.

16 Caroline Finkel, *Osman's Dream: The History of the Ottoman Empire* (New York: Basic Books, 2005), 321–23.

17 Daniel Goffman, *The Ottoman Empire and Early Modern Europe* (Cambridge: Cambridge University Press, 2002), 101.

18 Relihan, "Erasing the East," 92.

19 Relihan, "Erasing the East," 91.

20 See Parker, "Was Illyria as Mysterious"

21 Su Fang Ng, "The Frontiers of Twelfth Night," 175.

22 Shakespeare, *Twelfth Night*, 1.2.33; 42.

23 Shakespeare, *Twelfth Night*, 1.2.53–59.

24 Shakespeare, *Twelfth Night*, 1.1.1–3.

25 Susanne L. Wofford, "Foreign Emotions on the Stage of *Twelfth Night*," *Transnational Exchange in Early Modern Theater*, ed. Robert Henke and Eric Nicholson (London: Routledge, 2016), 157–74, (147).

26 Shakespeare, *Twelfth Night*, 1.4.1–4.

27 Halil Inalcık, "Ottoman Methods of Conquest," *Studia Islamica*, 2 (1954), 113.

28 Leslie P. Peirce, *A Spectrum of Unfreedom: Captives and Slaves in the Ottoman Empire* (Budapest: Central European University Press, 2021), 8–9.

29 Quoted in V.L. Ménage, "Some Notes on the 'Devshirme.'" *Bulletin of the School of Oriental and African Studies, University of London*, 29.1 (1966), 64.

30 Metin Kunt, "Turks in the Ottoman Imperial Palace," In *Royal Courts in Dynastic States and Empires: A Global Perspective*, ed. Jeroen Duindam, Tülay Artan, and Metin Kunt (Leiden: Brill, 2011), 292–93.

31 Knolles, *The generall historie of the Turkes*, 332–33 (italics mine).

32 Karen Barkey, *Empire of Difference: The Ottomans in Comparative Perspective* (Cambridge: Cambridge University Press, 2008), 124.

33 Jane Hathaway, "Ḥabeşī Meḥmed Agha: the First Chief Harem Eunuch (Darüssaade Ağası) of the Ottoman Empire," *The Islamic Scholarly Tradition: Studies in History, Law, and Thought in Honor of Professor Michael Allan Cook*, ed. Asad Q. Ahmed, Behnam Sadeghi, and Michael Bonner (Leiden: Brill, 2011), 179–96.

34 Palmira Brummett. "Placing the Ottomans in the Mediterranean world: the question of notables and households." *Osmanlı Araştırmaları* 36.36 (2010): 77–96. (79).

35 For more on Ottoman dynastic futurity see Leslie P. Peirce, *The Imperial Harem: Women and Sovereignty in the Ottoman Empire* (Oxford: Oxford University Press, 1993).

36 Jane Hathaway, *The Chief Eunuch of the Ottoman Harem: From African Slave to Power-Broker* (Cambridge: Cambridge University Press, 2018), 41.

37 Hathaway, *The Chief Eunuch of the Ottoman Harem*, 41.

38 Ottaviano Bon, *A Description of the Grand Signour's Seraglio, or Turkish Emperours Court: By John Greaves, Late Professor of Astronomie in the University of Oxford*, translated by Robert Withers (London: 1653), 74–75.

39 Kunt, "Turks in the Ottoman Imperial Palace," 293. For more about race, gender, and Ottoman eunuch enslavement see Abdulhamit Arvas, "Early Modern Eunuchs and the Transing of Gender and Race," *Journal for Early Modern Cultural Studies*, 19.4 (2019), 116–36; and George

H. Junne, *The Black Eunuchs of the Ottoman Empire: Networks of Power in the Court of the Sultan* (London: Bloomsbury, 2016).

40 Bon, *A Description of the Grand Signour's Seraglio*, 95–96. This specific description refers to the situation of the white eunuchs. Black eunuchs patrolled the harem, and in the sixteenth century their power greatly increased as the sultans began to take up residence in the harem. This led to power disputes between them and the white eunuchs, as discussed in Hathaway, *The Chief Eunuch*; and Junne, *The Black Eunuchs*.

41 Hathaway, *The Chief Eunuch*, 52.

42 Hathaway, *The Chief Eunuch*, 52.

43 I only use "mute" or "mutes" in this book if I am quoting from a source. I use "deaf people" to refer to those in the sultan's service who communicated through sign language. It is not clear from the literature whether these enslaved people were deaf or if they could not speak but could hear. This remains an important avenue for further investigation. For more on deaf people in the Ottoman Empire see, Mike Miles. "Signing in the Seraglio: Mutes, Dwarfs and Jestures at the Ottoman Court 1500-1700." *Disability & Society* 15.1 (2000): 115–34 and for Shakespeare and Disability Studies see Loftis, Sonya Freeman. *Shakespeare and Disability Studies*. Oxford University Press, 2021.

44 Shakespeare, *Twelfth Night*, 1.2.60.

45 M. Miles, "Signing in the Seraglio," 115–34.

46 Gülru Necipoğlu, *Architecture, Ceremonial, and Power: the Topkapı Palace in the Fifteenth and Sixteenth Centuries* (Cambridge, MA: MIT Press, 1991), 25.

47 Necipoğlu, *Architecture, Ceremonial, and Power*, 26.

48 See, for example, Richard Knolles and de Busbecq, Ogier Ghiselin. *The Turkish Letters of Ogier Ghiselin de Busbecq, Imperial Ambassador at Constantinople, 1554-1562*. London: Clarendon Press, 1968.

49 Seda Erkoç, "Repercussions of a Murder," *Practices of Coexistence. Constructions of the Other in Early Modern Perceptions*, ed. Marianna D. Birnbaum and Marcell Sebők (Budapest: Central European University Press, 2017), 35–70.

50 Knolles, *The generall historie of the Turkes*, 764.

51 Shakespeare, *Twelfth Night*, 1.5.142–43.

52 Shakespeare, *Twelfth Night*, 1.5.156.

53 Shakespeare, *Twelfth Night*, 1.5.270–72.

54 Necipoğlu, *Architecture, Ceremonial, and Power*, xvi–xx.

55 Necipoğlu, *Architecture, Ceremonial, and Power*, 91.

56 See, for example, Knolles; Nicolas de Nicolay, *The nauigations, peregrinations and voyages, made into turkie by nicholas nicholay daulphinois, lord of arfeuile, chamberlaine and geographer ordinarie to the king of fraunce conteining sundry singularities which the author hath there seene and obserued: Deuided into foure bookes, with threescore figures, naturally set forth as well of men as women, according to the diuersitie of nations, their port, intreatie, apparrell, lawes, religion and maner of liuing, aswel in time of warre as peace: With diuers faire and memorable histories, happened in our time. translated out of the french by T. washington the younger* (London, At the cost of John Stell] by Thomas Dawson, 1585); George Sandys, Richard Field, and William Barrett, *A Relation of a Iourney Begun an. Dom. 1610: Foure Bookes, Containing a Description of the Turkish Empire of Aegypt, of the Holy Land, of the Remote Parts of Italy and Ilands Adioyning.* (London: Printed for W. Barrett, 1615); and Sir Paul Rycaut, 1628–1700, *The present state of the ottoman empire containing the maxims of the turkish politie, the most material points of the mahometan religion, their sects and heresies, their convents and religious votaries, their military discipline . . . : Illustrated with divers pieces of sculpture, representing the variety of habits amongst the turks, in three books / by paul rycaut esq . . .* (London, Printed for John Starkey and Henry Brome .., 1668).

57 Peirce, *The Imperial Harem*, 3.

58 Peirce, *The Imperial Harem*, 4.

59 Peirce, *The Imperial Harem*, 5.

60 Peirce, *The Imperial Harem*, 5.

61 See, for example, alongside Knolles and Bon, Hugh Goughe, *The Ofspring of the House of Ottomano* (1553); Nicolas de Nicolay, *The Nauigations, Perigrinations and Voyages, made into Turkie* (1585); Samuel Purchas, *Purchas His Pilgrimage* (1613); Paul Rycaut, *The Present State of the Ottoman Empire* (1670).

62 The only notable exception being Sultan Süleyman's marriage to his former concubine, Hürrem, Peirce, 38.

63 Peirce, *The Imperial Harem*, 107.

64 Arvas, "Early Modern Eunuchs," 119.

65 Junne, *The Black Eunuchs*, 4.

66 Arvas explicitly points out this important quality of Ottoman eunuch enslavement: "Significantly, Ottoman eunuchs were racially marked and distinguished as either black or white. This racialization was a crucial—if under-analyzed—component of the depictions of eunuchs in Ottoman treatises, which reveal an emerging race-making process that constitutes blackness as intricately interlinked with non-normative gender." 117.

67 The homoerotic relationship between Cesario and Orsino displays similar potential.

68 Robert Burton, "*The anatomy of melancholy* (1621)," *Race in Early Modern England: A Documentary Companion*, ed. Ania Loomba and Jonathan Burton (New York: Palgrave, 2007), 204.

69 Burton, 204.

70 Nicolas de Nicolay, *The Nauigations, Peregrinations and Voyages, made into Turkie by Nicholas Nicholay Daulphinois, Lord of Arfeuile, Chamberlaine and Geographer Ordinarie to the King of Fraunce* [...] *Translated Out of the French by T. Washington the Younger* (London, 1585), 60.

71 George Sandys, "A Relation of a Journey Begun An: Dom: 1610 (1615)." *Race in Early Modern England: A Documentary Companion*, ed. Ania Loomba and Jonathan Burton (New York: Palgrave, 2007), 195.

72 Peirce, *The Imperial Harem*, v.

73 Peirce, 265.

74 Peirce, *The Imperial Harem*, 235.

75 Quoted in Peirce, *The Imperial Harem*, 236.

76 Twelfth Night (2.3.139).

77 Shakespeare, *Twelfth Night*, 3.3.64–67.

78 Parker, "Was Illyria as Mysterious," 212; Ng, "The Frontiers of Twelfth Night," 182–83.

79 Shakespeare, *Twelfth Night*, 2.5.75–76.

REFERENCES

Arvas, Abdulhamit. "Early Modern Eunuchs and the Transing of Gender and Race." *Journal for Early Modern Cultural Studies* 19.4 (2019): 116–36.

Barkey, Karen. *Empire of Difference: The Ottomans in Comparative Perspective*. Cambridge: Cambridge University Press, 2008.

Bisaha, Nancy. *Creating East and West: Renaissance Humanists and the Ottoman Turks*. Philadelphia, PA: University of Pennsylvania Press, 2006.

———. "European Reactions to the Fall of Constantinople." In *Routledge Handbook on Christian–Muslim Relations*, edited by David Thomas, 219–26. London: Routledge, 2017.

Bon, Ottaviano. *A Description of the Grand Signour's Seraglio, or Turkish Emperours Court.: By John Greaves, Late Professor of Astronomie in the University of Oxford*. Translated by Robert Withers. London: Jo. Ridley, 1653. Accessed via Early English Books Online.

Brockett, Gavin D. "When Ottomans Become Turks: Commemorating the Conquest of Constantinople and Its Contribution to World History." *The American Historical Review* 119.2 (April 2014): 399–433.

Brotton, Jerry. *Trading Territories: Mapping the Early Modern World*. Ithaca, NY: Cornell University Press, 1998.

Brummett, Palmira. "Placing the Ottomans in the Mediterranean world: the question of notables and households." *Osmanlı Araştırmaları* 36.36 (2010): 77–96. (79).

Burton, Robert. "The anatomy of melancholy (1621)." In *Race in Early Modern England: A Documentary Companion*, edited by Ania Loomba and Jonathan Burton, 201–04. New York: Palgrave, 2007.

Crang, Mike. *Cultural Geography*. London: Routledge, 2013.

de Busbecq, Ogier Ghiselin. *The Turkish Letters of Ogier Ghiselin de Busbecq, Imperial Ambassador at Constantinople, 1554-1562*. London: Clarendon Press, 1968.

Erkoç, Seda. "Repercussions of a Murder: The Death of Sehzade Mustafa on the Early Modern English Stage." In *Practices of Coexistence. Constructions of the Other in Early Modern Perceptions*, edited by Marianna D. Birnbaum and Marcell Sebök, 35–70. Budapest: Central European University Press, 2017.

Finkel, Caroline. *Osman's Dream: The History of the Ottoman Empire*. New York: Basic Books, 2005.

Goffman, Daniel. *The Ottoman Empire and Early Modern Europe*. Cambridge: Cambridge University Press, 2002.

Hathaway, Jane. "Ḥabeşī Meḥmed Agha: the First Chief Harem Eunuch (Darüssaade Ağası) of the Ottoman Empire." In *The Islamic Scholarly Tradition: Studies in History, Law, and Thought in Honor of Professor Michael Allan Cook*, edited by Asad Q. Ahmed, Behnam Sadeghi, and Michael Bonner, 179–96. Leiden: Brill, 2011.

―――. *The Chief Eunuch of the Ottoman Harem: From African Slave to Power-Broker*. Cambridge: Cambridge University Press, 2018.

Inalcık, Halil. "Ottoman Methods of Conquest." *Studia Islamica* 2 (1954): 103–29.

Junne, George H. *The Black Eunuchs of the Ottoman Empire: Networks of Power in the Court of the Sultan*. London: Bloomsbury, 2016.

Juric, Lea Puljcan. *Illyria in Shakespeare's England*. New York: Rowman & Littlefield, 2019.

Knolles, Richard. *The generall historie of the Turkes from the first beginning of that nation to the rising of the Othoman familie: with all the notable expeditions of the Christian princes against them. Together with the liues and conquests of the Othoman kings and emperours faithfullie collected out of the—best histories, both auntient and moderne, and digested into one continuat historie vntill this present yeare 1603.* London: Printed by Adam Islip, 1603. Accessed via Early English Books Online.

Kritovoulous, Michael. *History of Mehmed the Conqueror*. Trans. Charles T. Riggs. Princeton, NJ: Princeton University Press, 1954.

Kunt, Metin. "Turks in the Ottoman Imperial Palace." In *Royal Courts in Dynastic States and Empires: A Global Perspective*, edited by Jeroen Duindam, Tülay Artan, and Metin Kunt, 289–312. Leiden: Brill, 2011.

Loftis, Sonya Freeman. *Shakespeare and Disability Studies*. Oxford: Oxford University Press, 2021.

Marcus, Leah S. *Puzzling Shakespeare: Local Reading and Its Discontents*. The New Historicism, 6. Berkeley, CA: University of California Press, 1988.

Ménage, V. L. "Some Notes on the 'Devshirme.'" *Bulletin of the School of Oriental and African Studies, University of London* 29.1 (1966): 64–78. www.jstor.org/stable/611094

Miles, Mike. "Signing in the Seraglio: Mutes, Dwarfs and Jestures at the Ottoman Court 1500–1700." *Disability & Society*, 15.1 (2000), 115–34. doi: 10.1080/09687590025801

Necipoğlu, Gülru. *Architecture, Ceremonial, and Power: the Topkapı Palace in the Fifteenth and Sixteenth Centuries*. Cambridge, MA: MIT Press, 1991.

Ng, Su Fang. "The Frontiers of Twelfth Night." In *Early Modern England and Islamic Worlds*, edited by Bernadette Andrea and Linda McJannet, 173–96. New York: Palgrave Macmillan, 2011.

Nicolay, Nicolas de. *The Nauigations, Peregrinations and Voyages, made into Turkie by Nicholas Nicholay Daulphinois, Lord of Arfeuile, Chamberlaine and Geographer Ordinarie to the King of Fraunce Conteining Sundry Singularities which the Author Hath there Seene and Obserued: Deuided into Foure Bookes, with Threescore Figures, Naturally Set Forth as Well of Men as Women, According to the Diuersitie of Nations, their Port, Intreatie, Apparrell, Lawes, Religion and Maner of Liuing, Aswel in Time of Warre as Peace: With Diuers Faire and Memorable Histories, Happened in our Time. Translated Out of the French by T. Washington the Younger.* London: 1585. Accessed via Early English Books Online. Ousterhout,

Robert. "The East, the West, and the Appropriation of the Past in Early Ottoman Architecture." *Gesta* 43, no. 2 (2004): 165–76.

Parker, Patricia. "Was Illyria as Mysterious and Foreign as We Think?" In *The Mysterious and the Foreign in Early Modern England*, edited by Helen Ostovich, Mary V. Silcox, and Graham Roebuck, 209–34. Newark, DE: University of Delaware Press, 2008.

Peirce, Leslie P. *A Spectrum of Unfreedom: Captives and Slaves in the Ottoman Empire.* Budapest: Central European University Press, 2021.

———. *The Imperial Harem: Women and Sovereignty in the Ottoman Empire.* Oxford: Oxford University Press, 1993.

Relihan, Constance. "Erasing the East from *Twelfth Night*." In *Race, Ethnicity, and Power in the Renaissance*, edited by Joyce Green MacDonald, 80–94. Vancouver: Fairleigh Dickinson University Press, 1997.

Riche, Barnabe. "Apolonius and Silla." In *His Farewell to Militarie Profession*. London: Robart Walley, 1583. Ann Arbor: Text Creation Partnership, 2011. http://name.umdl.umich.edu/A68653.0001.00. [Accessed on 12/10/2022].

Şahin, Kaya. "Constantinople and the End Time: The Ottoman Conquest as a Portent of the Last Hour." *Journal of Early Modern History* 14.4 (2010): 317–54.

Sandys, George. "A Relation of a Journey Begun an: Dom: 1610 (1615)." In *Race in Early Modern England: A Documentary Companion*, edited by Ania Loomba and Jonathan Burton, 191–96. New York: Palgrave, 2007.

Stanivukovic, Goran. "Illyria Revisited: Shakespeare and the Eastern Adriatic." *Shakespeare and the Mediterranean: The Selected Proceedings of the International Shakespeare Association World Congress Valencia, 2001*, edited by Tom Clayton, Susan Brock, and Vicente Forés, 400–15. Newark, DE: University of Delaware Press, 2001.

Warren, Roger, and Stanley Wells. "Introduction," In *Twelfth Night*, edited by Roger Warren and Stanley Wells, 9. Oxford: Oxford University Press, 2008.

Wofford, Susanne L. "Foreign Emotions on the Stage of *Twelfth Night*." In *Transnational Exchange in Early Modern Theater*, edited by Robert Henke and Eric Nicholson, 157–74. London: Routledge, 2016.

Conclusion

"What is't to me?" or Muslim Worlds through Shakespeare

Shakespeare through Islamic Worlds has taken a varied itinerary through Shakespeare's works, from romance to history to tragedy and finally to comedy, yet it has rooted its inquiry in the geography of the Mediterranean, which is a prominent geography of Shakespeare's plays, to explore whether or not they engage with the real cultural presence of Islam and Muslims. No one book can cover the entirety of the vast and many worlds of Islam and Muslim societies and cultures and this book certainly does not try. Instead, I have focused my attention on the early modern Muslim Mediterranean because it was the most familiar geography in which English and European encounters with Muslim and other cultures occurred. The Mediterranean provided a contact zone wherein cultural contest, traffic, and exchange were the norm. By focusing on the multicultural Muslim Mediterranean of the early modern period, *Shakespeare through Islamic Worlds* highlights the deliberate exclusions, evasions, and excisions that Shakespeare effects in the cultures and societies of his plays. Islam and its cultures were both foundational and fundamental to this geography, and their erasure in his works not only belies the popularity of this material in the English culture of the period, but also reveals his investment in constructing a *globe* devoid of Islam. While Shakespeare does depict other religious and racial identities, these are banished to the peripheries, destroyed,

DOI: 10.4324/9781003213581-6

or transformed altogether in order to construct a Europe and a Mediterranean that is white and Christian, a geography safe from the looming threat of difference. Indeed, Shakespeare's omissions seem to be part of a larger worldmaking project that his works engage in and in which—for him—Islam and Muslims should have no purchase.

My investigation of Islam and Muslims in Shakespeare, then, has looked for the shadows, traces, and phantoms that haunt the margins of his oeuvre and materialize only through referents, keywords, and a coded shorthand. Islam appears through substitution and projection, in tropes that ambivalently circulate to remind his audience of the Muslim cultures that occupy their world yet have been deliberately removed from the place of the stage (and page). Mining the plays for these moments where phrases or allusions appear has sometimes felt like a futile exercise in overreading and overreaching, a magnification of sparse incidents that render their presence and subtext meaningful. However, putting pressure on these referents and contextualizing them throughout this study, unveils the broader social and political milieu in which they circulate and the specific ways that Islam and Muslims affected early modern English and European cultural production at large. I have had to dilate my evidence in order to apprehend why, for example, the trope of the "Turk" was accessible and legible to both Shakespeare and his audiences. If the "Turk" was such a radical Other—geographically, socially, religiously, and culturally distant—how was this referent meaningful in any way? What did the "Turk" convey beyond ideas of betrayal? By plumbing the depths of seemingly inconsequential rhetorical devices, *Shakespeare through Islamic Worlds* has resituated Muslims within the world that Shakespeare and his audience inhabited, where their troped constructions are subtended by the real, material, social, and cultural presence of Muslim cultures and regimes.

In addition, thinking spatially, with and through the geography of Shakespeare's locales, allowed me to harness the meaning-making possibilities of space. The geographies of Shakespeare's plays have traditionally been examined for their classical antecedents, circumscribing their meanings within a European cultural inheritance and excluding the influence of the Islamicate cultures that inhabited these places before and during the time of Shakespeare's writing. These scholarly and critical exclusions have obscured the ways that Muslim cultures may have influenced Shakespeare's mobilization of specific locales and have made geography and knowledge about the customs of these places the purview of whiteness and Europeanness. Reading through space has also allowed me to examine how identity construction in the period and Shakespeare's works is particularly rooted to geographic origin. My inquiry into the ways that "Moor" is often sutured to Muslim has emphasized the significance of Islamicate geographies in the construction of this identity. The "Moor" is one of the few recurring Others in Shakespeare's corpus whose racial and ethnic designation also contains a religious dimension, specifically historicized in and through Islam, and an identity that is often made legible through its own itinerant wanderings across Muslim societies and cultures. Indeed, my focus on the construction of the "Moor," has emphasized the centrality of Islam to early modern racial formations. I have in *Shakespeare through Islamic Worlds* made much out of very little, but by "speaking from a place in the margins where I am different, where I see things differently," I have been able to see that a little is quite a lot.[1]

Shakespeare through Islamic Worlds also represents my own journey through Shakespeare. As an immigrant Pakistani Muslim American woman, my work is influenced by my own social location, by who I am, where I come from, and where I am. All scholarship, as Edward Said so cogently reminds us, is subjected, meaning that it reflects the situatedness of scholars in bodies and geopolitical spheres:

> No one has ever devised a method for detaching the scholar from the circumstances of life, from the fact of his involvement (conscious or unconscious) with a class, a set of beliefs, a social position, or from the mere activity of being a member of a society. These continue to bear upon what he does professionally, even though naturally enough his research and its fruits do attempt to reach a level of relative freedom from the inhibitions and the restrictions of brute, everyday reality. For there is such a thing as knowledge that is less, rather than more, partial than the individual (with his entangling and distracting life circumstances) who produces it. Yet this knowledge is not therefore automatically nonpolitical.[2]

Some scholars have the benefit of being seen as more objective than others, and the assignment of such scholarly neutrality often rests on their normative identities, which include race, gender, class, sexuality, ability, and citizenship. Others of us, whose identities mark us as different from the majority, particularly in Shakespeare studies—which remains profoundly white and dominated by Anglo- and/or Euro-Americans—have a more tenuous hold on the label of scholar, let alone Shakespeare scholar.[3] These same identities mark our scholarship as having an agenda or as disrupting the heritage politics of early modern studies with our own identity politics.

My interest in Islam in Shakespeare is very much shaped by my own identity but is equally motivated by the historical amnesia of scholarship that has further marginalized Islam and Muslims from the plays and the places that they inhabited.[4] Much of this historical amnesia—the willful forgetting of the influence of non-white, non-European, and non-Christian people's contributions to the world—stems, I believe, from Orientalism, which, as Said defines, is a mechanism of controlling the Orient through discourse, a vital tool in the arsenal of imperial regimes of knowledge and power. Even though English and European powers did not have empires in Muslim geographies in the early modern period, Orientalism was a mode of intellectual practice inherited by scholars working on Shakespeare in later periods, scholars such as Samuel Chew, whose important study, *The Crescent and the Rose*, seemed to inaugurate, in the twentieth century, the field of Anglo-Islamic studies in early modern English literature. Despite performing vital recovery work, Chew's study is infused with Orientalist language that constructs the east, Islam, and Muslims in ways that reproduce the damaging and dehumanizing stereotypes so frequently encountered in texts from the high period of Orientalism. My point is not to castigate Chew, whose work has been necessary to my own, but rather to expose how Orientalism seeps into the very fabric of the work scholars do when they investigate Muslim cultures and geographies. It is part and parcel of our training, insidious and invisible in the core texts of the field.

Orientalism informs historical amnesia because it prioritizes Europe, and thus necessitates a constant recovery project of other peoples and societies who also influenced the development of early modern culture. *Shakespeare through Islamic Worlds* builds upon decades of such recovery projects, scholarship to which I am deeply in debt and have cited throughout this work. However, it is also scholarship that has often refused to engage with Said's thesis on its own terms: that knowledge-power is simultaneously discursive and material, that even without European empires controlling Islamicate geographies in the early modern period, their cultural productions were complicit in establishing and rehearsing stereotypes that became integral to Orientalism's ideological program.[5] Without thinking through how Orientalist epistemologies have influenced our own examination of Islam and Muslims in the early modern period, we remain in a constant cycle of historical amnesia and risk reproducing rather than challenging Orientalism.

Shakespeare through Islamic Worlds is a book that I would have liked as a student and then scholar. While I do not need to see myself in everything I read or watch, Shakespeare's work is positioned in a way that grants it unique claims of universalism, suggesting that everyone should be able to see themselves, in whole or part, in his ingenious framing of the human condition. However, early modern literature and Shakespeare have often not simply erased all or parts of my identity—a sign that I do not fit or belong here as a reader, audience member, or scholar—they also have denigrated and demonized all or parts of my identity. Muslims do not come off well in early modern English literature. They are often villains who need to be put in their places to effect a European Christian triumph. As a reader and scholar of these texts, they have harmed me, because they communicated that who I was did not align with ideas of beauty, virtue, civility, and humanity. As a reader and scholar, I have been tacitly asked over and over again to ignore and overcome that harm in the name of universal genius, the best that has been thought and said, and the aesthetic superiority of western civilization. I have had to separate who I am from what I do and to endorse cultural productions that have been the tools of my ancestors' and my own subordination and oppression. Such intellectual exercises are a heavy burden.

In writing *Shakespeare through Islamic Worlds*, I have attempted to lessen that load. My study is not a rescue project: it does not seek to recover Shakespeare and reposition the man and his work as universal, nor does it suggest that Shakespeare or western culture is a means through which Muslims can save themselves from their religion and societies. Instead, this book recuperates Islam and Muslims from the peripheries of Shakespeare's imagined world and puts them back in the place they had always been. *Shakespeare through Islamic World* asks and answers why Shakespeare undermines, diminishes, and erases Islam and Muslims from the places and cultures they occupied in the places and cultures about which he wrote. *Shakespeare through Islamic Worlds* talks back to Shakespeare and centuries of western tradition that have claimed that this religion and this culture are incommensurate with their modes of being and worldmaking by pointing out that Islam and Muslims were, in fact, already there, that they had simply been obscured by deliberate historical amnesia. *Shakespeare through Islamic Worlds* is my challenge to the myth of Islamic and Muslim incompatibility with Shakespeare and the values of the west. Finally, *Shakespeare through Islamic Worlds* extends an invitation to scholars to investigate Shakespeare and Islamic worlds beyond the Mediterranean, because the cultures, societies, and peoples of Islam are beautifully diverse and wondrously vast, and my study is not the end, but rather part of a larger and ongoing conversation about Shakespeare, Islam, and Muslims.

MUSLIM SHAKESPEARE

I want to end this book with a contemporary detour, an example of Muslim engagement with Shakespeare that resonates with the world we currently inhabit and issues that continue to affect our lives. Current social and political events in the United States—and globally—have made the "problem play" *Measure for Measure* (1604) particularly relevant and resonant.[6] Set in a vice-ridden Vienna, it exposes the hypocrisies of society, especially as they cohere around ideas of sexual morality. The play depicts the fall out from the Duke, Vincentio, abdicating his political responsibilities, and installing his rigidly moral deputy Angelo in his place to control the sexually riotous society of Vienna. Angelo's strict adherence to the law results, predictably, in a moral crackdown that catches citizens from all levels of Viennese society, from the well-born Claudio to the lowly Mistress Overdone, in its dragnet. The duke returns to Vienna in disguise and, after witnessing Angelo's shameful and misogynistic sexual advances upon Isabella, Claudio's sister, he masterminds an elaborate scheme to catch and dupe Angelo, while freeing those unmercifully tried by Angelo's rigorous execution of the law. The play ends with a kind of felicitous order restored, yet the ending remains problematic because the duke's eager assistance in aiding Isabella results in an unwanted eleventh-hour proposal that goes unanswered at play's end. Even as Shakespeare gives the Duke the last word, the ending depends on Isabella having the final say: Will she, a woman who had previously abjured marriage for a life of religious devotion, now be bound into a social contract with a man who deceived her about his identity and power and who mentally abused her by making her believe her brother was dead, all so that he could orchestrate a spectacular denouement where both his power and benevolence would be confirmed by the public display of his judicial mercy? Shakespeare's refusal to resolve the matter of marriage within such coercive conditions, might have baffled male critics of the play, leading to its "problem play" status; however, for women reading, watching, and analyzing Measure for Measure, the ending, rather than being problematic, is in fact a moment of liberation. It is a moment that opens up a myriad of possibilities and offers an opportunity for the construction of an alternative form of social and political female existence within highly regulated gendered regimes. The problem of the play is that Shakespeare gives a woman a choice to refuse, to withhold consent, to have her no mean no.

My broad sketch of Measure for Measure's action is meant to highlight those themes that make the play feel both current and urgent. On the one hand, this timeliness gestures toward Shakespeare's universalism. Of course, as that story goes, Shakespeare is able to both speak to and anticipate our concerns. On the other hand, the play's very contemporary resonance might have little to do with Shakespeare's transcendent universalism, and quite a lot to do with the longue durée of women's subordination and oppression under hetero-patriarchal regimes. In other words, sexism in one form or another has affected women and their social position from Shakespeare's time to ours. Sexism has always been current and timely. What our moment has allowed, however, is for patriarchy's insidious, pernicious, and underground operations to come out in to the open, to be exposed to the bright light of day, and perhaps to be both challenged and rectified.

Measure for Measure's contemporary popularity owes much, I believe, to the #MeToo movement, which went viral in the wake of the steady accusations of sexually inappropriate, predatory, and violent behavior by men in Hollywood, such as Harvey Weinstein and by powerful political figures, such as Donald Trump. Although the term #MeToo was created by activist Tarana Burke in 2006 as part of a "movement to interrupt sexual violence," particularly against Black women and girls, the phrase gained mainstream—meaning white— popularity when actor Alyssa Milano used it on Twitter in 2017 to call attention to unbridled sexual predation in Hollywood.[7] The following year, Donald Trump—a man who bragged on tape of sexual violence when he advised a cohort of male NBC television personalities to "Grab them by the pussy. You can do anything,"—before being elected president, nominated another sexual predator to the Supreme Court of the United States.[8] During Brett Kavanaugh's rushed confirm- ation hearing, a very credible allegation of attempted sexual assault was made against him by Dr. Christine Blasey Ford. Her visceral testimony of the attack; however, was overwritten by the petulant anger that Kavanaugh displayed, not in refuting those allegations, but in even being held to account for his behavior.[9] To him it was outrageous that he should have to answer for, let alone be held responsible for, engaging in the kind of behavior that is natural to and normal for men of his race and class. The fact that Trump was elected after admitting to sexual assault and given the power to seat Kavanaugh on the highest court in the land illustrates the truth of Angelo's confident words to Isabella in *Measure for Measure*, after she threatens to expose him for sexually propositioning her:

Who will believe thee, Isabel?
My unsoil'd name, the austereness of my life,
My vouch against you, and my place i' the state,
Will so your accusation overweigh,
That you shall stifle in your own report
And smell of calumny.[10]

Angelo knows, as do all powerful men who behave in predatory ways, that their social position not only shields them
from accountability but also facilitates this behavior.[11] They
are entitled to the bodies of those they desire, those they
seek to have power over, and this entitlement is fed by a
culture that accepts this behavior as a normative expression
of white masculinity.[12] The exposure of these scandals and
the few instances of legal accountability or repercussions
has made visible the gendered fault lines of western culture, which had been obscured through equal rights policies and the apparent social and political freedoms that
women in the Global North both earned and enjoyed for
almost a century. We are now at a moment when those
freedoms seem to be eroding, and #MeToo is one flash-
point that gestures toward the toxic ways in which masculine power, privilege, and patriarchy are rooted in
and dependent upon the oppression and subjugation of
women, even in societies that call themselves western and,
therefore, progressive.

Widespread cultural awareness of the precarity of women's
freedoms was not, however, the case when I taught *Measure for
Measure* for the first time in 2012. While I can safely say that
sexism was alive and well back then, I can also assuredly claim
that many of my students did not consider it to be salient to
their lives. When I asked my students how we might stage this

play now, one male student suggested that the play could only work in an Islamic setting, since those cultures were incredibly strict in policing sexuality *and* because those were also cultures where the capital punishments for sexual impropriety, such as those suggested in the play, "made sense." Many other students nodded along and affirmed my student's safe conclusion, that the play's implicit violence and its rigid sexuality had no place in the comfortable, egalitarian, and civilized western world that they occupied. Since 2012, I have witnessed similar proclamations, most recently, in the wake of the US Supreme Court's decision in June 2022 that overturned federal protections for abortions. Immediately after the Dobbs decision, images of the justices dressed as Muslim clerics or the female justices fully veiled in burqas proliferated on social media.[13] The intention behind such representations was to link the limitations on women's bodily autonomy and reproductive freedom to rigid Islamic "fundamentalism." The comparison revealed how easily accessbile demonizing stereotypes about Islam were to western liberals.

While I do agree that the gendered segregation that appears to be common in many Islamicate countries can tidily be mapped onto *Measure for Measure*'s gendered geographies and social positions, I heartily disagree with the ideological underpinnings of my student's argument. Implicit in his remarks was the notion that sexual predation and violence against women was the province of Islamicate cultures, just as the circulation of the SCOTUS image suggested that imposing mandatory reproduction on women and limiting the agency they have over their bodies is more appropriate to Muslim "fundamentalists," rather than the actual Christian ones on the court. By shifting the play's setting to an Other, foreign, and apparently barbaric culture, my student neatly solved the problem of having to attend to sexual violence at home. The same can be said for those gleefully sharing the SCOTUS image online. Western women are ostensibly free from patriarchal control because they do not have to wear the symbols of that control, such as the veil, upon their bodies as Muslim apparently women do.[14] This freedom also suggests a society that is freed from sexism. The freedom of dress and from gender segregation, signals the freedom from all forms of sex- or gender-based bias, prejudice, and discrimination. Freedom "to" easily slipped into freedom "from." Not only did the suggestion of an Islamicate culture allow my student to point the finger at those regressive regimes, but also it facilitated the unqualified valorization of the world, society, and culture of the Global North that he/we inhabited.

Another critique must also be mentioned here, that of the undifferentiated mass of the so-called "Islamic World" that my student so easily referenced. Islam and its cultures are global; they are diverse in religious belief, practice, culture, and custom. In the American imaginary, the worlds of Islam are overdetermined by the Orientalist geographic entity called the "Middle East." We can and should consider the diversity to be found within the real geography of Arab and Arabic-speaking nations and peoples; however, within American representations, the "Middle East" is flattened to a monolithic culture characterized by "fundamentalist" adherence to Islam and its attendant violence. Thus, when my student referenced the generic "Islamic World" to which *Measure for Measure* might easily be emplotted, he was not thinking of Indonesia, Sudan, Turkey, or Pakistan, but rather of those geographies made familiar, dangerous, and demonized by (at that time) over a decade of the War on Terror.

I meditate on this pedagogical encounter to highlight some of the stakes of Shakespearean universalism. Shakespeare was being used, in this instance by my student, to authorize uncritically Orientalist and imperialist framings of "the Islamic World." Shakespeare was going to illuminate the violence and barbarity of Islam and Muslims, and thus be a vital tool in the arsenal of the same ideology that underwrote the War on Terror, the invasions of Afghanistan and Iraq, and the countless drone strikes within majority Muslim nation states. In addition to rehearsing Orientalist tropes, the interpretation my student was advancing fell into what Moustafa Bayoumi calls "War on Terror Culture," which he defines as a western epistemological orientation toward Islam and Muslims that constructs Islam as Other, both theologically and culturally, and locates violence as inherent to Islam, which then explains not only Islam's "hostility" toward the west, but also its total incommensurability with western values, particularly as they cohere around individual and women's rights.[15] Islam's perceived hostility toward women, its fundamental and foundational misogyny, functioned as one of the pillars for the War on Terror: to rescue Muslim women from the tyranny of Muslim men. In this way, the logics of the War on Terror dovetail with Gayatri Chakravorty Spivak's claim about the deliberate muzzling of the subaltern's capacity to speak and represent herself, because she was always already positioned as needing rescue from the brutality of her own culture, never mind the dehumanizing ways that the colonizer culture denied her humanity.[16] The constellations of imperial, military, and cultural power in these representations of Muslims are often obscured by War on Terror Culture in order to identify and pathologize Islamic difference.

In the context of *Measure for Measure* and violent, repressive Islamic patriarchy, *Rahm*, a Pakistani adaptation of Shakespeare's play, disrupts these constructions and pushes back against the idea that Muslim women need protection from both Islam and Muslim men. The film further intervenes in such discourses by presenting the local as a site of subversion of Shakespearean universalism and the dominant Orientalist tropes that preside over the geography. Released in 2016, *Rahm*, which means mercy in Urdu, seems to have inadvertently anticipated the contemporary relevance of *Measure for Measure* that was to follow in the wake of the western #MeToo movement. A very faithful adaptation of Shakespeare's play, *Rahm* appears to ambivalently reflect Shakespeare's universality, particularly since the film requires no extraneous or unnecessary measures to make the play relevant to its local Pakistani audience. The facts of corrupt government officials, sexual misconduct, and the marginalized position of women in society are the material of the daily lived experience of most Pakistanis. Indeed, during a conversation with the film's director, Ahmed Jamal, he noted that one of the reasons why *Measure for Measure* was so compelling to him and his late brother, the film's writer, was that the plot was imminently translatable to and for Pakistani society.[17] According to Jamal, the plot echoed social policy which, in its aim to enforce a more religious and moral society, placed a disproportionate burden upon women to be the vessels of that order. Thus, not only was the play legible in this different social context, for Jamal it was *more* suitable to Pakistani culture than it was to the Global North or the English culture from which it originated.

Jamal's comments about the obvious ways that Shakespeare's plot makes more sense in his world might seem to reinforce Shakespearean universalism; however, I would say that the

232 Conclusion

hyper-local focus of the film, not only its Pakistani setting, but its choice of Lahore (a large metropolis in the northern region of the country) makes the play speak in the vernacular and grammar of this new geography. What I mean is that the local specificity of the film, its very deliberate provinciality, transforms the universal, which I characterize as a western imposition, into the particular.[18] The aim of global or universal Shakespeare is often to make the non-western both legible and translatable to audiences in the western former imperial metropoles of the Global North.[19] The hyper-local, however, eschews that colonizing gaze, opting instead to offer a social critique that speaks to the immediate and intimate concerns of the culture creating the representation. Shakespeare, here, functions merely as a plot, and significance lies in how the plot is executed through the idiom of the local geography, language, culture, and custom.

Set in Lahore, "at an imaginary time," *Rahm* opens with an aerial shot of the Badshahi Masjid, a Mughal-era structure, which along with the city's famed Shahi Qila, or Lahore Fort, signals not only the long and storied history of this culture and its religious heritage, but also tacitly points to the early modern affinities between this locale, the architecture, and its Shakespearean plot. With these establishing shots, the film indicates that this geography and culture have something to say to and about Shakespeare. Pakistan, of course, has been at the forefront of western global consciousness due to the War on Terror. While not an official theater of that war, Pakistan has served as a surrogate and proxy for that conflict, its border regions with Afghanistan often being targeted by US drones, and the discovery of Osama bin Laden's compound in the country suggesting its own shifting alliances in this long war. By refusing temporal exactness and specificity *Rahm* tidily side steps both Pakistani and western constructions of the War on Terror and its effects on this geography. Instead, the film argues for an understanding of its locale rooted both its magnificent history—emphasized through repeated shots of the historic Mughal landmarks and their early modern resonances—and its contemporary moment, where that particular history is in danger of being overwritten by another kind of foreign imposition: not Shakespeare but of imported religious extremism. The film depicts this tension through Qazi Ahad, its Angelo analogue, and his strict adherence to the rule of law, his adoption of external symbols of devotion, such as his beard and prayer beads, and his rigid unwillingness to bend and offer mercy. On the other side of the film's ideological divide are *Rahm's* Isabella analogue, Samina, and its symbol of religious piety and devotion, the Molvi Sahib or Imam, who opens the film, and represents the various Islamic practices that are native to South Asia.

Early on in the film, we are introduced to Samina through the Molvi Sahib, her religious teacher, who comes to her home which appears to be a boarding house of some sort, in order to guide her religious instruction not with the recitation of the Qur'*an*—as we might expect from such a man—but through song and mystical Sufi poetry. The short scene challenges dominant frameworks by highlighting the different pathways to spiritual enlightenment offered in Pakistani Muslim culture. Indeed, this specific, indigenous spiritual devotion becomes a recurring motif in the film, where we find a diversity of religious practices from traditional prayers in mosques, to musical evenings of ghazal (lyric meditation), and ritual prayers and alms given before the tombs of saints. Such culturally specific Islamic practices are increasingly challenged by the homogenizing import of stricter forms of Islam from places like Saudi Arabia. By depicting and even uplifting these practices, the film signals Islamic heterogeneity, but also a relation to religion that sees it as liberation rather than oppression. *Rahm's* presentation of Islam as redolent with personal and spiritual affirmation aligns with Shakespeare's construction of Isabella, who seeks personal freedom through her religious devotion, which manifests in her intention to join the cloister as a nun. Samina does not have or need such an intervention to enjoy religious practice in her daily life; indeed, such a possibility does not exist for her in the world she inhabits. A cloister or nunnery would be an unnecessary device within the film's social world because such a devout, secluded, and sex or gender-segregated life is easily possible for Muslim women in Pakistan. Samina's desires, as revealed through her spiritual practice and charitable works, suggest a woman searching for fulfillment outside of traditional social expectations of marriage and family but within and through her religion.

Figure 5.1 *Rahm*, Samina (Sanam Saeed) and Quazi Ahad (Sunil Shankar). Courtesy of Ahmed Jamal.

Rahm allows Samina some measure of agency, yet the film is at pains to demonstrate and critique how that power is contingent upon forms of patriarchal benevolence. The scene between Samina and the Molvi Sahib emblematizes the dependency that women have on men because her path to spiritual enlightenment is guided by her male religious teacher. Likewise, in all of her actions and schemes to rescue her brother from death, Samina must rely on the intercession of men, first the Lucio analogue, Kamal, then, of course, Angelo (Qazi Ahad) and finally, the duke (Governor Sahib). To be sure, the film's fidelity to its source mandates these plot developments; however, within its particular local setting, the film emphasizes the meager resources available to women across social ranks, from the lowliest brothel dancer to the elite upper-class woman. Women's social vulnerability and reliance upon men's goodwill is underscored through other marginalized female characters in the film, such as the bawd who demands payment from Kamal for services rendered, Gulzar, a hijra (transgender) pimp who is in the crosshairs of the judicial system, and the dancing girls in the red-light district who are subjects of over-policing on the one hand, and the lechery and solicitude of their customers, on the other.

Over and over again, *Rahm* emphasizes the precarious position of women and their enforced dependence upon the benevolence of men. In this way, the film exposes the rot at the core of sexist systems which victimize women and simultaneously blame them for their socially degraded condition. At the same time, it delineates the physical and corporeal danger that these women face should they misstep and challenge the coercive patriarchal power structure, such as imprisonment, flogging, and sexual assault. These moments are an indictment of a culture's failure to support the humanity and dignity of women. They are not, however, an indictment of Pakistani Muslim culture. The film does not position this culture as ontologically different from other patriarchal regimes. In other words, the film is not suggesting that there is something unique to Pakistani culture that makes it abuse and degrade women. Thus, the local idioms through which the disparate classes of women are presented bring a sustained and trenchant social critique to bear upon the injustices that these women face, but—and this is critical—without pathologizing the cause in Pakistani or Muslim identity, rather by pointing the finger at the toxicity of patriarchy which relies upon the social and political devaluation of women.

Rahm's focus on the local as a site for social critique manifests in its depiction of the two infamous moments in *Measure for Measure*: Angelo's propositioning of Isabella and the Duke's proposal to her at play's end. These two pivotal scenes are symptomatic of masculine entitlement and women's extreme vulnerability to resist the toxic effects of that entitlement. Although they go about it in different ways, one socially unsanctioned and the other socially validated, both men manipulate, lie, and coerce in order to claim and control Isabella. *Rahm's* transformation of these scenes successfully conveys the sexism inherent in the society it depicts while simultaneously launching an incisive critique of patriarchy and the abuses it fosters and encourages. Importantly, the film eschews Orientalist tropes around the veil and the veiled woman, especially in the scene with Qazi Ahad, where Samina must unveil in order to convince him to listen to her pleas for mercy toward her brother. One of the most common tropes of all Orientalist cultural production is the moment of the unveiling of the Muslim woman. The removal of her scarf or hijab is often hypersexualized, with her hair slowly cascading down from its ties and fetters, so that its forbidden sight can be luxuriantly enjoyed by the masculine (often western) gaze. This gaze and framing can, of course, be reproduced within an eastern culture, influenced as they are by internalized Orientalist representations and the desire to hypersexualize women.

Rahm rejects the sexual frisson that animates its source text in several ways: the business of unveiling is very much a business, with Kamal orchestrating the action in a brusque almost routine way. He first removes Samina's face veil and then helps her free her hair. Instead of tossing her head and displaying the opulent and forbidden beauty of hair in such contexts, Samina lets her hair simply tumble out of its clip and makes no move to adjust or tame it. The camera clinically focuses on this moment; indeed, it is shot from the back, denying the audience a view of Samina's face. Moreover, this is not a moment of disrobing for the audience because we have already seen Samina without her veil. Thus, Qazi Ahad and his reaction are the focus. The man's prurient thoughts are externalized through his flustered and dispossessed reaction. By refusing to play into, even for its local audience, the sexualized trope of the unveiled Muslim woman, *Rahm* defuses the eroticism attached to the veil and veiling in the Orientalist imaginary.

The film also affirms Samina's humanity in this moment and throughout. She is only ever objectified by Qazi Ahad, and so her chastity and modesty which are perpetually on display emphasize the violence of his unwanted harassment and aggression. Even as the figures of benevolent patriarchy and sexism, like Kamal, seek to transform her into an erotic object to suit their own ends, the film makes clear that the masculine gaze will not bind or control Samina. One of the ways it accomplishes this feat is by contrasting her with Mariam,

Qazi Ahad's spurned betrothed and the film's Mariana ana-logue. While Samina chooses to mostly veil and cover her head, Mariam, like many other Pakistani women, does not cover her hair, demonstrating that veiling and unveiling are choices allowed to Pakistani women, and that Samina's choice aligns with her more religious inclination, which has been stressed throughout the film. Nonetheless, the film does not direct any condemnation toward Mariam for not veiling. In a world where women's freedoms are tightly bound, *Rahm* advocates for their freedom of choice and agency.

Samina's refusal to participate in the erotic economy governing her society makes it quite fitting that the film does not depict Governor Sahib's proposal. Instead, once all has been revealed, he tells Samina that he would like to speak with her, but the audience is not privy to that conversation. All we see at the end is Samina, modestly veiled, walking the streets of her city alone. Casting might play an important role in informing the plot here, where the actor playing Governor Sahib is several decades older than the actor playing Samina and a proposal would be indecorous, transforming the ending into a truly comic plot with an old man reclaiming his youth by marrying a much younger woman. However, such a match would also reinforce stereotypes about Muslim women's lack of agency, especially in the arena of marriage and sexuality. Instead, the matter of the proposal is shunted off-screen, where if you know the play, you know what happened, and if you do not, then you imagine that the governor explained the reasons behind his unnecessarily convoluted plot. The film ends with Samina free and with the promise of her social and political emancipation from the benevolent patriarchy upon which she had to rely. Muslim women's freedom might be something that they can achieve, without global or western intervention and under conditions that allow them to live their lives without having to reject their religion, their customs, and their families—as western feminism demands that they do. *Rahm's* hyper-locale focus facilitates the terms and conditions of its feminist critique of Pakistani patriarchy. The film offers a hopeful ending that untethers Isabella from the Duke's proffered hand and, instead, allows Samina to walk alone on her own two feet.

I conclude *Shakespeare through Islamic Worlds* with this digression through a Muslim adaptation of *Measure for Measure* because it captures many of the tensions animating my project. Shakespeare's elisions of Islam and Muslims have suggested that there is no place for Muslims in Shakespeare's canon and worldmaking and that Muslim engagement with Shakespeare violates the norms of who Shakespeare is for even as those engagements buttress his universality. As a critical instrument of the British Empire in later centuries, Shakespeare was forcefed to many non-European, non-white, and non-Christian people across the globe. They had to adjust and adapt their comportment, mores, and values to fit the norm and form of humanity valorized by and celebrated in Shakespeare's works. *Rahm* eschews those contortions and shows how Shakespeare can seamlessly fit into its world and its anxieties and concerns. Even though Shakespeare may not have had much to say about Muslims, it is clear that Muslims have much to say to and with Shakespeare. I do not make this claim to reinscribe Shakespeare's universality or necessity to Muslim peoples; rather, I believe the future of Shakespeare lies in engagements like *Rahm* that localize, particularize, and provincialize Shakespeare to make his work speak in the vernaculars and idioms that are salient to them. Taking Shakespeare through their own worlds and on itineraries that he could never have imagined, these engagements expose the manifold routes that Muslims can open up for Shakespeare.

NOTES

1   bell hooks, "Choosing the Margin as a Space of Radical Openness," *Framework: The Journal of Cinema and Media*, 36 (1989), 22.

2   Edward Said, *Orientalism* (New York: Penguin Classics, 2003), 10.

3   Dennis Austin Britton, "Ain't She a Shakespearean: Truth, Giovanni, and Shakespeare," *Early Modern Black Diaspora Studies*, ed. Cassander L. Smith, Nicholas R. Jones, and Miles P. Grier (New York: Palgrave Macmillan, 2018), 223–28.

4   I borrow the term "historical amnesia" from Audre Lorde who developed it to demonstrate how white feminism colludes with other systems of oppression like sexism, homophobia, and ageism to stall advancement, so that marginalized people keep having to "reinvent the wheel." Audre Lorde. "Age, Race, Class, and Sex: Women Redefining Difference." in *Sister Outsider: Essays and Speeches* (Trumansburg, NY: Crossing Press, 1984), 110–119, 112.

5   For a cogent critique of such disengagements with Said's work, see Eric L. De Barros, "The Gatekeeping Politics of 'Good' Historicism: Early Modern Orientalism and *The Diary of Master Thomas Dallam*," *College Literature*, (2016), 619–44.

6   E.M.W. Tillyard, *Shakespeare's Problem Plays* (Toronto: University of Toronto Press, 1950).

7   "Social & Political Framework," Me Too Movement, updated 2022, https://metoomvmt.org/framework/; Harris, Aisha, "She Founded Me Too. Now She Wants to Move Past the Trauma," *New York Times*, October 15, 2018, www.nytimes.com/2018/10/15/arts/tarana-burke-metoo-anniversary.html

8   "Transcript: Donald Trump's Taped Comments About Women," *New York Times*, October 8, 2016, www.nytimes.com/2016/10/08/us/donald-trump-tape-transcript.html

9   Kate Manne, "Brett Kavanaugh and America's 'Himpathy' Reckoning: Rarely Has Society's Tendency to Sympathize with Powerful Men Been So Thoroughly on Display," *New York Times*, September 26, 2018, www.nytimes.com/2018/09/26/opinion/brett-kavanaugh-hearing-himpathy.html

10 2.4.169–74.

11 Laura Kolb, "The Very Modern Anger of Shakespeare's Women: What *Measure for Measure* Means to Us in 2019," *Electric Literature*, February 6, 2019, https://electricliterature.com/the-very-modern-anger-of-shake speares-women/

12 For more on white male entitlement see, Kate Manne, *Entitled: How Male Privilege Hurts Women* (New York: Crown, 2020).

13 Dobbs v. Jackson Women's Health Organization, 597 U.S. (2022). www.supremecourt.gov/opinions/21pdf/19-1392_6j37.pdf

14 There are many Islamicate regimes that mandate veiling for women, to the extent that women are violently punished and brutalized for violating those norms and laws. Such regimes do not value the dignity, humanity, and agency of women. In the west, those regimes have come to stand in for all Muslim societies and cultures, which is a misrepresentation of Islamic cultures and polities. On the issue of the veil, we should also consider western, liberal, and feminist positions that prohibit Muslim women from covering, circumscribing their political and religious agency in the name of empowerment.

15 Moustafa Bayoumi, *This Muslim American Life: Dispatches from the War on Terror* (New York: NYU Press, 2015), 12.

16 Gayatri Chakravorty Spivak, "Can the Subaltern Speak?" *Colonial Discourse and Post-colonial Theory*, ed. Patrick Williams and Laura Chrisman (New York: Columbia University Press, 1994), pp. 66–111.

17 Jamal Ahmed, Personal Communication. November 11, 2021.

18 Martin Orkin. *Local Shakespeares: Proximations and Power*. Routledge, 2007. (43).

19 Craig Dionne and Parmita Kapadia, eds. *Native Shakespeares: Indigenous Appropriations on a Global Stage* (Farnham: Ashgate, 2008), 6–11.

REFERENCES

Bayoumi, Moustafa. *This Muslim American Life: Dispatches from the War on Terror*. New York: NYU Press, 2015.

Britton, Dennis Austin. "Ain't She a Shakespearean: Truth, Giovanni, and Shakespeare." In *Early Modern Black Diaspora Studies*, edited by Cassander L. Smith, Nicholas R. Jones, and Miles P. Grier, 223–28. New York: Palgrave Macmillan, 2018.

De Barros, Eric L. "The Gatekeeping Politics of 'Good' Historicism: Early Modern Orientalism and *The Diary of Master Thomas Dallam*." *College Literature* 43.4 (2016): 619–44.

Dionne, Craig, and Parmita Kapadia, eds. *Native Shakespeares: Indigenous Appropriations on a Global Stage.* Farnham: Ashgate, 2008.

Harris, Aisha. "She Founded Me Too. Now She Wants to Move Past the Trauma." *New York Times.* October 15, 2018. www.nytimes.com/2018/10/15/arts/tarana-burke-metoo-anniversary.html

hooks, bell. "Choosing the Margin as a Space of Radical Openness." *Framework: The Journal of Cinema and Media* 36 (1989): 15–23.

Kolb, Laura. "The Very Modern Anger of Shakespeare's Women: What *Measure for Measure* Means to Us in 2019." *Electric Literature.* February 6, 2019. https://electricliterature.com/the-very-modern-anger-of-shakespeares-women/

Manne, Kate. "Brett Kavanaugh and America's 'Himpathy' Reckoning: Rarely Has Society's Tendency to Sympathize with Powerful Men Been So Thoroughly on Display." *New York Times.* September 26, 2018. www.nytimes.com/2018/09/26/opinion/brett-kavanaugh-hearing-himpathy.html

————. *Entitled: How Male Privilege Hurts Women.* New York: Crown, 2020.

"Transcript: Donald Trump's Taped Comments About Women." *New York Times.* October 8, 2016. www.nytimes.com/2016/10/08/us/donald-trump-tape-transcript.html

Orkin, Martin. *Local Shakespeares: Proximations and Power.* Routledge, 2007. (43).

Said, Edward. *Orientalism.* London: Penguin Classics, 2003.

Spivak, Gayatri Chakravorty. "Can the Subaltern Speak?" In *Colonial Discourse and Post-colonial Theory: A Reader,* edited by Patrick Williams and Laura Chrisman, 66–111. New York: Columbia University Press, 1994.

Tillyard, E.M.W. *Shakespeare's Problem Plays.* Toronto: University of Toronto Press, 1950.

Index

Note: Figures are indicated by *italics*. Endnotes are indicated by the page number followed by 'n' and the endnote number e.g., 20n1 refers to endnote 1 on page 20.